Transparency, Disclosure and Governance

About the Editors

Professor Ajit Kumar Singh (*b.* 1944) is a reputed economist with fifty years of teaching and research experience. He retired as Director of the prestigious Giri Institute of Development Studies in 2013. Presently, he is National Fellow, Indian Council of Social Science Research. Professor Singh has been a member of various working groups and Government Committees at the State and Central level. He has written extensively on different aspects of planning and development and has authored and edited over a dozen books.

N.S. Ravi (*b.* 1959) is a member of the Indian Administrative Service. He has worked in various high level positions in the UP Government. He is presently Director General, Deen Dayal Upadhyaya State Institute of Rural Development, Uttar Pradesh.

O.P. Pandey (*b.* 1959) has over three decades of experience in the field of research and training.

Presently, he is holding the position of Joint Director at the Deen Dayal Upadhyaya State Institute of Rural Development, Uttar Pradesh.

Transparency, Disclosure and Governance

Edited by

Ajit Kumar Singh
N.S. Ravi, *I.A.S.*
O.P. Pandey

Jointly Published
D.D.U. State Institute of Rural Development, Lucknow
and
CONCEPT PUBLISHING COMPANY PVT. LTD.
NEW DELHI-110059

ISBN-13: 978-93-5125-191-0

First Published 2015

Published and Printed by

Concept Since 1974

Concept Publishing Company Pvt. Ltd.
Regd. Office:
A/15-16, Commercial Block, Mohan Garden,
New Delhi-110059 (INDIA)
Phones : 25351460, 25351794, *Fax* : 091-11-25357109
Email : publishing@conceptpub.com
Website: www.conceptpub.com

Editorial Office:
H-13, Bali Nagar, New Delhi-110 015, India.

Cataloging in Publication Data—DK Courtesy: D.K. Agencies (P) Ltd. <docinfo@dkagencies.com>

National Seminar on Transparency and Disclosure (2013 : Lucknow, India)
Transparency, disclosure and governance / edited by Ajit Kumar Singh, N.S. Ravi, I.A.S., O.P. Pandy.
pages cm
Papers presented at the National Seminar on Transparency and Disclosure organized by Deen Dayal Upadhyaya State Institute of Rural Development, held at Lucknow during 29-30 May, 2013.
Includes bibliographical references and index.
ISBN 9789351251910

1. Transparency in government—India—Congresses. 2. Transparency in government—Law and legislation—India—Congresses. 3. Disclosure of information—India—Congresses. 4. Social justice—India—Congresses. 5. Human rights—India—Congresses. I. Singh, Ajit Kumar, 1944- editor. II. Ravi, N. S., 1959- editor. III. Pandey, O. P., 1959- editor. IV. Deen Dayal Upadhyaya State Institute of Rural Development.issuing body, organizer. V. Title.

JC599.I4N38 2013 DDC 352.880954 23

Preface

The recent decades have witnessed an increasing demand for ensuring transparency in the working of public institutions in all parts of the world including India. Lack of transparency in government decision-making and actions has been identified as the main reason for the prevailing corruption and mal-governance. It is realized that poor governance has been retarding progress towards economic development and poverty reduction. The United Nations has recognized integrity, transparency and accountability as the three cornerstones of good governance.

Democracy does not mean mere holding elections at regular intervals; instead the basic idea is participatory governance and a way of life. Active and meaningful participation in all spheres of governance is based on informed choices of the individual. The prerequisite for informed choice is transparency and disclosure in governance by state and the para statal and corporate entities. Democracy essentially implies inclusiveness and unless there is transparency and disclosure, meaningful participation of general public in governance is not possible. There is a widespread perception in India that the executive actions of the state are generally not carried out in a transparent and open manner and least regard is paid to transparency and disclosure when decisions are taken by the state.

Development has to be participative for inculcating the feeling of fairness, justice, ownership and accountability in the general masses. Racial, regional and gender-based inequalities can best be removed through a development process which is inclusive, based on transparency and disclosure. The extent of corporate greed witnessed in recent times is the result of the opacity in various domains, processes and programmes run by the state, its instruments and corporates. Transparency is of utmost importance for a society like India which is based on inherent biases, graded inequality and exclusion. Because of illiteracy, language barriers and urban-rural divide, inclusiveness requires optimum disclosure and transparency in various fields of public and private domain and that too in a language which can be comprehended by general masses. Transparency and disclosure are also important for ensuring human rights of the people. In order to ensure fairness and justness of executive actions we need to have a free, affordable and transparent justice delivery system. The processes and procedures followed by judicial and quasi-judicial authorities should be open, transparent and affordable so as to be accessible to the common man.

Recent technological advancements made in the field of communication have broken geographical and cultural barriers and simplified the task of transparency and disclosure. As information can be shared with the click of a button the problem of storage of information and records and transmission has also been solved to a large extent. Technology can further make transparency and disclosure simpler, realistic and cheaper.

Realizing the importance of transparency and disclosure for ensuring participatory and accountable government. The Deen Dayal Upadhyaya State Institute of Rural Development, Uttar Pradesh, organized a two-day National Seminar on Transparency and Disclosure on 29-30 May, 2013 in its premises at Lucknow. The aim of the seminar was to bring forward different views and positions to promote transparency and disclosure in governance and also to understand how it affects the relationship between the state and the people, how it helps in keeping alive the basic tenets of our Constitution and how does the lack of transparency and disclosure lead to weakening of the very foundations of our polity.

The deliberations of the seminar were organized under following themes:

1. Transparency and Disclosure and Democracy as a Political Concept
2. Transparency and Disclosure and Governance
3. Transparency and Disclosure and Human Rights
4. Transparency and Disclosure and Development
5. Transparency and Disclosure and Social Justice/Equality
6. Transparency and Disclosure and Justice Delivery System
7. Transparency and Disclosure and Consumer Protection
8. Role of Technology in Transparency and Disclosure

A large number of distinguished personalities from diverse fields and experiences including eminent scholars, jurists, administrators and social activists participated in the seminar and debated and discussed various aspects concerning transparency and disclosure. Well researched papers were presented in the seminar and discussed enthusiastically.

The present volume brings out together selected papers presented at the seminar. The sixteen papers included in this volume have been grouped under four parts dealing respectively with the concept and dimensions of transparency, disclosure, governance and development; the role of technology in transparency and disclosure; transparency, disclosure and social justice; and transparency, disclosure and human rights.

I would like to express my gratitude and thanks to all those who made this seminar a success and helped in bringing out this volume. But for their critical observations, comments and contributions in the form of their vast and varied experience of their respective fields, the seminar would not have achieved its objectives. Out of the galaxy of those illustrious and most ignited minds I would like to make special mention of Hon'ble Justice Virendra Singh, Chairman U.P. State Consumer Disputes Redressal Commission, Hon'ble Justice Vishnu Sahai, former Member, U.P. State Human Rights Commission, Mrs. Aruna Roy, Founder Mazdoor Kishan Shakti Sangathan, Rajasthan, Sri Nikhil Day, Co-founder, Mazdoor Kishan Shakti Sangathan Rajasthan, Sri R.C. Tripathi, former Secretary-General Rajya Sabha, Sri Shri Ram Arun, former Director General of Police, U.P., Prof. Girijesh Pant, Dean School of International Studies, JNU New Delhi, Dr. Amita Prasad, Director General, Administrative Training Institute Mysore Karnataka, Prof. (Dr.) S.S. Singh, Director, National Law Institute University, Bhopal, Prof. (Dr.) A.K. Singh, former Director, Giri Institute of Development Studies, Lucknow, Prof. Sushma Yadav, Dr. Ambedkar Chair in Social Justice and Public Policy, IIPA Delhi, Mrs. Suchitra Goswami, Project Officer, Common Wealth Human Rights Initiative, Delhi, Mrs. Jos Yula Laxmi, Centre for Good Governance, Dr. M. Chenna Reddy, HRD School, Hyderabad, Prof. Pranav Banerji, IIPA Delhi, Prof. Hari Krishna Mishra, Institute of Rural Management, Anand Gujarat, Prof. (Dr.) R. Srinivasan, University of Madras, Chennai, Prof. Pradeep Bhargava, Director, G.B. Pant Social Science Institute, Allahabad, Dr. D.N.S. Yadav, Dean Faculty of Law, Lucknow University, Prof. Dharmendra Singh Sengar, IIM Lucknow, Prof. Madhusudan Mishra, Mahatma Gandhi Kashi Vidyapeeth, Varanasi, Dr. G.G. Koppa, Director, Agricultural Rural Management Resource Group, Centre for Good Governance, Hyderabad, Prof. (Dr.) Dayanand Bidari, NIRD, Hyderabad, Dr. Mridul

Srivastava, Dr. Ram Manohar Lohia National Law University, Lucknow, Dr. Pamela Singh, Delhi University, Dr. S.M. Haider Rizvi, Director, 3eResearch, Bhopal, Dr. Nazeer, Director, Centre for Rural Development Studies, Bangalore University, Prof. (Dr.) Sheetal Kapoor Delhi University, Miss Kavita Srivastava, General-Secretary, PUCL Jaipur, Rajasthan, Miss Nirmita Mehrotra, School of Architecture and Built Environment, Gautam Buddha University, Noida, Dr. Yogesh Kumar, Executive Director, SAMARTHAN Bhopal, Sri C.R.K. Nair, Advisor, Ministry of Rural Development, Government of India, Dr. Ambreesh Kumar, Dy. Director General, NIC, Government of India, New Delhi, Dr. Surendra Kumar, Director, Giri Institute of Development Studies, Lucknow and Prof. Harsh Mohan, Prof. Arvind Mohan, Department of Economics, Prof. Rajesh Mishra, Sociology, Prof. Raj Kumar Singh, Social Work, Prof. R.K. Misra, Political Science Department, Lucknow University. My apology to those distinguished scholars whose names are left out for paucity of space.

We are highly grateful to Department of Rural Development, Ministry of Rural Development, Government of India and National Institute of Rural Development and Panchayati Raj, Hyderabad for their financial support and guidance for organizing the seminar.

I am also thankful to my colleagues in the SIRD particularly Dr. Lalit Mohan Joshi, Dr. Vardani, Dr. O.P. Pandey, Dr. D.C. Upadhyaya, Sri B.D. Chaudhary and other supporting faculties and officials. Without their tireless and selfless efforts the seminar could not have been possible. Even at the cost of repetition I would express my thanks again to Prof. A.K. Singh who has been a constant reference point for us relating to various aspects and issues concerning the seminar and bringing out this volume.

Finally, thanks are due to our publishers for their promptness and excellence in printing the volume.

We will feel amply rewarded if the present volume helps in spreading better awareness and concern for transparency and disclosure in governance at various levels and contributes to practical action in this direction.

Lucknow
14 April, 2015

N. S. Ravi, *IAS*
Director General
Deen Dayal Upadhyaya State Institute
of Rural Development, Lucknow
Uttar Pradesh

Contents

PART-3
Transparency, Disclosure and Social Justice

PART-4
Transparency, Disclosure and Human Rights and Justice Delivery System

List of Contributors

Arun, Shri Ram, IPS (Retired), former Director General Police, UP. shriram1940@rediffmail.com

Gopalakrishnan, T.R., Asst. Professor, Dept. of Journalism and Mass Communication, IDE, University of Madras, Chennai. trggopi@unom.co.in

Goswami, Suchismita, Project Officer/Moderator SARTIAN, Commonwealth Human Rights Initiative. suchiz08@gmail.com

Joshi, Rohan, Programme Director, Babasaheb Ambedkar Research and Training Institute, Pune. ruhaanj@gmail.com

Kapoor, Sheetal, Associate Professor and Convener Consumer Club, Department of Commerce, Kamala Nehru College, University of Delhi. sheetal_kpr@hotmail.com

Koppa, Gurulingappa G., Director, Agriculture and Rural Management Resources Group, Centre for Good Governance, Hyderabad. gg.koppa@cgg.gov.in

Kumar, Yogesh, Executive Director, Samarthan, Center for Development Support, Bhopal. yogesh@samarthan.org

Lakshmi, Joshyula, Programme Manager, Centre for Good Governance, Hyderabad. lakshmi@cgg.gov.in

Mehrotra, Nirmita, Head Department of Architecture and Regional Planning, Gautam Buddha University, Greater Noida. nirmita2006@gmail.com

Mishra, M.S., Associate Professor (Retired), Department of Economics, MGKVP, Varanasi.

Mishra, V.K., Assistant Professor, Department of Economics, MGKVP, Varanasi. vijayecon@rediffmail.com.

Pandey, O.P., Joint Director, Deen Dayal Upadhyaya Institute of Rural Development, Bakshika Talab, Lucknow. oppandey.upsird@gmail.com

Prasad, Amita, IAS, Director General, Administrative Training Institute, Mysore. amitaprasad@hotmail.com

Ravi, N.S., IAS, Director General, Deen Dayal Upadhyaya Institute of Rural Development, Bakshika Talab, Lucknow. dg@sirdup.in

Rizvi, S.M. Haider, Director 3e Research, Bhopal. smhaiderrizvi@rediffmail.com

Sah, D.C., Director Research, Samarthan, Center for Development Support, Bhopal. drdcsah_dcsah@yahoo.com

Singh, Ajit Kumar, Former Director Giri Insitute of Development Studies, Lucknow. aksingh101@rediffmail.com

Srinivasan, R., Asst. Professor, Dept. of Public Administration. IDE, University of Madras, Chennai. seenu242@gmail.com

Srivastava, Mridul, Assistant Registrar (Academics) and Faculty in Criminology, Dr. Ram Manohar Lohia National Law University, Lucknow. srivastavamridullko@gmail.com

Tripathi, R.C., Retired IAS and former Secretary General, Rajya Sabha. rameshctripathi2003@gmail.com

Yadav, D.N.S., Associate Professor, Department of Law, University of Lucknow, Lucknow. dnns_yadav@ymail.com

1

Introduction

Ajit Kumar Singh

The sixteen papers included in this volume have been grouped under four parts dealing with different aspects of transparency, disclosure and governance. Part-1 contains four papers dealing with the concept and dimensions of transparency, disclosure, governance and development. The opening paper by Ajit Kumar Singh elaborates on the concepts of transparency and disclosures and probes the relationship between transparency, right to information and development. He points out that during the last three decades or so the issue of good governance has emerged as a central focus in the development discourse. Movements have spawned the world over in recent decades for ensuring transparency in the working of public institutions and improving governance quality by making it people friendly. The movement towards good governance and openness in the functioning of government agencies was promoted by the efforts of the international donor agencies like the World Bank, IMF, DFID and Agency for International Development.

The concepts of integrity, transparency and accountability have been identified by the UN as part of the founding principles of public administration. Singh elaborates the concepts of governance, transparency and accountability and their interrelationships. It is generally agreed that good governance has to be participatory, responsive, non-discriminatory, transparent and efficient. Transparency is essential to ensure participatory and accountable government. This is possible only when the members of the public have access to the information held by public authorities. The movement towards Open Government Data (OGD) systems is as essential for ensuring transparency in government functioning and accountability of its actions. Open data regime require proactive role of government organisations and departments to make all relevant data available at all stages of policy formulation and implementation.

Singh argues that this shift from secrecy to transparency in government functioning involves a fundamental shift in the citizen-state relationship. The citizens are thus perceived as participants in government process with a legal right to all public information. This puts an obligation on the state to allow access of all public information to its citizens.

Singh then proceeds to examine the relationship between transparency, good governance and development. Cross-country studies of governance trends finds that transparency is positively and significantly correlated with many aspects of governance, including effectiveness, control of corruption, accountability, rule of law and bureaucratic efficiency. Studies also show that transparency is highly significant in explaining variation in human development indicators across countries.

The paper highlights how corruption adversely affects economic growth in various ways. Corruption in construction raises cost and lowers quality of infrastructure. Corruption promotes inefficiencies and reduces competition. Corruption can result in loss of government revenue, costs for businesses, missed opportunities for non-corrupt businesses, distortion of standards of merit, erosion of respect for the rule of law, higher costs and lower quality of infrastructure and mistrust of government. Corrupt practices impact on levels of poverty in various ways. Diversion of public funds meant for the poor undermines equitable economic development. Corruption contributes to income inequality through impacts on budgetary revenues and expenditure. The human cost of corruption is enormous. The paper points out that corruption is encouraged by the complex governmental regulations, discretionary powers and lack of transparency in government functioning. Fighting corruption is, therefore, of paramount importance for attaining faster and inclusive growth. It has to be at the centre of all governance reforms.

To ensure intended outcomes of public spending transparency in budget making process and public expenditures is most essential. Greater public participation in budget making would help in determining budget priorities and public spending according to the need of the people. Tracking public expenditure by the people would further help in improving the quality and effectiveness of government spending and check misuse and diversion of public funds. In recent years several governments have taken to make budgetary processes more participative and transparent. Several municipal bodies across the world have adopted participatory budgeting practices that allocate resources to programmes identified with the direct involvement of citizens and civil society groups.

Singh points out that the Government of India has repeatedly asserted its commitment to responsive, open and good governance. However, there are many challenges that must be addressed while moving towards opening up governmental data. The infrastructure of information gathering, processing and sharing remains inadequate. The challenge of open government data is especially great in a country where still a large number of people are illiterate and computer penetration is very limited. The need of expansion of ICT infrastructure remains a matter of high priority. The government has to follow a proactive approach to make available maximum possible information to the people. Singh ends the paper by asserting that the movement towards a transparent and accountable system of governance requires a firm political commitment towards these goals. The old colonial ways of secrecy in government functioning have to give place to a new value system wedded to the objectives of an open and participatory form of governance.

In his paper R.C. Tripathi draws attention to the vision of our founding fathers who gave to the people of India a democratic republic to secure social, economic and political justice combined with liberty of thought, expression, belief, faith and worship. India has all the features of a vibrant democracy—an elaborate Constitution, democratic institutions, regular elections, political parties, strong judiciary, a civil society and a vibrant print and electronic media. During the last over six decades, our democracy has faced crises yet come out each time more vibrant.

Lamenting the decline in the ethical behaviour and norms of public life over time, Tripathi observes that our country and society are faced with crises in governance reflected in lack of probity, violation of constitutional conduct and decline in ethical norms. There is growing disenchantment all-around with political parties and institutions. The gulf between the rich and the poor is widening. Redress of public grievances are getting remote and remoter. There is rampant crime against the weak, the poor, the child, women, old and the aged. The state has not been effective in controlling crimes and criminals. Money, muscle and *mafia* seem to have penetrated public life with little chance for redemption. The system of governance has been replaced by knee-jerk reactions with little consideration for long-term solutions.

He ends with a note of warning that if the governments fail to meet the expectations of people disillusionment is bound to set in. In a situation of gross disillusionment, democracy will have tough times to save itself and the country. Our political masters have to see the writing on the wall. They have severe trust-deficit and very little time to deliver what they promise through their manifestoes. Leadership and governance are critical. He ends by saying that commitment to public cause and service need to be deeply ingrained in the society and leaders in particular.

The paper by Amita Prasad dwells on role of transparency in good governance. According to her good governance is increasingly being advocated to improve service delivery. This is because of the realisation that the resources are not reaching those whom it has been intended to. According to her are good governance is participatory, consensus oriented, accountable, transparent, responsive, effective and efficient, equitable and inclusive and follows the rule of law. She argues that transparency and accountability are the main ingredients needed to achieve good governance. They are like the two sides of the same coin. One, without the other, is of no use. Transparency means that decisions are taken and their enforcement is done in a manner that follows rules and regulations. It also means that information is freely available and directly accessible to those who will be affected by such decisions and their enforcement. The existence of both conditions contributes to an effective, efficient and equitable management in public and private institutions.

She refers to the Service Guarantee Act passed by the different states in India to ensure service delivery to the people. '*Sakala*' in Karnataka is a good example of covering all the above said tenets of governance. It ensures that the citizens are guaranteed of their service within a specified time. Failing to deliver the services is to be compensated by the civil servant. It also ensures equity and inclusion as it provides equal opportunities for citizen in accessing the services.

Information is a key factor to ensure efficient and effective public services. It empowers the people to exert demand for better services. Right to Information Act 2005 in her opinion has ushered in transparency and accountability in administration and thereby has helped governments to engage citizens by providing information. It is recognized that the transparent and accountable measures would curtail corruption and help to hold governments responsible. Thus, by providing information to 'the citizens who desire to have it', emphasis is being placed on accessible and transparent governance.

She underlines the fact that machinery for redressal of public grievances has to be strengthened in every government office. An independent grievances redressal authority may oversee the action on redressal of public grievances. Examples of this are many in Karnataka, e.g. Bhoomi, Nemmadi and Banglore One. They combine IT enabled, e-governance mechanisms to heed to public grievances. Atal Bihari Vajpayee Janashree Yojana is another initiative of Government of Karnataka for getting governance at doorstep. Establishment of an Institution of Ombudsman to oversee redressal of grievances (as in Insurance and Banking Sectors) or a Public Grievance Commission, Strengthening of Consumer Courts and other institutions which helps redress complaints and grievances and provide local, quick and effective remedy is the next step forward in Good Governance.

In her view all these initiatives of transparency and Good Governance will only be realised if there is change of ethical culture in bureaucracy. This would require institutional reform of departments and continuous monitoring and assessment of service delivery. With the penalty/compensation clause introduced in the Service Guarantee Act, the culture of bureaucracy would certainly undergo change.

Joshyula Lakshmi in her paper focuses on the need for proactive disclosures and the provisions in this regard in the RTI Act 2005. Section 4 (1) (b) of the RTI Act pertains to proactive parting with information 'held' by the Public Authorities. This section indicates, for purposes of convenience and understanding of the Public Authorities, 17 sub-heads under which such information may be categorised and submitted for public view, scrutiny and usage. However, a stocktaking of the Right to Information Act shows that Public Authorities in our country have still to go a long distance in proactive disclosures. While many Ministries/Departments have put up information on their websites, the adequacy of the same, the quality and its amenability for further analysis and use merits a closer examination. She points out that the culture of proactive disclosure is lacking and needs to be cultivated.

The paper highlights the many deficiencies in the process and the system of information sharing from the government. The lack of attitudinal transformation and change over at different levels of governance is a major hurdle to be crossed. Fears and apprehensions of the information suppliers also need to be addressed in this regard. Lack of financial resources and insufficient manpower pose problems in providing the large volume of information sought. Public Authority is a broad term and needs to be pin-pointed for the general public. It is also important to relook at the institutional arrangements in place to ensure that the supply of information goes beyond the desired levels. Institutional arrangements have to be put in place in the form of rewards, awards, incentives like pay hikes and promotions and earning the goodwill of the public. The paper ends by observing that only a true commitment to the letter and spirit of the RTI Act by the Public Authorities can ensure that a transparent and participatory governance system is created in the country.

Part-2 contains three papers on the role of technology in transparency and disclosure. Srinivasan and Gopalakrishnan in their paper argue that while there are obvious benefits of e-transparency in governance there are also considerable risks and constraints in applying the concept in practice. Based on a case study of Computerisation of Land Records (CLR) initiated in the State of Tamil Nadu they point out that CLR has the potential to facilitate corruption rather than restraining it. The irony of CLR in Tamil Nadu is that over a decade of experimentation and use CLR has not had a significant impact on corruption in land transactions. There has been a tremendous increase in the cases of land grabbing and land document forgery in Tamil Nadu in the last five years. In addition to land grabbing, document forgery for obtaining loans is another major concern.

The paper points out the various channels through which CLR facilitates corruption. These include: (i) reification of default through improper data entry or glossing over historical contested claim over the land and by privileging default land owners the system reifies, freezes, the ownership rights; (ii) information asymmetry among different groups also facilitates corruption; (iii) re-intermediation has emerged as a new phenomenon in the land market; (iv) control of land information market creates opportunities for corruption; (v) compromising confidentiality of land record also leads to misuse of transparency; (vi) forgery and cloning and is another mechanism of corruption; (vii) many middlemen have used RTI Act to seek information on lands held by government, public and private trust and organizations; (viii) it has become easy to reclassify large tracks of conterminous farm land held by diverse small land owners into residential plots or consolidate them into single ownership; (ix) lack of inter-connectedness among departments is another source of corruption; and (x) malpractices of the revenue staff continue to subvert the reform.

They end by asserting that without an effective legal and institutional framework which guarantees oversight and is capable and willing of imposing sanctions ICT enabled transparency might increase the risk of "revenge effect". Hence, we should embrace transparency, knowing its limits.

Haider Rizvi in his paper presents a model for ensuring transparency and disclosure in governance structures using ICT. He starts by observing that in spite of the development efforts India as a nation has failed in improving the socio-economic health of the nation and solving the problems like mass poverty, unemployment, women empowerment and child protection, etc. The reason of the slow pace of development in India according to him is mainly human induced resulting in poor governance. There is a need of all round efforts to tackle the problems prevailing at various fronts. Few of the areas which are in need of immediate attention to make governance good and ensure inclusive development are: ensuring transparency in governance structures, making provisions of disclosure and access of information and making people accountable in their roles, responsibilities and functioning thereof besides participation and effectiveness.

Rizvi argues that there is a need to inbuilt the aspects of transparency and disclosures in the system and while managing the performance in government at least on the aspects of 'delivery of services' for the people. There is need of a framework which monitors and evaluates performances of the public service officers on ongoing basis with focus on 'results' and 'performance'. The e-governance had emerged as a tool to realize the application of Governance Framework of Administration to achieve overall objective of transparency, accountability, equity, responsiveness, effectiveness, efficiency and rule of law.

In this background Rizvi proposes a model taking into considerations the relevance and powers of existing structures and institutions and accompanied resources within those for ensuring people's participations through creating in-built systems of accountabilities at various levels using ICTs. The amalgamations of powers of ICTs and local governments i.e. Gram Panchayats in rural areas in particular the Panchayat committees besides the citizens at large have been kept at the centre of Socio-technological Publicness Model for Development (SPMD). The Socio-technological Publicness Model for Development is based on the premises that there is need to (a) share and disclose information at each tier of Panchayat, and (b) translate Acts, Schemes, and Programmes into action.

In SPMD Village Committees have been considered as the basic building blocks of development and as a medium to ensure people's participation. The system proposed to be kept at the Panchayats should be designed in a manner which besides managing the data should provide the information on needs of people. The work list would be generated for weekly and monthly execution and would be made available to the concerned people and functionaries. The other powerful feature of SPMD is the generation of weekly and monthly reports based on the generated web plan. The Web Stations at Panchayats would be designed using Participatory ICT Design Methodology with full participation of users and other stakeholders in the designing processes by providing them space of co-designers.

Rizvi ends by expressing the hope that the suggested model if applied in true spirit has powers to bring a culture of transparency in the Panchayat functioning and in fixing accountabilities at various levels. The model could also be used as a powerful tool in bringing a culture of 'Role Based Commitments' and making people accountable towards their roles.

M.S. Mishra and V.K. Mishra explain the role of technology and disclosure. In their opinion transparency is a monitoring device to ensure that all stakeholders understand and can influence organizations performance and operations in the stakeholder's interest. Transparency and disclosure serve as an instrument for prevention of fraud and corruption. Disclosure helps public understanding of an organization's objectives, policies and performance with regard to environmental and ethical standards, as well as its social responsibilities. In the emerging globalized scenario Information Technology (IT) is playing a decisive role in transparency and governance. Thanks to advancement in technology, information is now readily available in almost every shape and form to enable transparency and accountability to function to their full effectiveness. Technology helps in better management of risk and reduction of cost. Information technology has immensely altered the relationship between the internal and external customers of an organization. Cyber-space has broken the barrier of geographical boundaries.

The authors highlight various requirements of developing an effective IT based monitoring system. Effecting offline change often requires a shift in perception. In many areas, there is little public awareness and understanding of government activity, or of the power of citizens' oversight. Local mass media must be aware of and able to use the information collected by technology projects in order to hold governing authorities accountable. Lack or low engagement with governing authorities at various scales can also be a substantial obstacle in combating corruption through technology. Physical networks required for access to the internet is only one of many structures needed to realise the potential of technology-led transparency. Technology projects also rely on education, regulation, culture and social support. Language is another aspect of social infrastructure which, if overlooked, can significantly restrict the impact of technology-led transparency. There are often substantial communication, trust and knowledge gaps that exist as a result of low interaction and a lack of infrastructure. There is need by the government to develop learning networks to bridge these gaps.

The authors state that the realization of greater accountability in governance is long and complex. Online tools can definitely play a decisive role in this process, but can fail to generate the desired impact, if implemented without proper consideration and engagement of the relevant stakeholders and structures of governance.

Part-3 contains six papers on transparency, disclosure and social justice. In his paper Yadav looks at the issue of transparency and social justice from legal and constitutional perspective. The preamble of the Constitution of India makes it categorically clear that India is a democratic country committed to the ideals of justice and equality of opportunity to all people without any discrimination. The democratic set-up of governance visualizes that the government is accountable for the entire process of decision-making to the people who have elected them to rule.

Yadav asserts that the pillars of administrative accountability are 'transparency' and 'openness', which could be possible through the channels of sincere and honest disclosures. He stresses that development to be real and inclusive has to be participative and should inculcate the feeling of fairness, justice, ownership and accountability in the general masses. For understanding social justice in collective sense we need to understand justice, which is a concept of moral rightness based on ethics, rationality, law, natural law, religion and equity. The concept of social justice is based upon the principles of equality and solidarity among the people.

India experienced social injustice on a larger scale due to the caste divisions. Caste hierarchy feelings became a major issue of social justice in modern India. Gender-based exploitation are also a glaring instance of social injustice in the Indian society, where women had been the exploited lots at the hands of male dominated patriarchal social mentality. Rural India also faces graver social injustice situations in terms of gender issues, economic disparity, acute poverty conditions, poor educational facility, lack of basic health care infrastructure, nutrition, unemployment among youth, poor dwelling conditions in the villages and so forth.

Equality of opportunity is the most potential term, where it is the prime responsibility of the governance to make available to all equality of opportunity under ideal conditions so as to ensure social and economic justice. Yadav argues that the most significant aspect of rule of law initiative is the study and analysis of the rule of law's impact on economic development. The rule of law movement cannot be fully successful in transitional and developing country like India unless the rule of law honestly addresses to the economic development of Indian society.

Rule of law in India guarantees and promotes fundamental rights and freedom of the citizens and respect for the principles of the democratic state based on rule of law. The very Preamble of the Constitution enshrines within itself justice—social, economical and political and equality of status and opportunity to all its citizens. The concept of separation of powers is inbuilt in the form of establishment of three constitutional bodies i.e. the legislature, the executive and the judiciary. The Directive Principles of State Policy are not enforceable by the courts as is the case with the Fundamental Rights, but these are very crucial for the purposes of formulating and legislating social and economic policy considerations of the nation. Keeping this fundamental in mind the Indian Parliament enacted the Right to Information Act, 2005 with an avowed objective to ensure transparency and accountability through disclosures to its citizens.

The concept of distributive justice is essential for honest administration of social justice in India. Inclusive growth is the goal of social and economic development governance of the country. In the author's view poverty is the most important causative factor of social exclusion. It is the society as a whole which is squarely responsible for social inclusion and social exclusion. If a dalit is excluded and ignored by the society, then it is a social problem not a legal problem. Delay defeats the ends of justice. We come across the instances of undue delay and protracted trials in the Indian courts for years and years together.

Yadav points out that the concept of public interest litigation has been linked with matters of public importance and has proved to be a big instrument in the hands of judiciary for purposes of administration of social justice. There are matters of public importance which could not be resolved merely by judicial intervention unless there is a fair degree of people's participation. In the long-run for the administration of social justice judicial activism through PILs has proved to be an effective mechanism and would remain so for the sake of social justice as a last ray of hope.

Corruption in public life has become so cancerous that there is genuine and reasonable apprehension that the administration system would fail to deal with this incurable disease. The existing state of affairs is extremely dismal. He stresses the need to muster moral courage to deal with the situation. We cannot legislate for morals. It only comes from within and not from without. People should realise that they are morally accountable for the poor masses of the Indian society. He concludes by saying that unless honest participation of maximum number of people is ensured in governance it will not be possible to realize the dream of transparency and disclosure.

Kumar and Sah start by observing that of late ability of civil society to carry out social accountability initiatives has been strengthened dramatically, with sizeable community participation and involvement. In their paper they evaluate the strengths and limitations of social accountability work, taking Social Audit of MNREGA in Madhya Pradesh as a case. Based on extensive field level participatory studies the authors argue that the power of demand-side approaches in enhancing governance through the concepts of citizens' voice has serious limitations.

The evidences collected by the authors indicate that Social Audits in Madhya Pradesh have turned out to be a non-event. Social Audit

Committees exist only on paper in bulk of Panchayats. Members of the social audit committee are unaware about their inclusion in the committee and about their roles. Sarpanch and Panchayat secretary are not interested in opening-up the decisions for scrutiny in Social Audits. Even when Social Audit is able to bring issues of large scale fudging of muster rolls, work evaluation process and less payment, delayed payments, individual work remaining incomplete but shown completed in MIS, no one is accountable for these. This is because of the nexuses between Panchayat and higher levels officials. As long as prosecution of erring Panchayat officials is within the ambit of administration, prosecution against them is hard to initiate. This helps in avoiding accountability in development decision-making.

The authors feel that despite a lack of administrative support, the discussions at the Gram Sabha definitely showed a positive sign towards empowerment of the Gram Sabha as a key local self-governing institution. They have identified the following challenges in the social audit process. First, the MNREGA administration and the Panchayat officials are resisting Social Audits in Panchayats. Second, neither Gram Sabha members nor the members of Social Audit Committee are aware of the provision of Social Audit. Third, the necessary documents for social audit have to come from the Panchayats. But the Panchayat Secretary and the Janpad CEO are not ready to share information necessary for social audits. Lastly, the designated Nodal Officers for social audits do not participate in Social Audits; as a result, the proceedings of the Social Audits are not recorded, for further actions.

The authors suggest that there is a need to link personnel from C&AG office with social audit, to give the process some legitimacy. Awareness about social audit is a big concern and steps need to be taken for creating awareness for conducting social audit. Regular capacity-building trainings for the members of Social Audit Committee is a must for successful social audit to take place. Media Advocacy on grievances of labourers would also bring anomalies to the notice of the MNREGA administration. A block level support group is required to strengthen the implementation process by interacting and appraising the local implementing agencies including block level MNREGA administration.

The paper by Rohan Joshi presents an in-depth case study of Caste Scrutiny and Validation Process in Department of Social Justice and Special Assistance, Government of Maharashtra. This case study is used as a basis for discussion of transparency and governance and for developing a possible strategy for bringing transparency and good governance in government processes. In order to secure the benefits provided under the Constitution it is obligatory that every person who claims to be a member of Scheduled Caste or Scheduled Tribes produces a Caste Certificate signed by a competent authority as sufficient proof in support of a candidate's claim to make him/her eligible for various relaxations and concessions. In certain cases re-validation or authorization of a caste certificate of a person is necessary.

In Maharashtra, the process of caste scrutiny and validation of persons belonging to Scheduled Castes (SCs), Other Backward Castes (OBCs), Special Backward Castes (SBCs) and Vimukta Jati and Nomadic Tribes (VJNT) is handled by Caste Scrutiny Committees (CSCs) working under the Department of Social Justice and Special Assistance of Government of Maharashtra. Significant growth in number of applications for caste validation certificates led to accumulation of applications with Caste Scrutiny Committees. CSCs were not equipped with adequate number of competent human resources or infrastructure such as space, furniture and other office equipments to handle the increased number of claims As a result, thousands of applications received by each CSC remained unprocessed for periods ranging from a few months to several years, while ideally each application should only take about a fortnight to process. Many "agents" emerged in the system who ensured quick delivery of caste validity certificates on payment of commissions, which are meant to be issued free of cost.

In August 2012 Dr. Babasaheb Ambedkar Research and Training Institute (BARTI) Pune, an autonomous institute under the Department of Social Justice and Special Assistance, Government of Maharashtra, took charge of coordination of caste validation process in Maharashtra. BARTI decided to focus on the issue of pending applications first while also solving for others along the way. Series of Caste Validity Distribution Camps were organized throughout the state where all caste validity certificates that were ready for distribution with the CSCs, were distributed to the applicants. To streamline the work of CSCs, all CSCs were provided with basic furniture and office equipments such as computers, printers, stationary, etc. along with needed manpower. Data on the status of all pending and processed applications was collected from CSCs and the lists were published on a dedicated website. To support the applicants who were not savvy with the use of internet, a helpline was started which worked 16 hours a day and provided support to applicants in knowing the status of their applications. To check the malpractices such as the issue of forged caste validity certificates High Security Paper was introduced with the help of the Government Photozinco Press.

At each stage transparency was brought into the system. It substantiates the point that transparency is fundamental to bring good governance. Providing timely and free access to information is essential for bringing transparency. Another important factor of good governance that emerges here is that to practice good governance in systems such as this, it is important that the best interests of various disadvantaged groups are taken into account and that the needs of the most vulnerable in society are kept in mind during decision-making and implementation.

Gurulingappa G. Koppa in his paper looks at transparency and governance from the perspective of food security. He points out that food governance is an increasingly difficult task in a globalised world. The capacity of single households to ensure an adequate supply of food for its members is affected by developments from local to global levels. The paper presents a framework and a set of strategies for establishing open, democratic and transparent governance processes that lay the foundation for the policies with the overall goal of building a sustainable, healthy and just food system. Governance needs to consider not only how food is produced but also how it is processed, distributed, and consumed.

It is pointed out that food governance has become a complex web of often overlapping or contradictory formal policies and regulations, complicated by unwritten rules and practices that are not subject to political oversight. Koppa argues that although the productivist discourse is still very much with us, it is increasingly evident that the problem is not so much a technical one of producing more food as a political one of ensuring that food is available to those who need it. Moreover, we have a better idea of who are most in need. Majority of the hungry are poor rural food producers. Thus, fighting hunger in the developing world has to begin with supporting small holder food producers' capacity to feed their own families. At the same time, burgeoning problems of obesity and unsafe food are sensitising public opinion and policy-makers to the fact that there are problems with the food system in the North as well as in the South. Climate change and the energy crisis have shown that a food system based on the intensive use of petrol products and chemicals is not sustainable.

It is argued in the paper that the framework that gives direction to the planning and development of a process should be grounded in a vision for a sustainable, healthy, and just food system that provides adequate, healthy, acceptable, and safe food for all. We need food system that respects ecosystems as well as the people, animals, and organisms that depend on them. The pursuit of the vision of a sustainable, healthy, and just food enabling policy environment requires institutions and organizing structures that facilitate public participation in shaping policies, norms, values, and rules. Governance for food security should be put into relation with the right to food, while good governance as a general concept must be analyzed in relation to human rights based approach, i.e. beyond the right to food, and include all civil, political, social, economic and cultural rights.

To reach this development objective, governments should strive for enhanced access to food through transfers, safety nets and other social programmes on the one hand, and investment in development, in particular in support of agriculture and rural development, on the other. Good governance for food security constitutes the enabling environment that allows the two tracks to become effective. According to Koppa there should be more focus on the context and on actors and stakeholders in governance for food security. It is suggested to replace efficiency and effectiveness with professionalism, quality and evidence-based decision; to replace the principle of equality and fairness with gender equity and to add empowerment.

The paper by Nirmita Mehrotra discusses the role of transparency and disclosure in disaster management. The complex nature of disasters has led to recognition that risk reduction through increased resilience, which requires a strategy that is inter-disciplinary. True inter-disciplinarity only occurs where a number of separate disciplines surrender their own concepts and goals, and collectively move themselves by reference to a common set of strategic concepts and goals.

Mehrotra surveys the theoretical literature on the idea of resilience, which refers to the ability of an entity or system to 'recover from position elastically' following a disturbance or disruption of some kind. There are three key dimensions that differentiate resilience from traditional notions of disaster planning and recovery. First, the emphasis is on hazard mitigation and preparedness rather than post-disaster management. Second, there has been a widening of the emergency planning agenda to embrace security challenges in addition to natural hazards and technological accidents. The third dimension concerns the role of institutional resilience to protect key infrastructural systems.

She points out that disaster risks are actually driven by a number of unresolved, underlying causes such as vulnerable rural livelihoods, poverty, poor urban governance, lack of good governance, declining ecosystem services, and power inequality, which eventually lead to an uneven distribution of risk both socially and spatially, thereby increasing the risks faced by the poor and further amplifying poverty. In aftermath of Gujarat Earthquake, the persistent case of deliberate vulnerabilities pointed to lack of state's capacity to monitor and regulate housing construction. There have been perennial problems caused by low quality building material, deliberate non-compliance with building codes, regulations and safety norms, which has transformed the regions seismic hazard into disaster of catastrophic proportion. For example — the main earthquake affected parts of Ahmedabad was its affluent areas. Pointedly the root cause of enormous disaster in Gujarat was found to be lacuna in Institutional Framework. The Gujarat Earthquake of 2001 introduced local community as a vital component of successful disaster mitigation processes.

Mehrotra gives the example of the model of community participation in the direct leadership of the Surat Municipal Corporation that emerged in the aftermath of the outbreak of plague epidemics in the city of Surat in 1994. In face of the unprecedented crisis a seven-point action plan was launched for restoring normalcy at the earliest in collaboration with the non-governmental agencies, civil society, and the private sector working together. This model of urban management initiated changes at local level turned the city into second cleanliest city without any external financial or technical support.

Inter-organizational networks in emergencies can play an important role in facilitating the flow of information across organizational boundaries. In this context, local actors and agents from non-governmental organization play significant roles. Local actors have belongingness with the place and community, familiar with existing hazards, type of emergency needs and community in their neighbourhood, which require immediate support. They also help prioritization of immediate needs of the community and its specific members for example the people with disability, chronic illness or pregnant ladies.

According to Mehrotra transparency and disclosure can play a significant role in inducing flexible institutional structures, where decision-making can be actually decentralized at different levels with outcome oriented planning. Information revolution through means of mass communication like Twitter and Facebook has capacity to generate collective actions, which could be positively utilized to enhance Institutional resilience through collaborative and network of formal, informal organization. Transparency and disclosure can equip organization with a management system to support learning and facilitate continuous growth and development, as well as flexibility when managing diversity. She concludes by saying that transparency and disclosure has untapped potential as a means of Institutional learning and sharing of learning on a wider platforms for building networks of collective actions, rather than confining it as an accountability monitoring instrument for checking integrity of each other.

Sheetal Kapoor's paper examines transparency and disclosure in context of consumer protection. Consumers today want value for money, a product or service that would meet reasonable expectations, is safe in use and there is full disclosure of the product specification. These expectations are termed as 'Consumer Rights'. Indian Government has taken initiative to pass progressive legislation to safeguard the interests of the consumers. The most important milestone in Consumer Movement in the country has been the enactment of the Consumer Protection Act, 1986. The paper gives details of various provisions of the Consumer Protection Act 1986. The various kinds of unfair trade practices are highlighted. She points out that many rural consumers are illiterate and are easily vulnerable to the unscrupulous and unethical marketing practices of the greedy marketers.

The Act provides effective, people oriented, broad-based and efficient remedy to consumers against unfair dealings and exploitation. The Act postulates establishment of advisory and adjudicatory bodies to safeguard the interests of consumers. The Advisory structure is in the form of Consumer Protection Councils at Centre, State and District levels. The author traces the progress of implementation of the Act. It is pointed out that 80,014 cases were registered since inception up to 6-3-2013 with the National Commission, out of which 86.55 per cent cases were disposed of. In case of State Commission 6,00,097 cases were registered since inception up to March 2013 and 84.13 per cent cases were disposed of. A staggering number of 32.42,324 cases were registered throughout the District Consumer Forums in the country and 92.35 per cent cases were disposed.

In the end the paper gives some suggestions to improve the effectiveness of the Consumer Protection Act. The author pleads for a vibrant consumer movement, that is much closer to the people and is pro-poor, pro-women and pro-rural.

Part-4 contains three papers on transparency, disclosure and human rights. Shri Ram Arun starts by stating that privacy and transparency are tools of public good essential for the proper functioning of a democratic society, and both are defenses against abuses of power. The traditional expression of the relationship between privacy and transparency as a balancing act between the rights of the individual and the interests of the community is a false dichotomy that has led to a great deal of confusion in the operation of RTI laws. Elaborating the concept of human rights the author states that broadly speaking the Human Rights can be categorised as—(1) rights and freedoms to which all humans are entitled, (2) economic development, (3) social progress, and (4) achieving world peace. This concept he points out is enshrined in almost all the religions of the world.

The author traces the origin of modern concept of human rights to the *Magna Carta* issued by King John of England on 15 June 1215 to proclaim certain rights pertaining to freedom, respect of certain legal procedures, and accepted that his will could be bound by the law. It explicitly protected certain rights of the King's subjects, whether free or fettered, and implicitly supported what became the writ of *habeas corpus* allowing appeal against unlawful imprisonment. The modern concept of human rights developed in the aftermath of the World War II culminating in the signing of the Universal Declaration of Human Rights by the United Nations General Assembly in 1948. It recognized that all human beings are born free and equal in dignity and rights.

The author says that the scope of Human Rights is very large. The First-generation human rights are covered by the Universal

Declaration of Human Rights. They deal essentially with liberty and participation in political life and include, among other things, freedom of speech, the right to a fair trial, freedom of religion, and voting rights. Second-generation human rights are related to equality and began to be recognized by governments after World War I. They are fundamentally social, economic and cultural in nature. Secondary rights would include a right to be employed, rights to housing and health care, as well as social security and unemployment benefits. They were also covered by the Universal Declaration of Human Rights, and further embodied in Articles 22 to 27 of the Universal Declaration, and the International Covenant on Economic, Social, and Cultural Rights. Third-generation human rights are those rights that go beyond the mere civil and social, as expressed in many progressive documents of international law. The term "third-generation human rights" remains largely unofficial, and thus houses an extremely broad spectrum of rights. A number of international organizations have been established for safeguarding Human Rights.

Shri Ram Arun traces the various steps taken in India since Independence for ensuring protection of Human Rights of Indian citizens in general and certain groups like women, children, scheduled castes and scheduled tribes in particular. He goes on to elaborate the shortcomings in the criminal justice system in the country in ensuring Human Rights due to lack of transparency and disclosures at the level of various agencies like police and courts, which results in violation of Human Rights. These include: non-Registration of cases, minimisation and concealment of investigation of cases; lack of prosecution of accused and also of the State; infringement of their rights main problems faced by the under trials, etc.

According to the author, public access to and understanding of national law is crucial to any functioning democracy. In this context he refers to website *Indian Kanoon* launched in January 2008 by Sushant Sinha. The website indexes judgements from the Supreme Court, the High Courts and various tribunals and links them to the relevant statutes. Importantly, it provides all these tools free of charge.

Arun closes his paper by asserting the need of transparency and disclosure as the guiding principles of every Government for healthy administration, which will go a long way in ensuring the protection of Human Rights. Message should go to all that anybody who dares to violate this would not go unnoticed and unpunished. Human Rights violations could be ensured to a great extent if the Governments and the departments concerned make easy disclosure of information to the public and transparency and disclosure is ensured at every level. Those failing to ensure should be taken to task so that it becomes a lesson for other defaulters.

Mridul Srivastava in her paper discusses the features and merits of the formal and informal judicial systems. She first looks at the requirements of a just and transparent system of legal redress. The public has a right to expect the justice system to be swift and sure. According to her proper and timely disclosure is the lynchpin of criminal justice process. It provides the accused with knowledge of the case the prosecution proposes to make against them and so is the foundation of a fair trial. Timely disclosure minimises delay and supports the effective use of public resources. It fosters early pleas of guilty, founds negotiation and reduces wasting of resources. Technology has a critical role to play in delivering efficient criminal justice. Only when armed with the right information and given the chance to observe how the system works in practice can the public hold the criminal justice system to account. Accountability on the part of executive and judiciary is the most desired task in the criminal justice system. It is clear that our justice system must be strengthened by making it transparent, timely and balanced.

The formal legal systems being opaque, slow and costly fail to ensure justice to the poor. Hence, the poor prefer the informal legal systems to settle their disputes. The author explains the features of the informal legal system followed by tribals in the state of Madhya Pradesh. During the field visits, she found that tribal *panchayats* are far better in some areas in comparison of our formal justice system. Baiga and Gond people do not believe in formal justice system and do not at all want to refer their cases to police. Tribal people still strongly believe in tribal *panchayat* system. In more than 99 per cent of disputes, Baiga / Gond / Sahariya / Bhil / Bharia people do not approach police. People expressed overall satisfaction with the way tribal *panchayat* system is handling cases. People prefer the tribal *panchayat* system as the disputes are solved at village level and the dignity of both parties is maintained. Tribal Panchayat system is more easily accessible, resolves disputes in lesser time as compared to formal justice system. Thus, Tribal Panchayat system is better suited for tribal people. Women also feel that Tribal Panchayat system is better for them as they can easily approach it and their voice is heard. On the other hand, the negative points of the system are that the *panchayats* don't take proactive role when outsiders are cutting trees from jungle, spend money in the party, due to heavy fine the poor become more poor, interested parties including judges are in the direct link that can affect the decision. To pay the fine people might have to sell their lands, ornaments and need to borrow money from the money lenders.

The author concludes by saying that the informal norms evolve through social interaction and reflect customs and accepted behaviour within a particular group or community. The normative framework has the capacity to both protect and defend the interests of the poor, or to perpetuate injustices and inequities. A proper framework has to be evolved to engage with the informal justice systems while protecting the interests of the poor.

The last paper in the volume by Suchismita deals with international standards and local practices with respect to transparency, disclosure and human rights. United Nations at its very inception in 1946 recognised that "*Freedom of Information is a fundamental human right and the touchstone for all freedoms to which the United Nations is consecrated.*" Until and unless we have full information from the government it is difficult to realise other rights. The regime of secrecy needs to be replaced by the regime of transparency to ensure human rights to all.

Suchismita points out that the Right to information Act was first passed by Sweden in 1766. They granted public access to government documents and it became integral to the Swedish Constitution. This practice then gradually spread across the world. India passed its Right to Information Law in 15th June, 2005 and it came into effect on 12th October 2005. Right to Information Act is a tool for transparency and disclosure given to us by the state as a matter of right. In her view our democracy is made stronger by the presence of such an Act as now the citizens can keep a check on performance of the government. By not disclosing information to the citizens the government actually violates the right to participation, which is a major violation of right in a participatory democracy.

Suchismita points out that though Indian citizens have been given a legal right to information through the RTI Act 2005, several challenges remain in its effective use for ensuring transparency and disclosure in government's functioning. The delay in receiving information often violates the basic human rights of a person. The information that is given through RTI is usually in a very official language which is difficult for a person to decipher. To exclude more and more people from the purview of RTI it is seen that the application process to apply for RTI is itself made very difficult and expensive. Difficult process also discourages use of RTI. The overall attitude of the government is usually against transparency so it is much difficult for the civil society to fight against the backlash of this anti-corruption law. The pendency rate in the state as well as in the central commissions has been high. The RTI Act does not have a strong compliance mechanism to bring the law breakers to justice. In the recent times it is seen that a number of RTI activists have been killed or harassed because they dare to seek questions about the governance of the country and expose corruption.

According to the author the Right to Information Law has its own challenges, but it is a potentially powerful weapon for ensuring human rights. The basic human rights can only be successfully accomplished if we have a transparent and free flowing information system. In order to ensure the convolution we need to critically analyse the international standards and the local illustration of human right situation. Human Rights are now interpreted in a wider way and include among others the Right to Water, Right to Adequate Food, Right to Health, Right to Adequate Housing, Right to Education, etc.

Right to Information has opened up a new era of progressive democracy in our country, but to ensure human rights through transparent governance, it is not enough. To address the rights of the minorities, disadvantaged, women and prisoners we have to work on all systems of transparency to preserve their human rights. Under the RTI Act, it is the obligation of the public authority to proactively provide all information about the organization and its functioning and publish all relevant facts while formulating important policies or announcing the decisions which affect public. But these provisions are hardly implemented in reality.

The paper writer says that we should try to follow the best international practices for disclosing information proactively. She gives a number of suggestions for making information available to people in a comprehensible and timely manner at an affordable cost. The information provided should be easily findable. The information which are crucial and ensures human rights should be stored in such places which could be accessed easily without much problem. The information which is published should comprehensible and should be delivered in a manner which is well understood by concerned people and beneficiaries. The information needs to be updated to be of any use to the citizens. The information which are proactively disclosed should be by principle and by law done free of cost. The public authorities should be very particular to disseminate the information in local languages and in multiple languages which are prevalent in those areas so that maximum number of people can take advantage of the information.

According to her the biggest drawback of the Right to Information Act in India is that there is no agency to check the compliance of proactive disclosure as stated in 4 (b). In most of the countries there is a compliance mechanism to monitor the implementation of proactive disclosure. The lacking of such a provision makes the clause of proactive disclosure much week in nature.

The main lessons which emerge from the papers in this volume may be summed up as follows:

1. Participatory democracy is essential for ensuring that the fruits of development reach the common man.
2. An enlightened citizenry is essential for the functioning of the democratic government. This requires that the citizens have free and unrestrained access to information regarding public authorities.
3. The Right to Information is ingrained in our Constitution in the form of right of free expression.
4. This requires transparency in the functioning of public bodies and proactive disclosure of information on their part. Transparency and disclosures are thus essential for good governance.
5. Transparency is essential condition for promoting development and ensuring Human Rights to all citizens without discrimination of any kind.
6. The Right to Information Act 1985 is a major step in making government open and transparent. However, the full potential of the Act has not been realized due to a number of problems related to information infrastructure, widespread illiteracy of the people and lack of attitudinal change on the part of the bureaucracy.
7. Transparency is required for checking corruption in public life, but merely establishing right to information is not sufficient as the information is often misused and can give rise to new forms of corruption.

8. Information and Communication Technology (ICT) is an important tool of ensuring transparency. It needs to be strengthened to enable people to make its wide use. Necessary checks need to put in place.
9. We need to adopt the best international practices to ensure transparency and disclosure. The success stories from different parts of the country should be publicized so that they are adopted widely.
10. Social justice can be ensured only when various types of inequalities prevalent in our society are removed and the problems of poverty, unemployment and illiteracy are overcome.

To conclude, in recent years the issue of good governance has emerged as a central focus in the development discourse the world over including India. Movements have spawned for ensuring transparency in the working of public institutions and improving governance quality by making it people friendly. The citizens are now perceived as participants in government process with a legal right to all public information. This puts an obligation on the state to allow access of all public information to its citizens. International experience shows that transparency is positively and significantly correlated with many aspects of governance, including effectiveness, control of corruption, accountability, rule of law and bureaucratic efficiency and contributes to improvement in human development indicators. The shift towards a transparent and participatory government requires collaborative efforts on the part of the political leadership, bureaucracy and the civil society. It is hoped that the papers included in this volume will help in promoting awareness and debate in this direction.

PART-1
Transparency, Disclosure, Governance and Development

2

Transparency, Right to Information and Development

Concept and Experiences

Ajit Kumar Singh

Introduction

During the last three decades or so the issue of good governance has emerged as a central focus in the development discourse. This follows the realisation that the huge sums being spent by the governments in the developing countries on various development programmes are not reflected in the expected outcomes in terms of eradication of poverty and improvement in the quality of life of the people. Corruption prevailing at various levels of governments in the developing countries is perceived as a major factor acting a deterrent to faster and equitable development. Lack of transparency in government decision-making and actions is identified as the main reason for corruption and mal-governance. Movements have spawned the world over in recent decades for ensuring transparency in the working of public institutions and improving governance quality by making it people friendly.

In this paper we have examined the concept of good governance and its inter-relationship with transparency and right to information. We have first discussed the emerging trends towards open governments and the role of international agencies in promoting the same. We then discuss the concept of good governance and its linkage with transparency and right to information. The impact of good governance on development and equity is then examined. Various initiatives towards open government across the globe are highlighted.

Movement for Good Governance

The movement for good governance started in the eighties and picked up in the nineties as it was realised that poor government is retarding progress towards economic development and poverty reduction. The movement towards good governance and openness in the functioning of government agencies was promoted by the efforts of the international donor agencies like the World Bank, IMF, DFID and Agency for International Development (see *Saladin*). The World Bank came out with its report on Development and Governance in 1992 (World Bank, 1992). The report has been influential in shaping the thinking and programmes for governance reform. The IMF in its structural reform programmes has been emphasizing on good fiscal management. The Transparency International, a voluntary organisation, came into existence in 1993. It is campaigning for transparency in the working of public institutions. It has been publishing corruption index for a large number of countries.

The concepts of *integrity, transparency* and *accountability* have been identified by the UN countries, collectively and individually, as part of the founding principles of public administration (Armstrong, 2005). The United Nations Convention Against Corruption is the first legally binding global instrument related to corruption.

Within the country the civil society movements also started putting pressure on the government for greater transparency in its functioning. The *Jan Sunwai* and *Apna Paisa Apna Hisab* movements are example of the same (see Roy and Dey; Neelabh Mishra). More recently, Anna Hazare and Kejriwal are leading people's movement against corruption and pleading for a strong Lok Pal Act, which will serve as a watch dog for keeping corruption in check and punish the guilty. The media has been forcefully focussing on exposure of corruption in government.

Within the political and government circles the issues of corruption and need of integrity in public life are being hotly debated. The 73rd Constitutional Amendment provides for social audit of the working of the Gram Panchayats. After a prolonged public debate and pressures the Government of India adopted the Right to Information Act in 2005, which is a landmark in the movement towards transparency in government.

The national and state level Human Development Reports have emphasised the need of good governance for attaining human development targets. Tenth Five Year Plan devoted a full chapter to Governance and Implementation. The Twelfth Five Year Plan in the chapter on Governance re-iterated:

> "Good governance is increasingly viewed as an essential element of any well-functioning society. It ensures effective use of resources and deliverance of services to citizens and also provides social legitimacy to the system. Rising income levels in a democracy also bring with them rising expectations and a demand for good governance, both at the level of the Centre and the States, and also lower down in the third tier of government." (*Twelfth Five Year Plan*, Vol. I, p. 286).

What is Good Governance

According to the World Bank Report on Governance and Development (World Bank, 1992) governance "is the manner in which power is exercised in the management of a country's economic and social resources for development." The report defined three aspects of governance: (i) the form of political regime; (ii) the process by which authority is exercised in the management of a country's resources; and (iii) the capacity of governments to design, formulate and implement policies and discharge functions.

People have different notions of what is good governance. However, it is generally agreed that good governance has to be participatory, responsive, non-discriminatory, transparent and efficient. The Tenth Plan document sums up the principles of good governance in the following words:

> "The universally accepted features of good governance are the exercise of legitimate political power; and formulation and implementation of policies and programmes that are equitable, transparent, non-discriminatory, socially sensitive, participatory, and above all accountable to the people at large. There could however be aspects of governance that are contextually driven and geared to address the local concerns." (*Tenth Five Year Plan*, p. 177)

The World Bank has identified the following elements of good administration:

(i) Political accountability.

(ii) An established legal framework based on the rule of law and independence of judiciary to protect human rights, secure social justice and guard against exploitation and abuse of power.

(iii) Bureaucratic accountability ensuring a system to monitor and control the performance of government offices and officials in relation to quality of service, inefficiency and abuse of discretionary powers. The related determinants include openness and transparency in administration.

(iv) Freedom of information and expression needed for formulation of public policies, decision-making, monitoring and evaluation of government performance. It also includes independent analysis of information by the professional bodies, including the universities and others vital for establishment of a civil society.

(v) Cooperation between administration and civil society organisations is also essential.

As mentioned above the United Nations above recognises integrity, transparency and accountability as the three cornerstones of good governance (Armstrong, 2005). The UN defines the three terms in the following words:

> "*Integrity* refers to "honesty" or "trustworthiness" in the discharge of official duties, serving as an antithesis to "corruption" or "the abuse of office." *Transparency* refers to unfettered access by the public to timely and reliable information on decisions and performance in the public sector. *Accountability* refers to the obligation on the part of public officials to report on the usage of public resources and answerability for failing to meet stated performance objectives."

The report further underlines the inter-dependence of the three principles as follows:

> "*Integrity*, by requiring that public interest be paramount, provides the basis for transparency and accountability. *Transparency* without accountability becomes meaningless

> and makes a mockery of sound public administration. *Accountability* depends on transparency or having the necessary information. And transparency and accountability without integrity may not end up serving the public interest."

Transparency and Open Government Data Regime

Transparency is essential to ensure participatory and accountable government. This is possible only when the members of the public have access to the information held by public authorities (Wright *et al.* 2010). The movement towards Open Government Data (OGD) systems is as essential for ensuring transparency in government functioning and accountability of its actions. Open data regime require proactive role of government organisations and departments to make all relevant data available at all stages of policy formulation and implementation. More and more countries are expressing the commitment to the goal of OGD.

According to Open Government Data India Study the benefits of open government data include the following:

> "First, it will benefit government itself, by reducing the burden of locating information — both for internal use, as well as for responding to Right to Information (RTI) requests — and streamlining its own information gathering and processing procedures. It will expose incorrect and outdated data, which the government itself is often not in an easy position to detect. It will help citizens; the variety of CSOs in India currently working, despite difficulties, with government data — everything from electoral candidate data and legislations to municipal body phone numbers and public transport route information — is testament to this. Most importantly, OGD can be seen as a step in delivering the promises of the Right to Information (RTI) Act, and a step towards greater transparency and, importantly, accountability." (Wright *et al.* 2010, p. 4).

The Government of India has committed itself to make publicly available much of its data. Right to Information (RTI) Act was passed, after a prolonged campaign, in 2005. In its Tenth Five Year Plan (2002-2007) GoI announced its intention for India to become a 'SMART'

(Simple, Moral, Accountable, Responsible and Transparent) state. The National Knowledge Commission recommended using ICT for putting maximum possible data on the web. This has led to many e-governance initiatives. Much remains to be done in this field in terms of easy public access to uptodate, understandable and usable data (Wright *et al.* 2010).

Shift in Citizen-State Relationship

This shift from secrecy to transparency in government functioning involves a fundamental shift in the citizen-state relationship. As the authors of the report Open Government India observe:

> "This shift from a default of secrecy to transparency is a very important one. It not only indicates a concrete duty on the state to provide information as per the law, but can also be seen as an indication of a shift in the very conceptualization of the body politic. Formerly passive subjects of a state are re-imagined as active citizens with a legitimate interest in such information, and thus having an inherent right to it." (Wright *et al.* 2010, p. 14).

The citizens are thus perceived as participants in government process with a legal right to all public information. In fact right to information follows from the right of free speech. This puts an obligation on the state to allow access of all public information to its citizens. This is explicitly acknowledged in the Right to Information Act itself. Section 4 of the Act states: 'It shall be a constant endeavour of every public authority to take steps ... to provide as much information *suo motu* to the public at regular intervals through various means of communications, including Internet, so that the public have minimum resort to the use of this Act to obtain information.'

Governance, Transparency and Development

Several studies have examined the empirical relationship between good governance and better development outcomes. The Global Integrity and Transparency International has been publishing integrity and corruption index for countries for many years. These indicators show that governance quality varies greatly across regions and that poor governance continues to be an obstacle to poverty reduction and social development in many countries.

Cross-country studies of governance trends finds that transparency is positively and significantly correlated with many aspects of governance, including effectiveness, control of corruption, accountability, rule of law and bureaucratic efficiency. Studies also show that transparency is highly significant in explaining variation in human development indicators (including life expectancy, female literacy, and child immunization) across countries.

Twelfth Five Year Plan underlines the importance of good governance for ensuring expected outcomes from plan outlays in the following words:

> "Good governance is critical to translating plan outlays into significant outcomes on the ground. It is critical because without good governance, resources that are allocated are not efficiently utilised; management of public service delivery is sub-optimal; efficiency of public expenditure is affected; and finally, it impacts the effective management of natural resources which are sovereign wealth under sovereign ownership." (Twelfth Five Year Plan, p. 286).

According to the International Monetary Fund (IMF), every developing country that is committed to gaining the confidence of the international financial markets must dedicate itself to good governance. Good governance fosters a path for strong and stable economic development. Poor governance could adversely affect private market confidence and reduce private capital inflows and investment, retarding economic growth in developing countries (*Saladin*).

We will now discuss the links between transparency, right to information and development outcomes.

Transparency and Corruption

Corruption has been a persistent problem that has affected many, if not all, nations, be they emerging economies in Latin America, Asia and Africa, or the industrial countries of Europe and North America. Corruption has been identified as the major barrier to sustainable economic growth and development (*Saladin*).

Corruption adversely affects economic growth in various ways (see Earle and Scott 2010). Corruption in construction raises cost and lowers quality of infrastructure (Armstrong, 2005). Corruption promotes inefficiencies and reduces competition. Corruption can result in loss of government revenue, costs for businesses, missed opportunities for non-corrupt businesses, distortion of standards of merit, erosion of respect for the rule of law, higher costs and lower quality of infrastructure and mistrust of government (Everett *et al.* 2007). Khan (2006) notes that corruption disrupts the transparency of markets, increases transaction costs and creates uncertainty for investors. Cross country statistical studies show that reduction in the level of corruption has a positive impact on investment rate and GDP growth rate (Mauro 1998; Weiss 2008).

Corrupt practices impact on levels of poverty in various ways. Diversion of public funds meant for the poor undermines equitable economic development (Brown, 2007). Corruption contributes to income inequality through impacts on budgetary revenues and expenditure (Gupta *et al.* 1998). Wei notes that poor people are less able to pay bribes, and have much less political power to deal with corrupt bureaucrats (Wei 1999). The World Bank suggests that direct measures to reduce corruption in service delivery in Bulgaria and the state of Orissa in India have helped to improve access and efficiency.

The human cost of corruption is enormous. To quote a UN Report:

> "The devastating effects of the lack of integrity, transparency and accountability—leading to corruption and misconduct—cannot be underestimated. Unethical practices, bribery, and fraud have a very real human cost—whether it be in the lives and health of people who are robbed of quality health care and medicines or children who are not properly educated. The financial and even public safety costs of corruption are astounding. A lack of public trust undermines and even destroys political stability. And corruption remains the single most significant obstacle to achieving the MDGs." (Armstrong, 2005, p. 9)

Corruption is encouraged by the complex governmental regulations, discretionary powers and lack of transparency in government functioning. Fighting corruption is, therefore, of paramount importance for attaining faster and inclusive growth. It has to be at the centre of all governance reforms. A strong legal and institutional system has to be put in place to make corruption a high risk and low gain activity.

Transparency in Budget Making and Public Expenditures

To ensure intended outcomes of public spending transparency in budget making process and public expenditures is most essential. As a report of the Open Society Foundation observes:

> "Governments raise and spend public funds to meet public needs. To do this, they must make good policy choices, execute these effectively and be accountable for their decisions and actions. This is more likely to happen in budget systems that are transparent, i.e. those in which the government provides the public with comprehensive, timely, accurate and useful information. As a growing evidence base shows, open budget systems can enhance the credibility of policy choices, increase the effectiveness of policy interventions, limit corrupt and wasteful spending and facilitate access to international financial markets."
>
> (Open Society Foundation, 2011, p. 10)

A World Bank report observes that:

> "Effective Participatory Financial Management (PFM) systems are crucial to countries making progress in reducing poverty... partner countries increasingly recognize that problems in sectors such as health, education, and agriculture can have common origins in weak PFM. ... progress toward achieving the Millennium Development Goals (MDGs) has given additional urgency to improving PFM as an enabling condition for poverty reduction." (World Bank, 2004, p. 1).

Recent research has shown that greater access to public information together with effective public engagement can help reduce corruption and enhance socio-economic development (Open Society Foundation, 2011, p. 12). Greater public participation in budget making would help in determining budget priorities and public spending according to the need of the people. Tracking public expenditure by the people would further help in improving the quality and effectiveness of government spending and check, misuse and diversion of public funds.

In recent years several governments have taken to make budgetary processes more participative and transparent (see Open Society Foundation, 2011, chapter 3). In India, the Ministry of Finance holds pre-budget consultations with various interest groups and NGOs. The finance ministries in Kenya and Uganda have for many years conducted similar consultations on citizen budget priorities at the beginning of the budget drafting process. In South Africa the government has launched an initiative through which the public were invited to give tips on how to spend the country's money. Several countries publish or broadcast legislature budget deliberations on television. In the past few years, a number of countries have started to publish detailed transcripts of legislature budget debates.

Tanzania has established a review process through which civil society organisations regularly contribute reports and analyses. In the Czech Republic and the Philippines the public are invited to give testimony on the budgets of a number of key administrative units. In South Africa, the Finance Committee and sector committees regularly invite a range of non-governmental actors to testify in budget hearings.

Several countries are encouraging people participation in government audit. The South Korean Citizens' Audit Request System allows citizens to request that the supreme audit institution conduct audits of public agencies suspected of corruption or legal transgressions. In Philippines audit teams include employees of the audit institution and representatives of non-governmental organisations. The supreme audit institutions in the US and the UK maintain 'fraud hotlines' through which the public can report suspected malfeasance in the use of public funds.

Several municipal bodies across the world have adopted participatory budgeting practices that allocate resources to programmes identified with the direct involvement of citizens and civil society groups. The best-known example is Porto Alegre Municipality in Brazil, but similar participatory budgeting processes have been adopted in over 100 cities in Brazil, and in a number of countries around the world. The social audit system adopted in the PRI in India is another example of making local governments accountable to the people.

Transparency and Service Delivery

The public sector remains the main provider of social services like education, health and water services. The quality of these services affects the human development. Delivery of public services is the cutting edge where the common citizen comes face to face with the government. Massive and expanding public expenditure in these fields has not resulted in the desired outcomes as the quality of basic services remains very poor. Examples are poor infrastructure of government schools, missing teachers, dispensaries without medical supplies and trained personnel, non-functioning water supply systems, etc. The burden of poor public service mainly falls on the poor who do not have money or resources to obtain the services.

In these circumstances promoting greater transparency in delivery of public services and citizen participation in different stages of policy formulation and its implementation will lead to better use of public funds, greater responsiveness of service providers and improved service delivery. More importantly this will result in improved life of the poor and vulnerable sections of the society and contribute to the achievement of the the Millennium Development Goals (MDGs).

As the Tenth Plan document observes:

> "In a general sense, the ability to effectively target schemes/ programmes towards the most deserving depends critically upon the quality of governance. The better the levels of governance, the more precise can be the targeting. The corollary of this is that in the absence of acceptable levels of governance, it would be preferable to eschew targeted programmes in favour of more generally applicable schemes." (Tenth Plan, p. 180)

Role of Civil Society

In democratic societies civil society has an important role to improve accountability and governance. The individual citizens cannot do much to voice their grievances and expose wrong doings in public services. The CSOs are in a better position to monitor public expenditure and to make peoples' opinions heard on how public resources are used. However, the success of civil society organizations depends on free access to information on public expenditures. In the absence of transparency the CBOs cannot do much to act as watch dogs of public policies and expenditure. Another obstacle that the CBOs face in discharge of their duties is that of capability terms of resources and technical expertise.

The Open Society Foundation Report (2011) gives examples of several such initiatives in different countries. In countries like Uganda and Tanzania Education Public Expenditure Tracking Surveys (PETS) have been initiated. Kenya has introduced a system of medical stock-outs. Sweden provides right to information and government documents related to essential services to a very detailed level.

In Brazil, Cidade Democrática is an online platform that allows citizens, politicians, journalists and NGOs to collectively identify community problems and propose solutions. In Russia, TakTakTak, an initiative of Siberian journalists, works to connect citizens and to help them collaborate to solve social problems. The organisation's platform allows citizens to submit both problems and solutions. The project is intended to fill the gap between journalists, citizens, civil society.

In India, Praja, an NGO based in Bangalore, operates a similar platform to collect citizen input on civic issues of importance to them and to facilitate collaboration between citizens and government to develop solutions to these issues, and bring them to the attention of the proper authorities. Praja tracks the authorities' response to the complaints it raises by posting offline communication with government offices on its website. Praja's website tracks discussions, proposals, specific tasks and events related to specific issues. The organisation is also spearheading an open data project in Karnataka State.

The Accountability Initiative India collects economic and budgetary data through open government data sets as well as through official Right to Information requests. It then makes the information available online, where users can search for relevant information such as food subsidy information, education and health spending and water sanitation resources. The organisation also provides a 'How to Read the Budget' primer that describes the language used in government budget documents and the structure of the documents in order to facilitate better citizen understanding of these documents.

Kiirti is a platform where any individual or CSO can make a complaint or raise an issue by telephone or by using the website. That issue is then tracked, categorised, mapped and forwarded on to authorities. The issues can range from cleanliness to environment to sexual harassment. Kiirti enables aggregation of a number of issues in a single place so that they can be tracked and collaborated upon by anyone interested. It also maps and aggregates partner organisations that deal with civic complaints at the local level throughout India. It is a way to aggregate and integrate data from across platforms onto a single map that users can filter by location and topic.

Concluding Remarks

Integrity, transparency and accountability are universally accepted principles of public administration. Lack of transparency in government functioning breeds corruption, leads to misuse of resources, discourages investment, slows down growth rate, promotes inequality and affects the quality of life of the people especially the poor. Transparency is thus an essential requirement of good governance. Worldwide efforts are being made to make governments transparent and accountable by opening up maximum government data for public access.

The Government of India has committed itself to transparency by giving people the Right to Information. However, there are many challenges that must be addressed while moving towards opening up governmental data. The infrastructure of information gathering, processing and sharing remains inadequate. Though the ICT is expanding rapidly in the country, the computer literacy is still low and largely confined to the large urban centres. Power shortage especially in rural areas is a major bottleneck. The challenge of open government data is especially great in a country where still a large number of people are illiterate and computer penetration is very limited. New methods of providing people access to government data have to be adopted in these circumstances. Use of media, notice board displaying information, social audit have to be relied to a greater extent in these circumstances to ensure transparency and accountability particularly at the lower levels of administration.

The need of expansion of ICT infrastructure remains a matter of high priority. The issues of standardisation of formats and software for interoperability of data remain to be tackled. The issues of privacy are important. Steps for updating of government data and ensuring its correctness are also required.

The government has to follow a proactive approach to make available maximum possible information to the people including matters of appointment of public servants and judges, contracts for construction and mining, budgetary allocations, entitlement of the citizens to various services and benefits, etc.

Governments at different levels should promote a participatory form of decision-making in formulation of policies, budgetary processes and their implementation.

The capacity of CSOs to analyse government budgets and policies has to be improved through interaction with experts and technologists.

Most importantly, the movement towards a transparent and accountable system of governance requires a firm political commitment towards these goals. The old colonial ways of secrecy in government functioning have to give place to a new value system wedded to the objectives of an open and participatory form of governance.

REFERENCES

Armstrong, Elia (2005), *Integrity, Transparency and Accountability in Public Administration: Recent Trends, Regional and International Developments and Emerging Issues,* United Nations, Department of Economic and Social Affairs, New York.

Avila, Renata, Hazel Feigenblatt, Rebekah Heacock and Nathaniel Heller (2010), *Global Mapping of Technology for Transparency and Accountability: New Technologies,* Open Society Foundation, London.

Brown, Deryck (2007), *Foreword* to Sarah Bracking (ed.), *Corruption and Development: The Anti-Corruption Campaigns*, Palgrave Macmillan, Basingstoke.

Earle, Lucy and Zoë Scott (2010), *Assessing the Evidence of the Impact of Governance on Development Outcomes and Poverty Reduction: Issues Paper,* Governance and Social Development Resource Centre, University of Birmingham, Birmingham.

Gupta, Sanjeev, Hamid Davoodi and Rosa Alonso-Terme (1998), *Does Corruption Affect Income Inequality and Poverty?,* IMF Working Paper, Washington.

International Fund for Agricultural Development (1999), *Good Governance: An Overview,* IFAD, Rome.

Khan, Mushtaq (2007), *Governance, Economic Growth and Development since the 1960s.* United Nations Department of Economic and Social Affairs (DESA) Working Paper no. 54, New York.

Mauro, Paolo (1998),'Corruption: Causes, Consequences, and Agenda for Further Research', *Finance and Development,* March, IMF.

Mishra, Neelabh, *People's Right to Information Movement: Lessons from Rajasthan*, available at//data.undp.org.in/hdrc/dis-srs/Rajasthan/Right%20to%20Info.pdf.

Open Society Foundation (2005), *Opening Government: A Guide to Best Practice in Transparency, Accountability and Civic Engagement Across the Public Sector,* Open Society Foundation, London.

Planning Commission, *Tenth Five Year Plan*, Planning Commission, Goverrnment of India, New Delhi.

——, *Twelth Five Year Plan*, Planning Commission, Goverrnment of India, New Delhi.

Roy, Aruna and Nikhil Dey, *The Right to Information: Facilitating People's Participation and State Accountability,* MKSS Rajasthan *available at http://www.10iacc.org/download/workshops/cs54b.pdf*

Saladin Al-Jurf, *Good Governance and Transparency: Their Impact on Development.*

Wei, Shang-Jin (1999), *Corruption in Economic Development: Beneficial Grease, Minor Annoyance or Major Obstacle?*, World Bank Policy Research Working Paper No. 2048, Washington.

World Bank (1992), *Governance and Development,* The World Bank, Washington.

World Bank (2004), *World Development Report,* The World Bank, Washington.

Wright, Glover, Pranesh Prakash, Sunil Abraham and Nishant Shah (2010), *Open Government Data Study: India,* The Centre for Internet and Society, Open Society Foundation, London.

3

Transparency, Disclosure and Democracy

R.C. Tripathi

It is an opportune time to deliberate on issues of transparency and disclosure when our country and society are faced with crises in governance reflected in lack of probity, violation of constitutional conduct and decline in ethical norms. There is growing disenchantment all-around with political parties and institutions. The gulf between the rich and the poor is widening. Redress of public grievances is getting remote and remoter. The measures for social change and growth are barely scratching the surface. There are scams galore involving the high and the mighty, the rich and the feisty, making hapless masses wonder about the behaviour, conduct and commitment of powers that be towards the social, economic and political empowerment of the people at large. Promises on the eve of elections are usually superficial and vague only to muster votes and very seldom these get translated into reality.

It would be appropriate to begin with a quote from Machiavelli made for 'The Prince' in his book of the same title. According to him:

> "A prince will never lack for legitimate excuses to explain away his breaches of faith. Modern history will furnish innumerable examples of this behaviour, showing how the man succeeded best who knew best how to play fox. But it is a necessary part of this nature that you must conceal it carefully; you must be a great liar and hypocrite. Men are so simple of mind, and so much dominated by their immediate needs, that a deceitful man will always find plenty, who are ready to be deceived."

It was not relevant for Machiavelli whether his 'Prince' fulfilled promises made to his public, but in a democracy such conduct would be discovered sooner rather than later and would be duly addressed for corrective change through ballot in the course of elections. But such result or change is yet remote in our country. Much water in the Yamuna has flowed down denying the teeming millions what they aspired and looked for.

Rise of Democracy

During the first-half of the twentieth century, many tyrants and dictators lost their scepter and crown. The second part of that century was dominated by the concept of democracy, republicanism and democratic forms of government. 'Direct' democracy like a Greek city state was not feasible in the 20th century. Therefore, the 'representative' democracy became a common feature. There was a tendency to accept any country as a 'democratic' one, if that country so called itself. Democracy was largely understood as "the government of the people, by the people and for the people," as it was described by Abraham Lincoln in 1863. Like the 'serfs' in Greece, the USA of 1863 also did not include the non-whites and women in their very powerful democracy of those times. Hobbes, Locke, Rousseau, Bentham, John Stuart Mill and others provided venerable ideas about governance, sovereignty and representative forms of government. The US democracy has traversed a long distance since then.

People across the world opted and adopted democratic form of government as the best alternative having faith and belief that such a government would redeem masses and general public from oppressive autocracies and provide a stable, peaceful and prosperous society. The USA had sought representation in the British Parliament or else no taxation. Circumstances precipitated the War of Independence, eventually leading to liberation of the USA from the British colonial rule. The Americans did not adopt the parliamentary form of government of the British but opted for a Presidential form of government with a Congress having a House of Representatives and the Senate. The President is the chief executive and has a fixed term of four-years, unless removed by impeachment or death.

Vision of the Founding Fathers

Our country became Independent on the 15th of August, 1947. The

Constituent Assembly deliberated on diverse systems and adopted the parliamentary form of government largely based on the system as operating in Britain. It is argued that the system was adopted due to greater familiarity. This is a superficial argument. The Indian leaders, inspired by idealism, preferred parliamentary form which made the Executive, the Council of Ministers, collectively responsible to the House of People (Article 75) or the Legislative Assembly of the State (Article 164) believing that all future governments would be responsive and political parties would put public good superior to just holding on to power by any means.

The founding fathers gave to the people of India a democratic republic to secure social, economic and political justice combined with liberty of thought, expression, belief, faith and worship. The Constitution assured equality of status and opportunity and sought to promote among all Indians fraternity with dignity. All persons were equal before law and no discrimination was to be made on the basis of race, religion, caste, sex, place of birth, etc. Untouchability was abolished. The Constitution provided for affirmative action for the Scheduled Caste and Scheduled Tribes in the form of reservations with built-in probability to similarly provide for the Other Backward Castes so as to ensure social justice and empower the disadvantaged groups.

The spirit and philosophy of Mahatma Gandhi, Jawaharlal Nehru and B.R. Ambedkar deeply influenced the Constitution. Mahatma Gandhi was assassinated on 30th January, 1948 and did not live to see the document; but his spirit permeates the Constitution. Nehru firmly believed that political democracy without economic equality and good things of life to others had little purpose. Ambedkar was of firm opinion that in the absence of social democracy political democracy cannot last long. Liberty, equality and fraternity were not three separate items. These were integral part of the trinity and inseparably interdependent. Long ago, on the foundation ceremony of the Benares Hindu University (the erstwhile Central Hindu College founded by Mrs. Annie Besant) on 6th February, 1916, Gandhi spoke in unvarnished language about the bedecked Maharajah speaking about the poverty of India and decried the pomp and show and attributed all that as also their palaces coming out from the money of the agriculturists. The clarity of thought and expression of Gandhi found place in the subsequent land reforms; and his 'talisman' prescribing, when in doubt, to consider whether one's action was going to benefit the poorest of the poor or it was otherwise. What

Gandhi stated on the 27th January, 1948 for the Congress appears relevant and applicable to almost all the political parties: "The Congress has won political freedom, but it has yet to win economic freedom, social and moral freedom. These are harder than the political one if only because they are constructive, less exciting and not spectacular" and had gone on to suggest that the Congress could convert itself into a body dedicated to social service, exercising moral power over the government. Such moral power does not seem to appear in our country anywhere, under any political party or government.

Our founding fathers envisaged separation of powers between the executive, the legislature and the judiciary and created institutions like the Election Commission of India, the Comptroller and Auditor-General of India, the Public Service Commission for the Union and the States so as to provide for a sustainable democratic structure and buttress it for future growth. During the last over six decades, our democracy has faced crises yet come out each time more vibrant, unlike other countries that succumbed to martial law or dictatorial forms of government. There have been periodic and regular elections in India even the internal Emergency of 1975 was not able to reverse the trend; the emergency was withdrawn and general elections of 1977 followed, paving the way for the Janata Party Government.

India as a Democracy

There are some essential features of democracy and these should be found in any democracy. These essential features are:

1. Government chosen by the people,
2. Free and fair elections,
3. Freedom of expression,
4. Civil society, and
5. Rule of law.

It may be worthwhile to examine for a while how does our country fare on these parameters? We have in our country government chosen by people. Elections are regularly held and all efforts are made to ensure that the elections are free and fair and neither manipulated nor rigged. There is freedom of expression and all Indians are equal before the eyes of law. There is a vibrant civil society, with persons like Anna Hazare committed to the well-being of the general public. Thus, India is a thriving democracy on these parameters.

During the early seventies of the 20th century, the Supreme Court of India was faced with the question of amendments in the Constitution. Article 368 empowers the Parliament of India is to amend the Constitution. The question arose whether such power was unfettered, as was being assumed by the Parliament. In the Keshavanand Bharati *vs.* State of Kerala (1973) case, the Supreme Court delineated on the essential features of the Constitution and held these features as sacrosanct and these could neither be modified nor curtailed by any kind of amendment. The features enumerated were:

1. Rule of law,
2. Democracy,
3. Secularism,
4. Federation, and
5. Judicial Review.

Parliament and legislatures could only amend the Constitution observing sanctity and inviolability of the 'basic' features of our Constitution and, thus, it was obvious that the sovereign power rested in the Constitution as such. This was amply made clear in the Minerva Mills Ltd *vs.* Union of India (AIR 1980 SC 1789) wherein the Supreme Court declared clauses (4) and (5) inserted in the Article 368 giving the Parliament unfettered powers to amendment of the Constitution as invalid on the ground that these clauses sought to destroy and violate the essential features of the Constitution. The rule of law is firmly ingrained in the Indian society. This basic concept of the Constitution as the fountain-head of all powers must not be forgotten at any stage.

Nehru, the great visionary and idealist, laid the foundations of democracy deep and solid. Nehru would sit through the question-hour, debates and would ensure sittings of the Parliament for around one-hundred and eighty days year after year. During the sessions, touring outside the capital was abjured and Parliament was the sacred place for deliberating on issues relating to the welfare of the people. He laid the foundation of almost all the institutions we are proud of today. His commitment to democracy, its institutions, decentralization, community development, land reforms, agriculture, industrialization, harnessing of natural resources for irrigation and generation of power and so on was exemplary.

Nehru guided the destiny of the nation for seventeen long years during its formative period as the first Prime Minister of India. His sense of ethics, probity and high standards in public life were quite demanding. The expulsion of H.G. Mudgal in 1951 from the Provisional Parliament for asking questions and moving amendments in the Forward Contracts (Regulation) Bill in return for pecuniary benefits is an example. An Industries Minister of then Group 'C' State of Vindhya Pradesh was jailed for receiving Rupees ten thousand for renewing the contract of the Panna Diamond Mines. On an expose made by Feroze Gandhi in the Parliament, the then Finance Minister, T.T. Krishnamachari had to resign from the Council of Ministers for his indiscreet support to Hari Das Mundhra through the Life Insurance Corporation, a public sector organization. Nehru appointed the Santhanam Committee to go into the causes of increasing corruption and make recommendations for improving honesty and probity in public life.

His successor in office, Lal Bahadur Shashtri was scrupulously honest and had an overdraft of around four thousand with the Allahabad Bank when he passed away suddenly at Tashkent. Earlier, as a Rail Minister, Shastri had resigned for a train accident in Kerala owning up moral and constructive responsibility. Such cases of ethical behaviour and norms of public life became rare with the passage of time. One cannot even conceive of such behaviour in the present times.

Disclosure and Transparency

The concept of 'disclosure' and 'transparency' arise in situations when relevant facts are being concealed in the name of the Official Secrets or security of the State. Leaders of public, the parliamentarians, legislators, bureaucrats and all in civil society have to realize that straight and honest policy always pays in the long run. However, such is not the conduct of our leaders. "Disclosure" in simple dictionary meaning is making something known or public that was previously secret or private. Likewise, 'transparency' is a feature of making an event or a thing known. It is the quality of something, such as an excuse or a lie that allows somebody to see the truth. It makes situations easy and simple. In fact, transparency in conduct and behaviour would eliminate conjectures and wild goose chase by media. In the long run, it would improve credibility of the leaders among those whom they lead.

India has all the features of a vibrant democracy and on elaborate constitution, democratic institutions, regular elections, political parties, strong judiciary, a civil society and a vibrant print and electronic media. But we also have disparities and want. There is rampant crime against the weak, the poor, the child, women, old and the aged. The state has not been effective in controlling crimes and criminals. The criminal cases keep pending for years and for want of proper investigation and prosecution end in acquittals, bolstering up courage and haughtiness amongst the criminals. Many of these manage for themselves seats in legislatures and the Parliament.

Reflecting on this scenario, Vice-President Mohd Hamid Ansari, while delivering the Fourth B.R. Ambedkar Memorial lecture in December, 2012, had observed that 'our democracy is not the best.' He dealt at length the prevailing system of 'first-past-the-post', which does not promote the best candidate necessarily. A "Fifty-percent-plus-one" system would throw up better individuals, as also selection from below rather than from top of contesting candidates for elections. Big money has ousted sincere, honest and persons of average means from electoral contests. Gone are the days when 'conflict-of-interest' was enough for an elected member to withdraw from such a discussion.

Money, muscle and *mafia* seem to have penetrated public life with little chance for redemption. Occasionally, there are reports that media, both print and electronic, is manipulated by the high and the mighty. Legislations are conceived at the drop of a hat; the existing legislations are hardly being implemented with speed, urgency and deterrence required. The voice of the weak and the poor gets muffled. The Right to Information Act empowers for obtaining information. But the poor and the illiterate are too far removed from securing its benefits. The Consumer Protection courts are burdened with large number of cases and disposal stretches to years, much against the spirit of the Act. The courts in India are over-burdened with a large number of cases pending. The benefit of government sponsored programme is not making any impact. For example, education for all programme is not showing expected results. The malaise of absentee teachers is adversely impacting quality of education. Health care in primary health centres has a similar story to tell. The Public

Distribution System is reaching out insufficiently to provide for a healthy life and living. The system of governance has been replaced by knee-jerk reactions with little consideration for long term solutions.

Representatives are sent to the assembly or Parliament in the expectation of good governance, safety of life and property and appropriate opportunities to jobs for the young and the needy. If the governments fail to meet the limited expectations of people, disillusionment is bound to set in. In a situation of gross disillusionment, democracy will have tough times to save itself and the country. Our political masters have to see the writing on the wall. They have severe trust-deficit and very little time to deliver what they promise through their manifestoes, so nicely and attractively printed. Leadership and governance are critical. Our concern for these compels us to think that commitment (not merely lip-service) to public cause and service need to be deeply ingrained in the society and leaders in particular.

REFERENCES

Basu, D.D. (2008), *Introduction to the Constitution of India,* 20th Edition, Lexis Nexis Butterworths Wadhwa, Nagpur.

Chadha, Yogesh (1998), *Rediscovering Gandhi,* Arrow Books, London.

Kaul, M.L. and S.L. Shankdhar (1991), *Practice and Procedure of Parliament,* Fourth edition, Lok Sabha Secretariat, Parliament House, New Delhi.

Machiavelli, Niccolo (undated), *The Prince and the Discourses*, Carlton House, New York.

Naunihal Singh (2002), *Ethical Foundations of Freedoms: Economic and Political: A Law Beyond Law,* Anmol Publications Ltd., New Delhi.

Tichy, Noel M. and Andrew, R. McGill (2007), *Michigan Business School Guide to: The Ethical Challenge: How to Lead with Unyielding Integrity,* Wiley India Pvt. Ltd., New Delhi.

Tripathi, R.C. (2002), *Emergence of Second Chamber in India,* National Publishing House, New Delhi.

4

Transparency and Good Governance

Amita Prasad

Elements of Good Governance

UNDP defines governance in the following words: "Governance is the exercise of political, economic and administrative authority in the management of the country's affairs at all levels. It thus comprises mechanisms, processes and institutions. Governance thus encompasses government, private sector and the civil society organisations." Good governance is achieved when all the processes and mechanisms are exercised by concerned institutions following certain principles.

Good governance is increasingly being advocated to improve service delivery. This is because of the realisation that the resources are not reaching those whom it has been intended to. This is owing to the mismatch between what is needed and desired and what is being delivered. The World Development Report 2003, entitled *Making Services Work For the Poor*, points to a dismal picture of the development goals being reached due to the failure of service delivery mechanisms. This, the report says, has been due to the lack of accountability mechanisms, which hold the government responsible for its shortcomings.

There are many dimensions of good governance. The essential aspects of good governance are: participatory, consensus oriented, accountable, transparent, responsive, effective and efficient, equitable and inclusive and follows the rule of law.

Transparency and accountability are the main ingredients needed to achieve good governance. They are like the two sides of the same coin. One, without the other, is of no use. Transparency means that decisions are taken and their enforcement is done in a manner that follows rules and regulations. It also means that information is freely available and directly accessible to those who will be affected by such decisions and their enforcement. The existence of both conditions contributes to an effective, efficient and equitable management in public and private institutions.

Good governance also stresses on citizens participation, engagement of civil society in all aspects of governance. As has been seen in the micro planning processes on Kerala, citizen participant has been effective in giving results. Public consultations in budget preparations that are mandated by the urban local bodies is also an example of how the leaning is towards encouraging citizen's participation and engaging civil society organisations in governance.

With the leaning of the administration towards Right based initiative, citizens and citizen centric governance are taking the centre stage in the development discourse. An example of this is the Service Guarantee Act passed by the different States in India. In Karnataka, this initiative is called as "*Sakala*", colloquially meaning in time. It ensures that the citizens are guaranteed of their service within a specified time. Failing to deliver the services is to be compensated by the civil servant. "*Sakala*" is a good example of covering all the above said tenets of governance. It also ensures equity and inclusion as it provides equal opportunities for citizen in accessing the services. And all of this is done under the purview of the legislation. Thus, it meets the basic the tenet of good governance that it follows the rule of law.

Increasingly, India is witnessing scams being exposed and civil society in agitation. The civil society movement is also an important principle in transparency and accountability. Government and Governance must be open to civil societies.

Trust in public bodies is affected by two things: (1) the quality of services that citizens receive; and (2) how open and honest organizations are about their performance, including their willingness to admit to and learn from their mistakes.

Transparency and Good Governance

Transparency implies openness, clearness and lack of obstruction in the vision. Transparency helps not only to inform the public about development of ideas and proposals, but also to convince citizens that the public agencies are interested in listening to their views and responding to their priorities and concerns. This in turn enhances the legitimacy of the decision-making process and strengthens democratic principles. The holding of Ward *Sabha* and *Gram Sabha* thus become important in ensuring articulation of views by people.

Transparency in governance depends on the availability of information. Information—the empowering tool—was hitherto kept in the fists of a few. With this, corruption and misuse of power increased. The relationship between the information giver (the State) and the information receiver (the citizen) underwent change with the passing of Right to Information Act 2005. The Act has ushered in transparency and accountability in administration and thereby has helped governments to engage citizens by providing information. The transition from an opaque system of governance to one of a transparent system—from one of 'confidentiality' to openness is a progressive move. It ensures that all governmental activities are transparent, fair and open.

Role of Right to Information (RTI)

The concept behind the passing of the RTI Act, 2005 is the acknowledgment that informed citizenry and transparency of information are vital to the functioning of a democracy. It is recognized that the transparent and accountable measures would curtail corruption and help to hold governments responsible. Thus, by providing information to 'the citizens who desire to have it', emphasis is being placed on accessible and transparent governance.

Transparency would require an appropriate information disclosure mechanism. Information is crucial to good governance as it reflects and captures government activities and processes. Every citizen of the state has right to access information under the control of public authorities consistent with public interest. The main objective of governments providing information to its citizens is not only to promote openness, transparency and accountability in administration, but also to ensure participation of people in all matters related to governance.

Information is a key factor to ensure efficient and effective public services. It empowers the people to exert demand for better services. People are entitled to an apology, explanation and remedial action if the promised standard of service is not delivered. Public services should be provided economically and efficiently. Also, the implementation of citizen's charters must be monitored publicly and public service report cards be published to ensure efficiency and effectiveness.

All procurement in government must be regulated by transparency through legislation. This law may be enacted for ensuring transparency in public purchase of goods and services, in selecting tenderers, or inviting, processing and acceptance of tenders by procurement entities including e-procurement agencies. It is meant to provide a legal framework for all public procurement and should be applicable to Government Departments, Public Sector Undertakings, Universities, Panchayats, Local Bodies, Statutory Boards, and those who receive money from Government, etc. Karnataka Transparency in Public Procurement Act 2000 is an example worth emulating.

Redressal of Grievances

Machinery for redressal of public grievances has to be strengthened in every government office. An independent grievances redressal authority may oversee the action on redressal of public grievances. Examples of this are many in Karnataka, e. g., Bhoomi, Nemmadi and Bangalore One. They combine IT enabled, e-governance mechanisms to heed to public grievances. Atal Bihari Vajpaee Janashree Yojana is another initiative of Government of Karnataka for getting governance at door step. Establishment of an Institution of Ombudsman to oversee redressal of grievances (as in Insurance and Banking Sectors) or a Public Grievance Commission, Strengthening of Consumer Courts and other institutions which helps redress complaints and grievances and provide local, quick and effective remedy is the next step forward in Good Governance.

The principles of Good Governance are applicable to all areas of Government. The present machinery is found to be stagnant, unaccountable and corrupt and hence there is need to change processes. Good Governance also looks at Public Private Partnership in governance. The role of private sector is very important as they help in creating jobs and employment. The private sector and the government need to work together for providing better opportunities. Transparent corporate governance is a must for a responsible private sector.

All these initiatives of transparency and Good Governance will only be realised if there is change of ethical culture in bureaucracy. This would require institutional reform of departments and continuous monitoring and assessment of service delivery. With the penalty/ compensation clause introduced in the Service Guarantee Act, the culture of bureaucracy would certainly undergo change.

The rule of law will be protected in India only if it is ensured that those who violate it are given the punishment that is appropriate for that violation. The effort to establish independent Institutions like Lokpal and Lokayukta is thus important due to the need to fight against corruption.

Government in general and bureaucracy in particular need to look within and find answers to problems of governance. The process needs to be streamlined. The norms should be available in public domain so that there is less room for corruption, discretion and delays. There is need for maintenance of fair play at all levels for ensuring transparency in Governance. There is need for deregulation, extensive use of technology and continuous improvement in Public Policy Initiatives and process in Government. The initiatives started by State Governments need to be accelerated and should be recessed at regular intervals.

5

Proactive Disclosure and the Right to Information

Joshyula Lakshmi

Introduction

Democratic system of governance presupposes a well informed citizenry. Citizens in a democracy always want to be well informed but they had to obtain information through sources other than the government. Conventional political institutions have lagged in co-opting citizens into the political processes, through their legacies of secrecy and bureaucratic oneupmanship. What separated the rulers from the ruled was coveted administrative information that was in the possession of the former. This situation leads citizens to believe that administration is distant from the people. This situation is changing now with democratization of society, growth of literacy, proliferation of print and visual media which have made it difficult for governments to keep any information secret. In such a situation it is wiser for the governments to part with requested information than to keep it under wraps. Governments the world over too have realized the fact that information will have to be revealed sooner or later.

Transparency and Disclosure in India

Disclosure of official information in India was governed by the Official Secrets Act (OSA) of 1889 enacted during the British rule. The Act was amended in 1923. The OSA, 1923 restricted information related to security of the State, sovereignty of the country and friendly relations with foreign states from being made public. It contained provisions prohibiting disclosure of non-classified information. This official secrecy was compounded by the legacy of British Civil Service attitudes inherited by all civil servants recruited post-Independence. Official transactions in the government were many times veiled in secrecy as these were 'policy matters'

This situation has been changing now under peoples pressures and intervention of Courts broadening the scope of right to freedom of speech and acknowledging the citizen's right to know. In 1975, the Supreme Court delivered a landmark judgement on the citizen's Right to Know. The Supreme Court judgement delivered by Mr. Justice Mathew in the State of UP *vs.* Raj Narain (1975) case, ruled that 'in a government of responsibility like ours, where all the agents of the public must be responsible for their conduct, there can be but few secrets'.

Article 19 (1) (a) of the Constitution guarantees the fundamental rights to free speech and expression. As a prerequisite for enjoying this right it is important that people have the knowledge and information about what they speak and express. Especially, in the context of absence of authentic information on matters of public interest, the citizens will not be able to exercise their freedom of speech and expression. Enabling the right to know would be necessitated for this and to quell rumours and uncalled for speculations. Thus, by interpretation, the right to know becomes a constitutional right, being an aspect of the right to free speech and expression and thereby includes the right to receive and collect information.

In this context, the RTI Act makes it clear that the supply of information through Section 4 (1) (b) is to be such that the citizen is spared the hardship or effort to apply for information and seek the same. This means that the Public Authority shares the information before it is asked for or demanded.

Since, The Right to Information (RTI) Act 2005 has come into being, one has seen its usage by citizens, groups of citizens, media, academia and individuals. Its success lay in Public Authorities sharing coveted government held information to the persons that demand for it. The Mahatma Gandhi National Rural Employment Guarantee Scheme (MGNREGS) proposes mandatory social audits through the effective usage of the RTI Act. Through this access to information several cases of corrupt practices, small and large scale scams have been unearthed. However, of late we have been hearing about concerns pertaining to frivolousness of information sought by citizens, intrusion of individual privacy, usage of such information to target individuals and groups, etc. This paper deals with one of the important obligation bestowed upon the Public Authorities to put forward information. A prerequisite for the same is to improve the record management practices that seem to be lacking.

RTI Act and the Need of Proactive Disclosure

We may refer to some of the important provision of the RTI Act, Section 4 (1) (b) that has got sidelined in the nine year journey of the Act. Section 4 (1) (b) of the RTI Act pertains to proactive parting with information 'held' by the Public Authorities. This section indicates, for purposes of convenience and understanding of the Public Authorities, 17 sub-heads under which such information may be categorised and submitted for public view, scrutiny and usage. While 16 of the sub-heads are meant to share generic information, the sub-head 17 indicates 'such other information as may be prescribed', either by themselves or by the government as it may deem fit to make public. The information to be published therein is one of basic nature and is information that the Public Authority 'holds'. It is in no way 'out of the ordinary' information. *Suo motu* disclosure gives information about the rationale and basis of the existence of the Public Authority its *raison d'etre*. If the Public Authority appreciates the intent of Sec. 4 (1) (b) in letter and spirit and thus makes transparency an article of faith all efforts to drive in the message are achieved. Let us examine critically, the issues of openness and the journey of Section 4 (1) (b).

Section 4 (1) is the core of the RTI Act with reference to the responsibilities of the Public Authorities to keep their records in order and to ensure that maximum information is placed in the public domain preferably electronically or else in hard copies and provide information pertaining to policy matters affecting people and to convey administrative or quasi-judicial decisions to the 'affected' persons. The idea is that the citizens are not inconvenienced in accessing the information that they seek or are kept in ignorance of the policies likely to affect them and their lives. As per the interpretation of this Section, Public Authorities have to proactively (and not necessarily reactively) provide information as per the mandated sub-sections that reflect the basic information about the organisation. They are required to update it annually and also if possible furnish information beyond the items indicated. The idea is that more the information in the public domain, less would be requests for such information from the public.

Under Section 4 (1) (b), the Act mandates Public Authorities to furnish information compulsorily on the following 17 sub-sections, while not restricting information over and above these:

(i) *Particulars of its Organization, Functions and Duties:* The disclosure of the basic particulars about the Public Authority such as the name of the Public Authority, the nature of its works, vision, mission and strategy, functions and duties of the organization would basically give a rationale to its existence and purview. A look at some of the websites of Public Authorities shows that several organsiation take their existence as understood and hence this information is not provided. Without knowing the larger context of the organisation, it becomes difficult to a citizen to place it in proper context.

(ii) *Powers and Duties of its Officers and Employees:* Proactive disclosure of the powers and duties would help public know the level of authority and jurisdiction of each officer and help them understand the working of the Public Authority in that context. Often we find the powers and duties presented on the websites are vague and make no sense. For example, the roles and responsibilities of staff in a Block Development Officer's office, duties and functions of staff listed clearly would help citizens approach the appropriate officer or its representative to get their benefits and redress their grievances.

(iii) *Procedure followed in the decision-making process, including channels of supervision and accountability:* There are very-well laid out documented procedures in the government that guide officers of different level function in their roles and with each other in a coordinated manner. Divulging this on the proactive disclosure explains the rules of decision-making, the levels of decision-makers and pin-point authorities whose decisions prevail. They also explain the hierarchy in a Public Authority and help in identifying with clarity, efficient role-players from the inefficient ones. Not divulging this information could lead to a wrong person being held responsible for another persons' mistake and made a scapegoat for others vices. The cycle of accountability should ensure that those responsible for making vital decisions are also held responsible for wrong decisions. In practice there are very few Public Authorities that articulate this well. Procedure for decision-making is very vital in a representative democracy and arbitrary and discretionary decisions can be avoided if these are mentioned.

(iv) *Norms set by it for the discharge of its functions:* Norms are normally laid out like the timing of the office, reporting to duty procedures to take after leave etc. to which the personnel are required to adhere to. Similarly, norms of service delivery through application, forms and formats are also spelt out, so that intended beneficiaries have a fair chance to going through properly laid out procedures and do not break the line. In this regard preparation of Citizen Charters would help citizens know the procedures and their likely timelines of delivery. For the Public Authority, laying down the norms minimizes the scope for manipulation by individuals and thereby public allegations of manipulation. We find, however, that there are serious allegations afloat both in the media and from Civil Society Organsations that Public Authorities seldom mention the norms of functioning leaving a lot of scope for nepotism and corruption. This allegation could be reversed with a well laid out Citizen Charter and its implementation. The non-mention of this gives undue discretionary powers to officers to do works as per their whims and fancies and convenience. Governance and service delivery are two sides of the same coin.

(v) *Rules, regulations, instructions, manuals and records, held by it or under its control or used by its employees for discharging its functions:* Disclosure of all information pertaining to this aspect has to be in the public domain so that citizens understand the context of the functioning of the Public Authority. Once the rules are made, they are amended from time to time in a bid to improve and rationalize the functioning of the administrative system. All such amendments made need to be in public domain so that the sequential understanding of policy matters is transparent and known to all. Secrecy on this matter raises doubts about the

Public Authorities functioning and suspicion about its activities. It is, however, a matter of grave concern that today the Right to Information Act is bringing forth information regarding 'skipping the procedures', 'bending the rules' and cases of 'lost files' due to non-disclosure of this information from earlier times. Keeping the information under wraps has the potential to expose the real and perceived manipulations. The rule books, circulars used in discharge of duties will be very helpful for citizens to understand what the law is and what the rule book says. All memos, circulars, rule books including file notings are to be disclosed.

(vi) *Statement of the categories of documents that are held by it or under its control:* A disclosure statement with a listing of the various categories of documents held by a Public Authority would help the Public Authority in keeping its records in order as well as help the citizens in identifying the exempt and the non-exempt categories of information held by the Public Authority. However, unless the categories of documents held by the Public Authority are disclosed, the burden of transferring applications cannot be avoided.

(vii) *Particulars of any arrangement that exists for consultation with or representation by the members of the public in relation to the formulation of its policy or implementation thereof.* Where a Public Authority is engaged in a project/policy matter that requires consultation with the public, it requires to be made known to the public through this disclosure. It would equip the public represent its views and opinions and actively participate in better implementation. The idea is to give ample notice for consultation, to ensure preparation on the project/policy matter, participation in maximum numbers, and with well-discussed quality inputs for successful implementation. We find that several actions of resistance from the 'likely to be affected' persons in the recent past have emerged because this disclosure was lacking. The consultation processes have neither been initiated and if so have been nominal and inconsequential to the outcome, thereby rendering the process null and void. The disclosure of this information is vital because websites and computers are not available in rural areas and in remote locations. Thus, publicity for the consultation process has to be through local indigenous means of communication

— through the Panchayat, through wall writings, through public announcement systems, through plays, songs, etc.

(viii) *Statement of the boards, councils, committees and other bodies consisting of two or more persons constituted as its part or for the purpose of its advice, and as to whether meetings of those boards, councils, committees and other bodies are open to the public, or the minutes of such meetings are accessible for public*: Where a Public Authority is mandated/required to constitute boards, councils, committees and other such bodies it has to disclose such information. This would explain implicitly the financial burden on the Public Authority for constituting the same. Detailing of these, we find is not adequately done at all levels, leaving the ordinary citizens with apprehensions about misuse of offices and the finances of such offices. Instances of these were evident in the press, regarding constituting Sports bodies, their membership and management.

(ix) *Directory of its officers and employees*: Disclosure of the contact details of officers and staff in a Public Authority would ensure that these are accessible and within reach. Moreover, where the medium of communication—either a landline or a mobile is allocated by the office and its expenses borne by the Public Authority, it is meant to be used officially and hence, citizens must have access to this information for official purposes only. Secondly, Public Authorities are not always located in the same premises—the contact details help the citizens in accessing the nearest possible location to reach them or for them to reach it. This information is disclosed by Public Authorities but is sometimes partial. It does not cover all the staff, but the highest officers and their contact details only. There should be no apprehensions of victimisation or frivolous calls as citizens using the contact details are meant to do so with due discretion to the privacy of the staff and the propriety of the call.

(x) *Monthly remuneration received by each of its officers and employees, including the system of compensation as provided in its regulations:* This is a very basic of information that ensures transparency within and outside the Public Authority. Often the budgets of running a Public Authority are mostly spent on salaries, perks and privileges of the employees. Only the balance is spent on running the projects, programmes and services. Distinguishing the constant from the variable expenses would help a citizen know and understand the mechanisms of expenditure made by the Public Authority. Salaries and compensation are expected to be transparent and based on a laid out rational system. Hence, a disclosure of the system of compensation would alley doubts about financial irregularities. Public Authority's receive increments on a yearly basis and any change over the years will have to be reflected on this item of their proactive disclosure. Since, many Public Authorities are not updating their websites on a regular yearly basis, one does not know for sure if the item mentioned under (ix) on their RTI disclosures is current or dated.

(xi) Budget allocated to each of its agency, indicating the particulars of all plans, proposed expenditures and reports on disbursements made. Disclosure of financial position of the Public Authority in terms of its income and expenditure as well as its sources of funds is required to understand the financial state of the Public Authority. It helps one understand its financial health (profitability or loss making) as well as amounts sanctioned for beneficiaries under various schemes. An important concern is that budgets are never mentioned (planned and unplanned) by several Public Authorities. This information is also more often than not, dynamic and hence, whatever is available on the sites that uploaded their *suo motu* in 2005 and never updated it later, the information is dated. It should be made mandatory right from the *Gram Panchayat* level to disclose the budgets, how it is spent (proposed and actual) and details of various disbursements made. This can greatly reduce the number of applications.

(xii) *Manner of execution of subsidy programmes, including the amounts allocated and the details of beneficiaries of such programmes:* Public Authorities executing subsidy programmes and disbursing welfare schemes have the responsibility to describe the manner of execution of the subsidy. It helps to give clarity on the same because welfare schemes are meant to reach the targeted population. States run such schemes and subsidies with an intention to support the disadvantaged and deprived communities and groups in society. We find that while the state's responsibility and intent are socialist, its execution has to be open and transparent. A pro-people policy cannot be executed in a clandestine manner. Thus, a disclosure policy is mandated in such schemes with a list of the various beneficiaries mentioned in the disclosure. If the eligibility criteria, and list of beneficiaries (updated regularly) of various schemes is disclosed proactively, corruption as well as number of applications will greatly reduce.

(xiii) *Particulars of recipients of concessions, permits or authorisations granted by it:* The disclosure under this items calls for total transparency and a strict adherence to the Rule book. The state as an administrator has the powers to grant concessions, permits (for works, products and services) and authorizations granted by it. These are based on rational procedures and are laid out clearly. The fact that Public Authorities are not privy to scuttling the procedures and favouring some over the others, it is important to disclose such particulars. This disclosure reflects upon the Public Authorities' adherence to the principle of equity and fairness. This is an important clause as the disclosure eliminates arbitrary and discretionary use of power and authority in their allocation. It also greatly reduces corruption and clandestine deals. Unearthing of scams and large scale siphoning of resources of recent times are a reflection of insufficient disclosure of this aspect.

(xiv) *Details in respect of the information, available to or held by it, reduced in an electronic form to the extent possible in disclosing this item, the interest and the resources of the Public Authority would be served:* The aim is to let the citizens know the availability of information held by it in an electronic format, so that citizens can view it, access in a similar format or access it electronically. This works out to be economical for the Public as well as precious time of the PIO and financial resources of the Public Authority could be saved. By furnishing information in an electronic form, the citizen's resources are economized as well. Because an applicant of the APL category will have to pay 'further fee' for hard copies of information sought.

(xv) *Particulars of facilities available to citizens for obtaining information, including the working hours of a library or reading room, if maintained for public use:* Disclosure of working hours for citizens to consult (open *darbars*, weekly contact days, etc.), for obtaining information, mechanisms for grievance redressal, library and reading room facilities, etc, if maintained have to be publicly displayed and changes if any need to be regularly updated. Citizen-friendly facilities are maintained by some Public Authorities, but their utility for the citizen and their satisfaction have not been ascertained.

(xvi) *Names, designations and other particulars of the Public Information Officers who is to be contacted for accessing information:* The information about who is the Public Information Officer in a particular Public Authority, what is the PIOs designation, etc. enables the citizen applicant the persons they could approach with an RTI application. It is sad that the exact number of Public Authorities is not enumerated and thereby a database of PIOs is also not available for reference at this stage. This is very often neglected by Public Authorities. In fact, many designated PIOs are not aware of their being PIOs. Several PIOs trained in RTI and its execution have either retired or been transferred out. The new entrant is untrained and hence tentative in its approach to demand-based information. It is unfair to expect the second generation of untrained PIOs to take a stand and influence the Public Authorities *suo motu* disclosures. Where boards are put up with this information, the board should be a permanent one and should not display a mere print-out with the names. This is in fact the first thing that should be done by Public Authorities.

(xvii) *Such other information as may be prescribed; and thereafter update these publications every year*. This sub-item expands and enlarges the scope of proactive disclosure to a vast extent. It, in fact, gives room for discretionary disclosure of information subject to its relevance for the public. It is one un-explored area where the head of the Public Authority could share its innovative practices, be enterprising in asking citizens to give feedback on its disclosure policy or establish a mechanism for the same. The sub-section (xvii) has enormous potential to share all other information hitherto not shared under sub-sections (i) to (xvi) above. Citizen's charters, Public Disclosure Laws where available and applicable, etc. could be shared under this sub-section. Yet it is the most neglected of all sub-sections. Where Public Authorities have done well in their *suo motu* disclosures on (i) to (xvi), (xvii) is left blank and unattended. While its potential is not tapped, its significance to the proactive disclosure is also misunderstood, because the subsection calls for yearly updation of the above (xvii) and the other information (under xvii). This sub-section is like the soul and spirit of the RTI Act. Its neglect is a cause for concern. It draws a definite timeline for the proactive disclosure made. Not updating it every year is like cutting short the lifeline of *suo motu* disclosure.

Implementation of RTI Act

Let us now examine the critical aspects of the Section that have come forth during the implementation of the RTI Act. At a stocktaking of the Right to Information Act in 2010, the Prime Minister Dr Manmohan Singh said that Public Authorities in our country have still to go a long distance in proactive disclosures. The Prime Minister hoped that the Government Plan of e-governance for computerization of all Central Government Organisations would ensure that the mandated Section 4 is taken care of by all Public Authorities.

While many Ministries/Departments have put up information on their websites, the adequacy of the same, the quality and its amenability for further analysis and use merits a closer examination. An examination of the websites of some public authorities shows the following:

- Not all Public Authorities maintain website in the first instance.
- Among those that do, the RTI disclosure is there on the websites of few Public Authorities.
- The RTI disclosure is sometimes not easily traceable on the site as it is embedded within the grievance redress mechanism icon and needs some element of web search.
- Where the RTI disclosure is uploaded on the PA website and is prominently visible, the items disclosed are not complete and nor comprehensive. Most sites continue with partial information disclosure
- The RTI disclosure put up on the websites of Public

Authorities are outdated and not up to date. A large number of Public Authorities have put up the RTI information in 2005 and have not updated it since then.

What could be the reasons for this unmaking of the RTI Act? Public Authority, unlike a common citizen without resources, is better placed to make provisions for putting up all information held by it in the public domain instead of; The focus has by far been on giving information rather than on making provisions for making it public in the first instance. Do Public Authorities have an ulterior motive in not publishing information on their own and would rather want to wait and watch? Is this not a priority with the Public Authorities? Once done, the information does not seem to be updated annually.

Seven years since the enactment of the RTI Act, it has been recognized at the highest level that the culture of proactive disclosure is lacking and needs to be cultivated. The reasons largely are that the governance system by and large has been dominated by secrecy and closed behaviour rather than transparency and openness and it continues in spite of the Act. It is hence a matter of concern and a priority to change the attitude and behaviour to ensure proactive information sharing.

The Key Aspects in *Suo Motu* Disclosure

In making possible the process of *suo motu* disclosures, it is important that certain aspects of the disclosure are ensured so that the disclosure is comprehensive enough and not partial, is citizen-centric and citizen friendly. It is recognized that Section 4 (1) (a) on record management is found deficient in its maintenance and retrieval and needs equal prioritization. Record management has a direct bearing on the information disclosure process especially when the information is demanded. Section 4 (1) (b) is current, doable and futuristic and its immediate understanding among the Public Authorities is a priority.

How to prioritise and popularize *suo motu* disclosure among Public Authorities? Foremost, it is important to establish responsibility for Section 4 (1) (b). To identify one person who is going to be responsible for regular updates on the same. The decision to create and publish proactive disclosure the Public Authority must adhere to the generic (indicative) format as given by the Act. The onus for non-compliance would lie on the Head of the Department and the person in-charge who is at the helm of affairs with regard to that Public Authority. The common confusion about the PIO taking the initiative on this does not arise. The items to be covered have been indicated by the RTI Act. The idea is to adhere to a format covering the 17 items of *Suo motu* disclosure. The list shall not be treated as exhaustive. These 17 items give out the basic information about the Public Authority and its activities.

The key aspects in *suo motu* disclosure that need reiteration are:

1. Understanding the extent and quality of the information to be disclosed as per the stipulations of Sec. 4 and its key requirements.
2. Actual translation of the understanding into actions and its execution in practice.
3. Repetition of the procedure to ensure its proper utilization with a practice of proper and periodic updation of the various components of Section 4 (1).
4. Periodic self-assessment by the PA of its mandatory disclosure.
5. Attention to detail in terms of comprehensiveness, simplicity, coherence, and usefulness of the *suo motu* disclosures so as to be citizen-centric in nature and citizen friendly in its presentation.
6. Adopting different means for dissemination of the disclosures.
7. Use and infusion of appropriate technology for *suo motu* disclosure for the convenience of the Public Authority as well as the Citizen-Applicant.
8. Process reform/re-engineering that could be carried out in operationalising Sec. 4 and innovations and openness to experiential learning from within or outside.

In ensuring that *suo motu* disclosure is made comprehensively and in its totality, it is important that the information that is largely dynamic is updated as and when necessitated. As seen from sub-sections under Section 4 (1) (b), more often than not the nature of information sought to be published is subject to changes. This dynamic aspect of information/data needs to be captured and updated as and when changes occur. Today, websites of most Public Authorities are static with a monolith of information published as a response to the enactment of the RTI Act in 2005, staring at the viewer. The dynamic information is not being updated and the result is that a purposeful facilitating action of proactive disclosure by Public Authorities is being defeated in its letter and its spirit.

Issues and Way Ahead

It is found that the deficiencies in the process and the system of information sharing from the government are manifold:

(i) *Attitudinal Deficiencies:* The attitudinal transformation and change over at different levels of governance is a major hurdle to be crossed. The journey from secrecy to transparency, from small group closed door transactions to openness and public viewing and participation in policy-making is one large leap that should be taken. These attitudinal changes need to be brought about at different levels of the administration right from the top to the bottom.

(ii) *Fears and Apprehensions:* Fears and apprehensions of the information suppliers need to be addressed in this regard. Large chunks of information sought by citizen applicants, the fee rate differences, the fear of giving away critical information, inviting the ire of the boss, the weighing down of several responsibilities hinder the PIOs from airing their difficulties in facilitating sharing of information. If the fears of the PIOs and the FAAs are addressed in this regard, then the burden of supply of information felt at this stage (when the information is being provided on demand), would be offset and the spirit of the RTI Act would prevail.

(iii) *Improper or lack of awareness:* Knowing and understanding that supplying information proactively would alley much of the fears of the citizen applicants as well about the processes within the Public Authority would help in charting a course of full and updated *suo motu* disclosures.

(iv) *Lack of financial resources:* This is one reason why Public Authorities refuse to take up supply of information proactively. There is some truth in this as well and needs to be appreciated. For long, the administrative matters have been transacted on paper and do so to this day. The dream of complete computerization of all offices is yet to be realized. Thus retrieval of information from paper-based records, not stored as per the stipulations and cast away in decaying corners is a true story of some of the government offices to this day. Computerisation of office records and their systematic maintenance holds the key to proper holding of information.

(v) *Insufficient Manpower:* It is seen that the responsibility of supply of information on demand is currently given to a person already holding a post in the Public Authority. The PIOs job is thus an additional responsibility of one of the existing officers in the PA, and is unrewarding monetarily. It has no incentives attached to it and is hence not handled many a times with the kind of seriousness that it deserves to be handled. It would help to incentivise PIOs for every citizen application well handled with satisfactory supply of information within the stipulated time and economically.

(vi) *Quantum of information sought is huge:* It has been the experience of many PIOs that large quantum of information through one application or through multiple applications calling for a greater amount of their time devoted to furnishing that information. This also offsets job responsibilities and impinges on their work time. In the process the RTI application and the work related to it gets relegated to the bottom of the priority list. For this the remedy is to know and understand the RTI Act in its totality and to bring it to the notice of the higher-ups for decision-making on the cost effectiveness of supplying information proactively so that all the information is furnished in one place and is available for viewing or downloading.

(vii) *Defining the levels of Public Authority:* By Public Authority it has largely been held that any organization or body 'substantially' funded by the Government however, this has created a lot of confusion for the public as it is unable to place and locate a Public Authority that would address its concerns. Hence, for the convenience of the citizen applicant it would be helpful to slice down the Public Authority as defined under the RTI Act. The proactive disclosure of each Public Authority laterally and sliced down by their hierarchical levels/regional ambit of their authority need to be provided separately. Thus the proactive disclosure of a Public Authority at a district level read in conjunction with its parent Departments' proactive disclosure should make sense and be intelligible to anyone.

(viii) *Positioning the highest level of the Public Authority:* Public Authority, as mentioned in the point above, is a broad term and needs to be pin-pointed for the general public. In the context of RTI the Public Authority for the general citizen applicant is an unseen body. The only identifiable persons within are the PIO, the APIO and the FAA. Decisions for proactive disclosure for public display are, however, not taken at their levels and decisions are taken more than one notch higher than the FAA. There is a need to identify the highest authority in a Public Authority and ensure that such person holding that post is made responsible for monitoring and reviewing the proactive disclosure of the Public Authority.

(ix) *Institutional arrangements for proactive disclosure:* Mandating proactive disclosure under RTI has not yielded much from the Public Authorities. It is hence important to relook at the institutional arrangements in place to ensure that the supply of information goes beyond the desired levels, institutional arrangements have to be put in place. These could be Rewards, Awards, Incentives – hikes and promotions – and earning the goodwill of the public.

(x) *Institutional deterrents:* Information Commissions may reprimand PAs for non-compliance in their various decisions and under Section 25 of the RTI Act in its Annual Reports. Information Commissions have recommended immediate, time-bound and full compliance to Section 4 (1); eminently visible display of details of APIOs/PIOs/FAOs; making such information available on electronic network and high-level monitoring necessary.

The Report of the National Sub-Committee constituted by the Central Information Commission recommended in 2008 that every Administrative Secretary should be held responsible for assuring proactive disclosure and capacity building by all Public Authorities within his purview.

Some of the other ways to take up proactive disclosure effective are suggested below:

1. To prioritize good record management practices and regularly (frequently or at least annually) update web disclosures.
2. Revive and mandate inspections beginning with inspection of Record Room.
3. Digitalise State Archives and have it under the purview of the GAD or the nodal Department for RTI in the state.
4. Mandate uploading of all PIO/APIO/AA information and update frequently.
5. Have a single web-window for all such disclosures.
6. Have legislation for the maintenance of State Records.
7. The need for the Appropriate Government(s) to not leave this issue un-addressed any more.

If the government is concerned about the feasibility of implementing proactive disclosure across the whole of the bureaucracy, consideration could be given to identifying pilot proactive disclosure departments, which could be given priority for implementing proactive disclosure first, to develop robust systems that can then be used by other departments. The following departments could be prioritized in this context:

- *Finance Ministry*—in particular by publishing the budget; regular and detailed updates on expenditure broken down by line item; details about development assistance received from donors, broken down into projects/programmes.
- *Education and Health Departments*—in particular by publishing basic budget information and expenditure updates; details on the release of monthly grants to local health services and schools; information on special programmes.
- *Public Works Department*—in particular by publishing all public contracts entered into by Public Authorities.

Only a true commitment to the letter and spirit of the RTI Act by the Public Authorities can ensure that a transparent and participatory governance system is created in the country. Strict adherence to Article 4(1) of the RTI Act has to be ensured.

REFERENCES

Ansari, M.M. (2008), *Impact of Right to Information on Development: A Perspective of India's recent Experiences*, lecture delivered at UNESCO Headquarters, Paris, France, on May 15.

Centre for Good Governance (2009), *Best Practices in the Implementation of Right to Information Act*, Hyderabad.

Centre for Good Governance (undated), *Significant Decisions of Information Commissions*, prepared by CGG for RTI Gateway, Hyderabad.

CHRI (2006), *Information Disclosure Policy, A Toolkit for Pacific Governments*, Study commissioned by the Pacific Media and Communications Facility (PMCF).

World Bank (2004), *Legislation on Freedom of Information: Trends and Standards*, Poverty Reduction and Economic Management (PREM) notes, The World Bank, Washington.

World Bank (2005), *Fostering Trust and Transparency through Information Systems*, Poverty Reduction and Economic Management (PREM) notes, The World Bank, Washington.

PART-2
Role of Technology in Transparency and Disclosure

6

Potentials and Pitfalls of Computerization of Land Records in Tamil Nadu

A Case Study of 'Tamil NILAM'

R. Srinivasan and *T.R.Gopalakrishnan*

Introduction

The concept of transparency has been a central guiding principle in public administration reforms in the country. The Right to Information Act and many initiatives to make government documents available to public are a few examples of the attempts to operationalise the concept of transparency. More recently the Central and State governments are investing in e-governance projects that seek to use new Information and Communication Technologies (ICTs) to enhance the goal of achieving what some scholars have called "radical transparency". This notion of transparency has been inspired by developments in Free and Open Source Software (FOSS) movement.

Most of these projects work on the assumption that increased transparency would reduce corruption. The expectations is that open and free access to information available with the government would empower citizens, enable participation and thus act as a check to abuse of power, which is one of the key sources of corruption. We call this ICT—enabled transparency as e-transparency.

In this paper, we argue that while there are obvious benefits of e-transparency in governance there are also considerable risks and constraints in applying the concept in practice. The main argument that we forward is that ICT based application can increase transparency in governance, but its outcome in relation to reducing corruption cannot be taken for granted. Based on a case study of Computerisation of Land Records (CLR) initiative in the State of Tamil Nadu, this paper argues that CLR has the potential to facilitate corruption, rather than restraining them.

The Card Project

Computerisation of Land Records has been one of the earliest efforts for the realisation of e-transparency. The need for reform land information management has been recognised as a significant challenge within the overall land reform policies in India and the potential of computer application to facilitate this process is well understood. As a result some of the earliest efforts in land reform included a consideration of extending e-governance model to land record maintenance and management. Bhoomi in Karnataka and CARD in Andhra Pradesh are some the examples of successful projects. All state governments now have invested in CLR with the support of full funding from the central government.

In Tamil Nadu, the Tamil NILAM (Tamil Nadu Infosystem on Land Administration and Management) project was started with following major aims:

(i) To implement comprehensive and transparent Land Information System capturing entire work flow of land records maintenance with a provision to store, retrieve and process land records data containing ownership, tenancy rights, crop details, land revenue, source of irrigation, mutation, its updating and dispute resolution.

(ii) On demand distribution of computerised copies of Record of Rights to the landowner at reasonable charges with a provision of on-line mutation module for ownership changes, seasonal crop updating, etc. at this level.

(iii) Provision of legal sanctity to computer generated certificates of Land Records title documents after authentication by authorised revenue officials.

(iv) To generate and integrate various levels of data for purposes of planning, monitoring, evaluation of development programmes.

The Land Records System Tamil NILAM (Tamil Nadu Infosystem on Land Administration and Management) is implemented in 194 taluks. Touch Screen Kiosks have been installed in 127 taluks, which have been used by more than 6 lakh people in the last four years. Collab land software for generating field maps have been implemented in two taluks and the software is approved by the government for use in all the taluks in the State.

The Centrally Sponsored Scheme on Computerisation of Land Records (CLR) was started in 1988-89 with 100 per cent financial assistance to remove the problems inherent in the manual systems of maintenance and updating of Land Records and to meet the requirements of various groups of users. It was decided that efforts should be made to computerise CORE DATA contained in land records, to assist development planning and to make records accessible to people/planners and administrators.

As of 2011, out of 220 Taluk offices 216 offices have been computerised with over all records in the system. However, as the CAG report (2009) on CLR shows, the implementation of Tamil NILAM has been uneven with some taluks (such as those in the district of Kancheepuram, Krishnagiri) better adopted to new system than those in other districts (Ramanathapuram, Villupuram)

Despite these differences, the state of Tamil Nadu has progressed in adoption of CLR to the extent that the government banned all manual documentation through its GO of 2003. Since, then most land related transactions in Tamil Nadu (Issuance of RoR, EC, Mutation, etc.) have been facilitated through CLR.

More recently National Land Record Modernisation Project has made more central funds available for standardisation and up-gradation of CLR in the state, even though there are some concerns over proper utilization to these funds, as pointed out by CAG.

Most of the studies have been focusing on the technical efficiency of CLR to delivery end-user services and consequently paid less attention to the long term outcomes, especially in relation to reducing corruption. So the question still remains as to what is the impact of CLR in bringing greater transparency and reducing corruption.

The E-Transparency Paradox

The irony of CLR in Tamil Nadu is that over a decade of experimentation and use of CLR has not had a significant impact on corruption in land transactions. Data gathered from the Police Department as well as media reports suggests that the problems of corruption in land dealings are deep rooted and depend crucially on access to information. There has been a tremendous increase in the cases of land grabbing and land document forgery in Tamil Nadu in the last five years. For several months since then, there was at least one high profile land grab story in a week. Such cases forced the new government under J. Jayalalitha to initiate several measures to contain and reverse land grabbing and forgery cases.

Land grab has topped all crimes in the state with complaints and allegations still pouring in. According to the policy note of the home department of Tamil Nadu government, the "anti-land grabbing cells" that it established have received more than 34,000 complaints across the state.

The government established 39 anti-land grab cells, one each for each district and one each with each Police Commissioner; and 25 fast track courts for the quick disposal of cases. 1,225 criminal cases have been registered by landowners since June 2011, mostly on charges of forgery or forcible possession. The cases registered stood at 111 in 2005, 127 in 2006. So far, 3,070 acres of land and 14, 77,424 sq ft of housing plots (which were grabbed) worth Rs. 1,156 crore have been retrieved and returned to the rightful owners.

1,178 cases had been filed and 2,034 people arrested since May 2011. In addition to land grabbing, document forgery for obtaining loans is another major concern. RBI in a circular to banks warned of increase in such forgery cases estimating that 3-4 out of 10 documents submitted to banks might be forged.

The Revenue Department which is responsible for implementing CLR is considered the most corrupt department in the state. The Revenue Department has topped in the number of corruption cases booked by the Directorate of Vigilance and Anti-Corruption (DAVC) in the last two years. Of the total 319 trap cases registered by the agency between April 2010 and October 2011, Revenue Department officials were involved in 69. The Tamil Nadu Electricity Board and Police Department followed with 29 and 28 cases, a source in the DVAC said.

This leads us to conclude that CLR has the potential to facilitate corruption rather than containing it. Such incidences suggest that computerization facilitates land grabbing on the one hand and if properly implemented could mitigate land document forgery by enabling record checking. Lack of co-ordination between police department and registration department meant that computer records themselves are forged. How can we explain the increase in corruption and to what extent CLR can be held responsible for these. Of course, we need to remind ourselves that corruption is a complex issue and multiple factors are involved in the process of corruption. Manual system of land record maintenance has also lead to corrupt practices.

However, it is clear from these cases that the stated objective of reduction in corruption has not taken place in land management and we need to consider aspects of CLR that might have contributed to this process.

How does CLR Facilitate Corruption?

There are various channels through which CLR facilitates corruption as elaborated below:

Reification of Default through improper data entry or glossing over historical contested claim over the land and by privileging default land owners the system reifies, freezes, the ownership rights. This increases the scope for dispute and thus increases the opportunity for corruption. One estimates claims that over 70 per cent of the cases in the courts in TN are land-related. Over 40 per cent of the land titles are disputed

Re-centralisation of records at Taluk level, reduces the role of village administrative officers and hence shifts the corrupt practices from village level-where the bribe amount was small to Taluk level where it has become higher. CLR has shifted corruption from diffused state to consolidation.

Information Asymmetry among different groups also facilitates corruption. Realtors, brokers, advocates and other middlemen are regular "users" of information available through CLR. Since the vast majority of the land transactions are one-off deals-most of the owners engage in land selling/buying only once or twice in a life time and hence it might not be worth the efforts to learn all the procedures. This is especially true for first time land owners. On the other hand, most middlemen and big realtors are heavy users of the system and hence have an inherent advantage. This creates an information asymmetry that privileges the heavy-regular users of CLR at the expense of poor, illiterate and rationally ignorant citizens. More transparency benefits those comparatively more capable of taking advantage of increased available information, reinforcing already existing social inequalities

Re-intermediation has emerged as a new phenomenon in the land market. Since the boom in reality market since the late 1990s, the amount and volume of land transaction has increased and hence has opened new employment opportunities for land transaction related services. As a result there are more middlemen now than ever before. There are now part-time, full-time and even freelance land brokers and service providers. Muscleman and powerful land *mafia* have emerged in high value locations—suburban, peri-urban and locations proximate to the cities. These people have often resorted to violence and intimidation to subvert this process. More importantly their business depends on having access to land related information

Control of Land Information Market creates opportunities for corruption. Increase in demand for land for housing, industries and investment has intensified the competition amongst middlemen and intermediaries. As a result there is new demand for information about potential marketable land. So, there is increased temptation on the part of the people who have access to this information through CLR (like the staff of revenue department) to selectively part with information for financial consideration. There is a clear case of collusion with the administrative staff in exchange of information. Anyone can get the copy of the records of rights, tenancy, and crop inspection register (RTC) by paying a fee. Thus, records become transparent, as it is easy for landowners to verify data on the landholdings of neighbours. e-Transparency increases the ability of groups to manipulate such data and thus increases the risk of misinterpretation or misuse.

Compromising Confidentiality of land record also leads to misuse of transparency. With the emergence of new land information market, the middlemen are desperately on the lookout for large parcels of land that are vulnerable to appropriation-especially lands that are under dispute. Information on such properties is very valuable. For instance, lands under family disputes, with no clear titles, lands with incomplete records, land registered under the name of dead people, absentee landlords, NRI owned lands and lands belonging to old people. This information is easily retrievable and tradable in the market. Small land owners are especially vulnerable. Many middlemen even offer to negotiate with other family members to bring the disputed land to the market. Transparency is becoming increasingly misused. Transparency is not a self standing good to be embraced under any circumstances; one should consider that privacy may have a place when making sensitive information transparent.

Forgery and Cloning is another mechanism of corruption. It has become easy to gain access to details of land records either through impersonation or through privileged leaks by inside staff. As a consequence, forged and cloned documents can be easily created. Thus, CLR facilitates the risk of forgery leading to outright land grabbing. Of course, this was possible even under the old manual system, but with CLR the process is more efficient, fast and less detectable, especially when the records themselves can be changed. Banks now are facing the problem as same documents are given as collateral/surety for multiple loans and it becomes hard to distinguish between the real and the fake documents.

Misuse of RTI for seeking information. Many middlemen have used RTI act to seek information on lands held by government, public and private trust and organisations. With these information they are able to reconstruct the details of vulnerable lands (e.g. 1-5 acre, but not too large parcels of land to avoid suspicion). If the land has not been marked out for any other purpose or has remained inactive for long, then they are easy targets for land grabbing.

Misuse through Land Use Conversion. It has become easy to reclassify large tracks of conterminous farm land held by diverse small land owners into residential plots or consolidate them into single ownership. Under manual system such undertakings were very difficult. Especially lands that are distributed under various land reform schemes are vulnerable to re-classification. Farmers who have received lands through such schemes apply for changes/updating/reclassification of their land and resell it given the attractive market prices they can receive. At worst these changes could be carried out without their knowledge. If mutation records are not reflected in CLR, the scope for such conversions is very high. This is especially evident in locations close to cities. Even though as per rules all mutation requests must be logged into the system by an operator, and such requests may subsequently be rejected after formally recording a reason, in practice this does not happen.

Lack of inter-connectedness among departments is another source of corruption. Tamil NILAM has not been networked to Registrar department and hence the information available at registrar might not match with that recorded in Tamil Nilam. Further there is no interconnection with anti-corruption or police department, thus limiting preventive measures. The lack of inter-connectivity means that lands can be registered with forged documents and the scope for validation of data is limited.

Malpractices of the revenue staff continue to subvert the reform. The staff of the revenue and Registrar departments, while getting trained in the new CLR, have also learnt to subvert the new systems so that they can continue their old practice of bribe. By continuing the physical separation of counters for issuance of computer outputs and payments of fee the scope of corruption increases.

Conclusion

To conclude, while CLR has achieved transparency, it has failed to reduce corruption. Computerisation alone cannot be a sufficient tool to tackle corruption. Outcomes of transparency depend not only on what is revealed, but also on how the information is assessed, used and acted upon. More importantly who gets access to the system is critical.

Tamil NILAM project design provided little focus on reducing corruption. The system design did not take into account forms of corruption and ways to minimise it. Instead it was taken for granted that computerisation will automatically lead to transparency and since transparency was assumed to reduce corruption, it was uncritically concluded that the systems technical superiority would automatically ensure mitigation against corruption. The application was focused on the narrow purpose of increasing revenues and administrative efficiency. The commitment to reducing corruption was never reflected in the design stage. It was used as rhetoric to justify the investment in CLR.

Transparency might also put powerful land owners at risk as their data too can be obtained by motivated individuals. But small land owners are at greater risk from transparency than large owners.

The fundamental problem that we see in e-governance model is not that the ICT-applications would fail to provide a transparent system. Rather because the model enables transparency the old corrupt practices would quickly adopt new tool and even reinvent new modes of corruption. The problem is with the uncritical belief that increased transparency would lead to reduced corruption. The relation between transparency and reduction in corruption is contingent on how social and organisational systems are transformed, rather than how they could be translated from analogue to digital or manual to automatic.

Perhaps CLR and e-governance in general might work if we have a stronger punitive system like Lokpal, because major factor that contribute to corruption is the low probability of discovery, and perceived immunity against prosecution. The weak character of institutions which are supposed to investigate charges of corruption and prosecute the guilty as well as an inefficient judiciary further exacerbate the problem of corruption and facilitate immunity against prosecution. Even those who are convicted would get not more than six months of imprisonment or penalty.

Transparency by itself does not amount to much as a democratic reform agenda, without an effective legal and institutional framework which guarantees oversight and is capable and willing of imposing sanctions ICT enabled transparency might increase the risk of "revenge effect". This leads to a larger question: Is transparency always good? The point is not to dismiss transparency as a failed ideal, but underscore the importance of balancing transparency with confidentiality, privacy and secrecy. We should embrace transparency, knowing its limits.

7

Exploring Model for Ensuring Transparency and Disclosure in Governance Structures Using ICT

S.M. Haider Rizvi

> "A popular Government without popular information or the means of acquiring it, is but a Prologue to a Farce or a Tragedy or perhaps both. Knowledge will forever govern ignorance, and a people who mean to be their own Governors must arm themselves with the power knowledge gives."
>
> —James Madison, Letter to W.T. Barry, August 4, 1822

Introduction

India, like any other nation, has kept inclusive development among its top priorities. It has been an active partner in various development debates, discussion and efforts internationally. Important and sizable efforts have been made by the country to raise the social and economic well-being of people. The State governments besides responding promptly to the calls from the Centre, too, have taken certain innovative measures for development of the people through legislation of policies and formulation of programmes and schemes. There seems no dearth of policies, programmes and schemes initiated at the Central and State levels.

There are many who would believe that India as a nation has failed in improving the socio-economic health of the nation and solving the problems like mass poverty, unemployment, women empowerment and child protection, etc. though these issues always been on the radar of policy-makers and other stakeholders. It would be unwise to reject the efforts made at the levels of visioning for lessening of these problems and bridging the development gaps and the formulations of policies and programmes thereof. One has to examine the reasons for the failures of these efforts with independent and impartial diagnostic tools. This paper is an effort in that direction. The need of the hour is effective implementation of the existing policies and programmes in their true letter and spirit with genuine political will accompanied with transparent and accountable systems of governance at various levels. It is needed to shun the inhibitions at the level of people and enable them to participate in efforts and interventions for their development.

The Development Efforts in India Since Independence

When India became Independent in 1947, it was resolved to focus on ending poverty, ignorance, diseases and inequality of opportunity. It is in this background the Planning Commission was set-up to work for the development of the country through formulating Five-Year Plans (FYPs). The First FYP was meant to assess the available resources, augmenting deficient resources and determining priorities for development. The focus and approaches of the FYPs got changed from time to time. In Second FYP the principle of 'socialistic pattern of society' was adopted to plan strategies and emphasize social gains whereas during the 1960s, 1970s and 1980s, the primary focus remained on accelerating economic growth, savings and investments.

The 1990s saw a major shift when economic reforms through liberalizing the economy were introduced in India. It was also a time when there were lots of debates and discussions on 'Human Development Index (HDI)' as parameters for determining development of nations and other units within countries. In India, too, the importance of human development as an approach for development was realised to put direct focus on human development and from Eighth FYP onwards the Five-Year Plans have been set within the human development paradigm. This paradigm shift has resulted in addressing inequalities and accelerated growth in the 2000s. During this time several landmark rights-based legislations such as Mahatma Gandhi National Rural Employment Guarantee Act (MGNREGA), Right to Education and Right to Information emerged as the foundations of poverty reduction strategies. The Mahatma Gandhi National Rural Employment Guarantee Scheme (MGNREGS) that got started in 2006 brought the 'right to work' to the front stage of the discussion on social protection. The National Rural Health Mission (NRHM) has strengthened public health systems by increasing community participation, adding to human resources in the system, improving health infrastructure, public health management and increasing public expenditure on health. The Jawaharlal Nehru National Urban Renewal Mission has led to construction of around 1.5 million houses for the poor and slum dwellers. The Jawaharlal Nehru National Solar Mission, launched in January 2010 aims to create a capacity of 20,000 MW grid solar power, 2000 MW off-grid solar applications and 20 million square metres of solar thermal collectors by the year 2022. There have been significant efforts to provide electricity, safe drinking water, telephones and broadband connectivity to remote villages.

As far as the achievements of targets set under Millennium Development Goals (MDGs) are concerned the results have been mixed with significant progress in 10 of the 22 indicators. There have been impressive gains in improving primary education, enrolment rate, promoting gender equality and increasing forest cover. The UN MDG Report 2012 points out that overall, three important targets on poverty, slums and water have been met three years ahead of the 2015 deadline. The share of people living on less than $1.25 a day has reduced to less than half as compared to 1990.

The Development Gaps

India's high growth rate has been accompanied with persistent poverty, inequality and many other deprivations on the socio-economic front. The findings on various development fronts are not very encouraging. The GDP growth rate is declining. It was 9.5 per cent during 2005-06 but decreased to 8.0 per cent in 2009-10 and to about 5.5 per cent in 2011-12. The GDP growth couldn't significantly impact some of the major areas of development. As per the estimates of Human Development Report 2011, the Human Development Index (HDI) Rank for India is 134 out of 187 countries. On the Gender Inequality Front (GII), India ranks 129 out of 146 countries. The literacy rate is 74.04 per cent. The female literacy rate is still only 65.46 per cent, meaning that still about 35 per cent women are illiterate. On poverty and hunger indicators, about 53.7 per cent population is multi-dimensionally poor and in absolute term the number of multi-dimensional poor is 612 million. 21 per cent of the total population in India is undernourished and 43.5 per cent children under 5 five years of age were undernourished in 2004-05.

The overall performance of India as a nation in achieving MDGs might be called satisfactory, but at the same time, the country's lacklustre performance in reducing overall poverty and health indicators has dragged down the performance of the South Asian region. India, compared to most nations in the Asia Pacific, has made very slow progress in eradicating poverty over the period of 10 years (Asia-Pacific Regional MDG Report 2011-12). With 49.4 per cent people living on less than $1.25 per day in the country, the metric for poverty used by MDGs, in 1994, the country was able to reduce it to only 41.6 per cent in the ten years to 2005. The rate of reduction in poverty is much lower than in other south Asian countries, e.g. Bangladesh which has brought down proportion of extremely poor people from 66.8 per cent in 1992 to 49.6 per cent in 2005. India's poor population is much higher than that in Pakistan (22.6%), Sri Lanka (7%) and Turkey (2.7%).

According to The National Millennium Development Goal Report 2011, much work remains to be done in reducing hunger, improving maternal mortality rates and enabling greater access to water and sanitation targets as well as reducing social and geographic inequalities in achieving these targets. The rising gender inequality continues to remain a concern hampering progress on achievements of other development goals. Women continue to be excluded in social, economic and political domains.

India has reduced MMR significantly from 437 per one lakh live births in 1999 to 212 now, yet one maternal death reported every 10 minutes. At present, the Maternal Mortality Rate (MMR) of India is 212 per one lakh live births, whereas the country's target is 109 per one lakh live births by 2015. There is a need to hasten the pace under National Rural Health Mission to achieve targets set under MDG 5 to reduce maternal mortality (MMR) from 437 deaths per 100,000 live births in 1991 to 109 by 2015. Till date it has only reached the 212 mark.

The proportion of people with improved access to drinking water has gone up from 76 per cent in 1990 to 89 per cent in 2010. As many as 237 million Indians are still living in hunger though India has managed to meet the first MDG of reducing people in extreme poverty by half between 1990 and 2015. The performance of India, with a population of 1.21 billion people, impacts the global achievement of the MDGs.

The Inequality in Development Outcomes

Though addressing inequalities has been the prime focus for the accelerated growth of the nation, yet persistent inequality continues. The level of human development attainment is much lower in case of the country's most marginalized groups including scheduled castes, tribal and rural populations, women, people living with HIV and migrants. The gender inequality in India persists despite high rates of economic growth with the outcomes lower among *Dalits* and *Adivasis*. Participation of women in employment and decision-making remains far less than that of men and the disparity instead of getting lessened are persistent. India's poor performance on women's empowerment and gender equality is reflected in many indicators, the most telling of which is the sex ratio which has in some parts of India dropped to 833 females per 1000 males. India ranks very low on Gender Inequality Index (129 out of 146 countries) with a value of 0.617). India is second from the bottom, above Afghanistan, in the South Asian countries.

The effectiveness of rights-based legislation such as the Mahatma Gandhi National Rural Employment Guarantee Act, the Forest Rights Act and Panchayat Extension to Scheduled Areas has been hampered by weak implementation. India's poor record on governance is reflected in its 87th rank on the corruption perception index among 178 countries with a value of 3.3 on a scale of 1 to 10 in 2010. Sustained focus on attaining high GDP growth rates with inadequate attention given to revisiting development patterns and inclusiveness of growth lies at the heart of India's paradox.

Growth rates, inclusiveness and sustainability are further constrained by the impact of climate change and vulnerability to disasters. Diverse factors, natural and human induced, adverse geo-climatic conditions, topographic features, environmental degradation, population growth, urbanization, industrialization and unscientific development practices play a huge role in accelerating the intensity and frequency of disasters resulting in huge economic losses and human casualties.

Strategies to Achieve Inclusive Development

The reason of the slow pace of development in India is mainly human induced resulting in poor governance. There is a need of all round efforts to tackle the problems prevailing at various fronts. Some of the areas which are in need of immediate attention to make governance good and ensure inclusive development are: ensuring transparency in governance structures, making provisions of disclosure and access of information and making people accountable in their roles, responsibilities and functioning thereof besides participation and effectiveness (OHCHR, 2004 and 2007; Choudhury and Skarstedt, 2005). These issues are discussed below.

Transparency in Governance Structures and Access to Information

The role of governance in the functioning of the government services should be visualized in terms of the delivery of services. Governance signifies "a change in the meaning of government, referring to a new process of governing or a changed condition of ordered rule; or the new method by which society is governed" (Stoker, 1998). In this way governance should be concerned with creating the conditions for ordered rule and collective action.

Stoker (1998) has summarised various propositions of governance as follows:

- Governance refers to a set of institutions and actors that are drawn from but also beyond government.
- Governance identifies the blurring of boundaries and responsibilities for tackling social and economic issues.
- Governance identifies the power dependence involved in the relationship between institutions involved in collective action.
- Governance is about autonomous self-governing networks of actors.

Governance recognizes the capacity to get things done which does not rest on the power of government to command or use its authority. It sees government as able to use new tools and techniques to steer and guide.

The analysis of governance structures in India in relation to the propositions made by Stoker suggests that there have been efforts at the level of government to make governance effective, e.g. to facilitate access of information to citizens and establish a culture of transparency in public offices and other government establishments. The Right to Information (RTI) Act promulgated in 2005 makes it mandatory for the public agencies to share and disclose information to each and every citizen on demand. The RTI Act, 2005 has certainly paid dividends especially in urban areas, yet the ordinary citizens in rural areas and small towns have not benefited much from it.

The finding of a study conducted on implementation of RTI Act in 12 States by PRIA in 2008 reveal that in 90 per cent districts information about designated Public Information Officers (PIOs) were not available and in equal number of districts the self-disclosure mandated under Section 4 of the RTI Act was not made. There was lack of cooperation from the PIOs on giving the information.

Making Governance Structures Accountable

The accountability aspects in ensuring good governance to achieve desired outcomes of the development programmes and schemes are taking front seat in government policies, procedures and services. It has always been prevalent in some form or other but because of lack of clarity on the concepts and absence of their direct relationship with different people in different roles, it was difficult to ascertain, individual as well as collective responsibilities, in case of non-achievement of performance and desired results.

In India, the focus of performance management have confined to confirming and regulating the processes with less emphasis on results. The Second Administrative Reforms Commission, 2005 has summarized it as follows by:

> "Traditionally governance structures in India are characterized by rule-based approaches. The focus of the civil services in India is on process-regulation. With such focus on processes, systems in government are oriented towards input usage — how much resources, staff and facilities that are deployed in a scheme, programme or project and whether such deployment is in accordance with rules and regulations. The main performance measure thus is the amount of money

> spent; and the success of the schemes, programmes and projects is therefore generally evaluated in terms of the inputs consumed."

The need is to inbuilt the aspects of transparency and disclosures in the system and while managing the performance in government at least on the aspects of 'delivery of services' for the people. There is need of a framework which monitors and evaluates performances of the public service officers on ongoing basis with focus on 'results' and 'performance'. It needs to be made more direct where the people in governance structures holding different portfolios are directly accountable for the results that are associated with their roles. In finding out various ways to bring transparency and accountability to regulate risks in public life, it is needed to work for developing a transparent and accountable culture and it is possible only when everyone is committed towards the demands of their roles and answerable for the performance of tasks assigned to them (Tandon, 2012). This will automatically bring a culture of accountability. Of late the efforts made in the direction of transparency and accountability by government and civil society is making the individuals and institutions/organisations accountable and answerable for the lapses in their achievement of performance and results.

Tandon (2012) has suggested ways to determine accountability that includes clearly specified tasks-allocation of time and budget for completion of the task, clarity on the responsibilities for task performance against the person/position/team, clearly laid down procedure for reporting progress and completion of the task to an authority upward in the hierarchy and a mechanism for course-correction for effective task performance exists.

The Right to Service Guarantee Acts enacted by different states for ensuring public services in time bound manner to citizens have strengthened the accountability dimensions in public agencies and institutions. Madhya Pradesh has taken a lead in this direction by effective implementation and streamlined processes and putting necessary ICT tools in place. On the lines of Madhya Pradesh eleven States have enacted Public Service Guarantee Acts and five have proposed appropriate legislations. The Government of India through Citizens Right to Grievance Redress Bill 2011 is trying to ensure right to service to the citizens.

The Conceptual Framework

Fig. 7.1 shows the conceptual framework suggested to ensure accountabilities in governance structures.

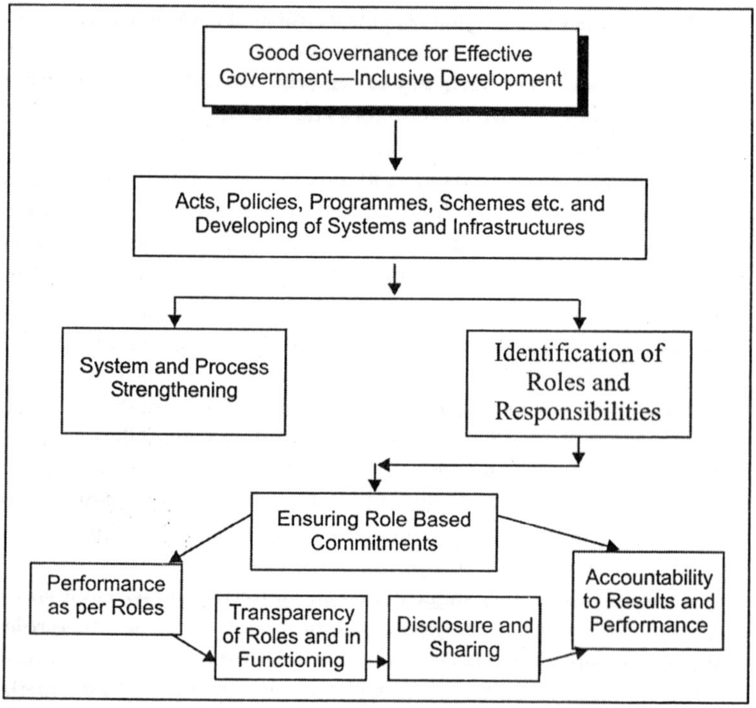

Fig. 7.1: Conceptual Framework for Accountability and Good Governance

Role of ICT in Ensuring Accountability

In the modern era where expectations are rising, it is difficult to govern, at various levels, without making changes in traditional approaches of governing. It is a gigantic task to ensure access of services to people without using the applications of Information, Communication and Technologies (ICTs). In order to achieve good governance, it has become mandatory on the parts of the institutions involved in governance at various levels to have requisite infrastructures and use ICTs to realize the development goals. The e-governance had emerged as a tool to realize the application of Governance Framework of

Administration to achieve overall objective of transparency, accountability, equity, responsiveness, effectiveness, efficiency and rule of law. The structures/processes that have been created under the rubric of e-Governance focus upon the realization of these objectives. The proposed socio-technical model under e-governance framework is an attempt to provide alternatives to achieve these goals.

The Socio-Technological Publicness Model of Development (SPMD)

In a political and democratic set-up like India, the processes have been built to incorporate opinion of citizen in policy formulations, programme designing and implementation at various levels—national, state and local. At national and state level there are, mainly, indirect processes to seek opinion of the intended beneficiaries in the designing of policies for their welfare in the form of discussions in legislature by the elected representatives, whereas at the local level it is direct participations through Gram Sabhas and Gram Panchayats in rural areas and municipalities in urban areas. However, it has been seen that there is gap between the expectations of the intended beneficiaries and the policy objectives finalized after different levels of discussions and consultations. In the process it has been seen that the intended beneficiaries play a little role in designing process and the centre stage has been taken by bureaucracy to a large extent with support from civil society, media, academia and interest groups. The role of common man in local level planning and executions is negligible and creates gaps between the designed programme and expectations of people.

In this background there is a need to design citizen driven model of e-governance where citizens play a significant role not only in designing of programmes for their own welfare but have space to check and monitor the programme designing, execution and outcomes in relations to their contexts and needs. There are evidences that when given the opportunities and space the *Gram Sabhas* have worked successfully to meet the need of local people for their development (MPRLP, SGPA, 2010). Direct participation of people plays a major role in the fulfilment of their expectations which can not be replicated by other mediums. These efforts need to be accelerated and supplemented through e-governance.

The proposed socio-technical model under e-governance framework is an attempt to provide alternatives to achieve these goals. It has used the 'Government-to-Citizen-to-Government (G2C2G) Model of e-governance. It is based on paradigm shift which advocates for bi-directional and multi directional approaches of Government to Citizen and Citizen to Government (G2C2G) instead of the unidirectional approach of governance in Government-to-Citizen or Government-to-Consumer (G2C), Government-to-Business (G2B), Government-to-Government (G2G) and Government-to-Employees (G2E) where the focus is on the government supported initiatives rather than the citizen initiated and driven initiatives. The major objective of the proposed model is to enhance 'publicness' in the governance structures and processes. The relevance of the model lies in its reliance on the existing structures, institutions, resources and infrastructures. The mechanisms, structures and roles suggested in the proposed model have powers to accommodate many factors which otherwise hinder the smooth running of e-governance initiatives e.g. accessibility of ICTs, people's technological assets, connectivity, real time interaction with government personnel with transparency and disclosure mechanisms, change management and ensuring of role based accountability.

The proposed model has been developed taking into considerations the relevance and powers of existing structures and institutions and accompanied resources within those for ensuring people's participation through creating in-built systems of accountability at various levels using ICTs.

The model has been confined for rural areas with building on the powerful provisions as a result of 73rd CAA in 1992 the Government of India has tried to fulfil the wishes of the people by involving them in planning and execution of developmental programme. It is focused upon fulfilment of grassroots expectations and to effectively develop ownership of the common man towards interventions for their own development. Their participation in the designing and execution of the programme would enhance their active participation in the government supported programmes.

Empowering of *Gram Sabhas* as institutions for strengthening democratic governance locally has created forums where people can take part in direct democracy through collective decision-making for their development. It has encouraged and strengthened leadership at the grass roots. They not only understand the problems of the people but also work towards finding a viable solution through allocating required resources. It is enabling the society to move towards *'Gram Swaraj'* as envisioned by Mahatma Gandhi.

The formation of Village Level Committees as intended in Part-IX of the Constitutions helps in grounding participation at grassroots. It brings about 'devolution' in the form of democratic decentralization. In this aspect various committees have been formed keeping in view the spirit of decentralization and proper functioning of Panchayats. The model is banking upon the powerful structures and provisions of Panchayat Committees. The representation of women, SCs/STs and OBCs in the committees would bring the diversity of issues raised and worked upon by committees through participatory planning at Panchayat level for attaining the goals of economic development with social justice.

The amalgamations of powers of ICTs and local governments i.e. Gram Panchayats in rural areas in particular the Panchayat Committees besides the citizens at large have been kept at the centre of Socio-technological Publicness Model for Development (SPMD) (Fig. 7.2). It is because of obvious reasons of the constitutional legitimacy of Panchayats as the third-tier of governance with local participations and ample resources from national (MMNREGS, BRGF, FC grants) and state (SFC, Grants-in-aid, Assigned Revenue) programmes and schemes, contributions and locally generated revenues through own funds like tax revenue, non tax revenue, service delivery etc.

Premises of SPMD

The Socio-technological Publicness Model for Development (SPMD) is based on the premises that there is need to:

- Share and disclose information at each tier of Panchayat.
- Translate Acts, Schemes, and Programmes into action.
- Ensure, at least, the basic functioning of the systems and processes such as village committees, Panchayats, District Planning Committees and functioning of para-statal bodies at the district and state levels besides establishments of a web station with internet connectivity.
- Employ or restructure the manpower deployments at the Panchayats to get them engaged in the roles envisioned under SPMD.

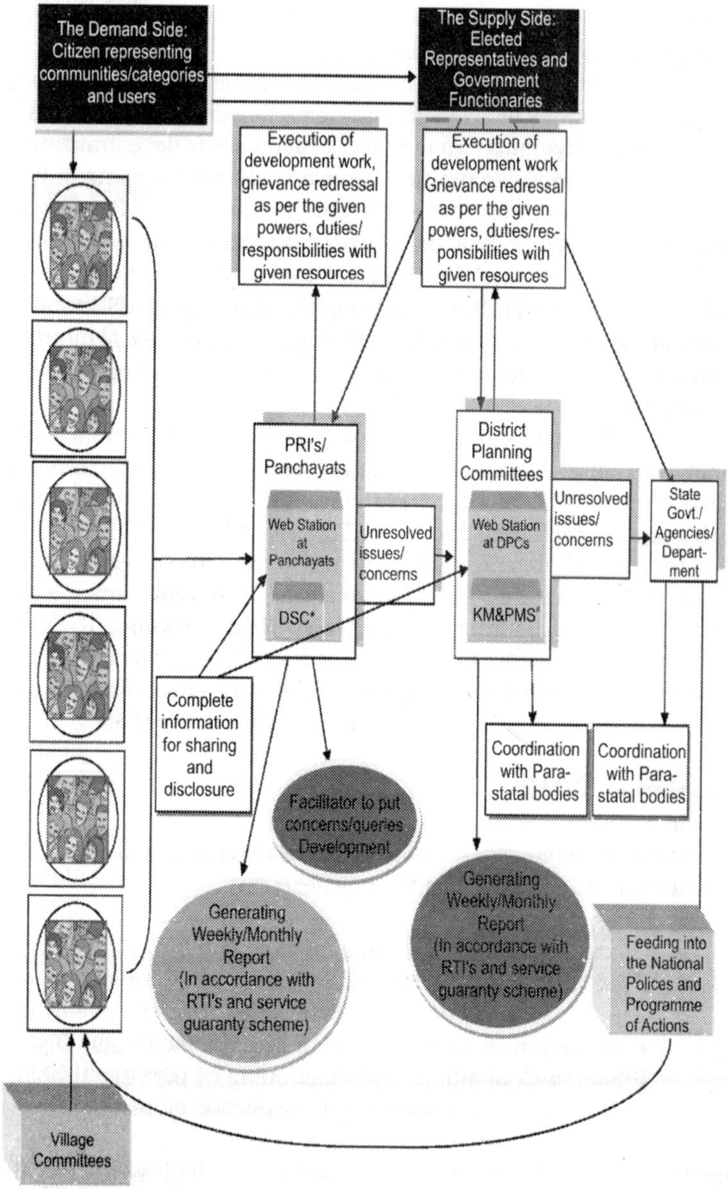

* Development Communication Specialist,

\# Knowledge Management and Programme Monitoring Specialist

Fig. 7.2: Socio-technological Publicness Model for Development

- Ensure two way direct and full participations of the citizens in the designing and implementation and evaluation of development programme and schemes.
- Facilitate, mediate and have checks on the governance structures and processes using ICT's to enhance transparency and accountabilities and attain desired development outcome

Features of SPMD

In the SPMD citizens have been kept at the centre to drive processes and also to make the processes themselves empowering for them (Oakley, 1991) and making the supply side accountable with their participation. The increased accountability would help in validating the participation to hold people in governance structures responsible for their actions (World Bank, 1992).

The basic constitutional entities, i.e. Gram Panchayats and Village Committees (VCs) have been given a prominent role in it. The VCs which otherwise have been mandated as the basic entity for development have largely been found idle. The awareness about the formation and functioning of the VC is very low. One could find the formations of the VCs on paper but most of the times members themselves are not aware about their being member of the committees and the envisaged functioning of these committees remains a distant dream. As per the visualisations these could have supplemented greatly in overall functioning of the Panchayats and local development. The concerns of the people and area could have been reflected well with the help of VC's.

In SPMD and VCs have been considered as the basic building blocks of development and as a medium to ensure people's participation. VCs have scope to accommodate a sizeable number of people from various socio-economic categories. As the core of the SPMD, the VCs have to be made functional with required capacity building to represent the concerns of the citizens as per the local socio-economic realities. As per responsibilities and powers given to members of the VCs, they would be putting or feeding the concerns in the system/portal/web station at the Panchayats. Though it will primarily the responsibilities of VC members to puts the data in the system with the help and facilitation of Development Communication Specialists (DSC's), the citizens and other stakeholders—elected representative, members of CSOs/NGOs, academia, media should also be encouraged to use the system to put their concerns and contribute to local development.

The system proposed to be kept at the Panchayats should be designed in a manner which besides managing the data should provide the information on needs of the people. The work list would be generated for weekly and monthly execution and would be made available to the concerned people and functionaries. The other powerful feature of SPMD is the generation of weekly and monthly reports based on the generated web-plan. These reports would also help in fixing accountability for persons given responsibilities for the execution of plans. The reports would give a clear cut picture of the work completed, in progress, under planning phase and work not attempted with the reasons thereof. These would automatically be circulated to the people engaged with the tasks in various capacities at various levels. The responsibilities assigned and the roles envisaged to Common Service Centres could very well be added to web stations at the Panchayat and *vice-versa.*

The SPMD has visualized having similar arrangement at the DPC level with a Knowledge Management and Programme Monitoring Specialist appointed from within the existing manpower. It would help in planning of interventions for the districts and the report generated at the district level would help in developing accountabilities towards the tasks coming under purview of various stakeholders. This would help in making DPCs more functional, relevant and accountable as per the roles envisaged for them instead of being a customary and ornamental body. The system would have features to supplement the plans and reports generated at the Panchayats and District Planning Committees.

Designing of the System for Web-Stations at Panchayats

The Web-Stations at Panchayats would be designed using Participatory ICT Design Methodology with full participation of users and other stakeholders in the designing processes by providing them space of co-designers (Rizvi and Dearden, 2008). The areas to accommodate during designing of the ICT solution would be as follows:

- MIS for Panchayats including powers and duties of the three-tiers of Panchayats — elected and appointed officials.

- The committees in Panchayats and their roles and responsibilities.
- Availability of resources through various sources and the allocation of funds.
- The manpower deployments in VC's, Panchayats and DPC's and their roles and responsibilities.
- The plans and priorities for the Panchayats/DPC's.
- The schemes and programmes for the local development from the Centre and State besides Panchayat's own development programmes and schemes.
- Provisions to assess progress made against various plans and development activities in Panchayats.
- Inter-linkages amongst different agencies at different levels i.e. Village, Block, District and State
- The monitoring mechanism in VC's, Panchayats and DPC's.
- Reports and other features and documents—As per needs and requirements

Strengths of SPMD

The SPMD would be far more advantageous in comparison to the other models because of the following salient features of the model:

- The model would help in enhancing the flows of information not only within Panchayats but would also enhance working linkages with other stakeholders and institutions. As envisaged in RTI Act, 2005 it would help in making people disclose information on their roles and responsibilities in public domain that would enable citizens to demand services and claim rights due to them from appropriate authorities and officials.
- The model would help in the direct participation of the citizens. There being no restrictions in the nature and kinds of information to be fed in the system, it would help in getting more and more information on the local needs and issues.
- In RTI Act 2005 citizens are to take initiatives for making the system respond to their demands instead of going to the specially created centres and getting engaged in various procedures, filling of forms and in case of non-availability of services and following-up with the centres. The SPMD, unlike Right to Service Guarantee Schemes, make the system

accountable in their spheres with regular monitoring and evaluations of the desired results and performance as envisaged as per their roles. There is no need on the part of the people to put checks and balances on them as their designated roles put checks and balances on them.

- The appointment of Development Communication Specialist would help in channelizing the information from the last mile and moving those upwards for the necessary follow-ups and actions.
- The model would help in generating transparency and accountabilities at various levels. It would also play a prominent role in fixing the accountabilities against the task assigned to various roles.
- The model would help in keeping track of the functioning of the Panchayats in terms of the progress made, achievements and delays with reasons and failures with responsible factors. It would help in reducing bureaucratic intricacies, red-tapism and controlling of corruptions.
- The model will help in translating the vision of the father of nation Mahatma Gandhi into action on *"Gram Swaraj"* by devolution and democratization of powers in the hands of actual beneficiaries as they are at the forefront of the designing of programmes for themselves.
- It would help in evolving mechanism for other departments not connected directly with the rural populations to have their opinion on the issues of their importance.
- It would strengthen the ownership on the part of people towards the government programmes/policies since they would be actively participating in the process.
- It would strengthen the faith of people in the government and would strengthen democratic governance processes at the grassroots.

The SPMD has been developed keeping the legal, operational, social and technical feasibilities into considerations.

Conclusion

The SPMD model is an effective tool developed under rural e-governance framework which is very pragmatic and feasible. It has tried to accommodate and optimally utilise the resources available locally with the Panchayats. It is not demanding things in an over ambitious manner. The only demand it puts forth is the genuine political will on the part of the people who are already involved in the planning and executions of development programmes. It not only emphasizes the 'accomplishments of the developments' tasks through Panchayats and other responsible agencies, but also has scope for making 'corrections' in the existing approaches. At the top of everything, the model if applied in true spirit has powers to bring a culture of transparency in the Panchayat functioning and in fixing accountability at various levels. The model could also be used as a powerful tool in bringing a culture of 'Role Based Commitments' and making people accountable towards their roles.

REFERENCES

Administrative Reforms Commission (2008), *Refurbishing of Personnel Administration: Scaling New Heights, Tenth Report of Second Administrative Reforms Commission*, Government of India, New Delhi.

Central Statistical Organization (2011), *Millennium Development Goals—India Country Report*, Ministry of Statistics and Programme Implementation, Government of India available on www.mospi.nic.in.

Choudhury, N. and C.E. Skarstedt (2005), *The Principle of Good Governance.* CISDL, Oxford, United Kingdom.

Dearden, A. and H. Rizvi (2009), "A Deeply Embedded Socio-Technical Strategy for Designing ICT for Development," *International Journal of Socio-technology and Knowledge Development*, Vol. 1, No. 4, IGI Publishing, USA.

http://en.wikipedia.org/wiki/Governance accessed on 9th August 2010.

http://planning.up.nic.in/annualplan0203/part1/chap-10.htm accessed on 31st August 2010.

http://www.tnrd.gov.in/reports/firstsfc/english/1-2.pdf accessed on 25th August 2010.

http:economictimes.indiatimes.com/topic/poverty. Accessed on 25/09/2012.

Ministry of Rural Development, *rural.nic.in/22_JULY/PlanPlus.../PlanPlusfoRDWorkshop22nd-23rd.ppt* accessed on 31st August 2010.

Oakley, P. (1991), *Projects with People: The Practices of Participation in Rural Development*, International Labour Organisation, Geneva.

Odugbemi, S. and T. Jacobson (2008), *Governance Reform under Real World Conditions: Citizen, Stakeholders, and Voice*, The World Bank, Washington D.C.

Planning Commission, Government of India, *Five Year Planshttp://planningcommission.nic.in/plans/planrel/fiveyr/welcome.html* accessed 12th September 2012.

PRIA (2008), *Implementation of RTI Act in 12 States*, Pune.

Report on National Consultation on Strengthening Delivery and Accountability Frameworks for Public Services 8-9 December 2011, supported by the GoI-UNDP Pathways for an Inclusive Indian Administration (PIIA) Project, Bhopal.

School of Good Governance and Policy Analysis (2010), *Assessment of the Improvement in Quality of Life of Beneficiaries under Madhya Pradesh Rural Livelihood Project*, Bhopal.

Sonalde B., A. Desai, A. Dubey, B. Joshi, M. Sen, A. Sharif and R. Vanneman (2010), *Human Development in India — Challenges for a Society in Transition*, Oxford University Press, New Delhi.

Stoker G. (1998), "Governance as Theory: Five Propositions," *International Social Science Journal*, Vol. 50, No. 1.

Tandon, R. (2012), "Transparent and Accountable Governance," *India Todayhttp://indiagovernance.gov.in/files/transparent_accountable_governance.pdf* accessed on 25th May 2013.

White, J.D. (2007), *Managing Information in the Public Sector*, M.E. Sharpe, New York.

World Bank (1992), *Governance and Development*, World Bank, Washington D.C.

8

Role of Technology in Transparency and Disclosure

M.S. Mishra and *V.K. Mishra*

Introduction

Transparency implies openness, communication and accountability. Transparency and disclosure is a process by which information regarding the existing conditions, decisions, and actions are made accessible, available and understandable. It helps to encourage accountability, by promoting decision-makers to make their decisions and further more to be answerable for such decisions. Transparency is thus a monitoring device, to ensure that all stakeholders understand and can influence organizations performance and operations in the stakeholder's interest.

Transparency and disclosure serve as an instrument for prevention of fraud and corruption. Disclosure helps public understanding of an organization's objectives, policies and performance with regard to environmental and ethical standards, as well as its social responsibilities. Reliable and timely information enhances confidence among the key players i.e. decision-makers and the stakeholders within an organization and helps in making rational decisions directly affecting growth and profitability. The information provided shows the decision-makers and the interested public whether and to what extent an organization meets the legal requirements.

Role of Information Technology

In the emerging globalized scenario Information Technology (IT) is playing a decisive role in transparency and governance. An organization head who has dealt with the pains of computerization must have realized that the transition from a paper-based structure towards a paperless modern IT-integrated knowledge-based institution is full of challenges. The challenges are in the nature of organization's objectives, standards of performance, internal controls and data-based management. Those who computerized old paper-based systems without proper thought have led to chaos and confusion which further affected the efficiency of the organization. The concept of paperless office cannot be thought of without fuller computerization. This not only enhances efficiency but also helps in improving the transparency in the working of the organization.

Thanks to advancement in technology, information is now readily available in almost every shape and form to enable transparency and accountability to function to their full effectiveness. The ever expanding technological development makes possible the processing and transformation of huge quantities of complex data and information at an economical cost. It is forcing standardization of objectives, measurement, processes, and setting benchmarks so that units of operations can be monitored and controlled more quickly and efficiently. Standardization of reporting formats enable performance to be monitored functionally and across time and geography in a short span of time. Technology helps in better management of risk and reduction of cost.

Information technology has immensely altered the relationship between the internal and external customers of an organization. Organizations are now forced to be more open in order to reach to the global markets. Data availability through the Internet ensures that stakeholders have better and faster information to hold the organization's directors and managers more accountable for their action. Through technology, no director of an organization can have an excuse that they do not have access to the right information at the right time.

Cyberspace has broken the barrier of geographical boundaries and hence geographical governance whereas the national laws and regulations are still grappling with. Like all tools IT is only a means towards an end, namely, the objective of an organization's governance with transparency as its core characteristics.

Turning online activity into offline change continues to be a struggle for digital activists all over the world, and projects aimed at addressing issues of corruption are no exception. Low involvement of people and a lack of infrastructure are commonly cited as obstacles for many technology projects. However, they are particularly relevant in the case of transparency, where participation from diverse players is mandatory to the success of most initiatives.

Peoples' Participation

Effecting offline change often requires a shift in perception. While several technology projects attract substantial interest from citizens, some, particularly those focusing on disseminating government information rather than on collecting citizen input, have difficulty gaining and sustaining citizen's involvement. In many areas, there is little public awareness and understanding of government activity, or of the power of citizen's oversight.

When data is being collected from individuals and communities, low citizen involvement could also be a result of distrust or poor relationships between the intended users of the information and the disclosed information.

In this globalised environment mass media is an important tool which impacts our lives in every sphere especially in the decision-making. Involvement of mass media is also an essential component for achieving wider social impact by technology-led transparency. This is an important aspect in utilization of technology for enhancing the transparency. Local mass media must be aware of and able to use the information collected by technology projects in order to hold governing authorities accountable.

Lack or low engagement with governing authorities at various scales can also be a substantial obstacle in combating corruption through technology. Distrust and secrecy are commonly cited issues for technology-led projects working towards accountability, often enhanced by a lack of communication and consultation on both sides. Government officials can be an essential partner in increasing government transparency. They can push for legislative reform based on data available due to disclosure.

One of the most commonly raised issues among technology projects is the need for clear outcomes from citizen's involvement. In many cases there was significant interest from communities, but when the project was unable to effect change, interest and support for the project diminished. Conversely, when participants felt that their input had led to a definitive outcome, even if that outcome did not translate directly into accountability, confidence in the tool improved.

Infrastructure Deficit

While dealing with technology, infrastructure is often understood as the physical networks required for access to the internet. But this is only one of many structures needed to realise the potential of technology-led transparency. Technology projects also rely on education, regulation, culture and social support. These structures are very much tied into issues of engagement, and in some cases it may be necessary to build up adequate infrastructure before effectively engaging various participants. Ideally, technology-led transparency projects should have clear frameworks for implementation and progression, which ultimately depend on the existing and emerging technology infrastructure.

Language is another aspect of social infrastructure which, if overlooked, can significantly restrict the impact of technology-led transparency. This has become vital now with the availability of more online content in local languages in the country. But still many people prefer to receive information orally at face-to-face meetings, which generate the need for proper demonstrations and follow-ups.

Learning Networks

Online tools provide an important opportunity for "enhanced transparency", where the users of data create and shape information content, allowing for interactions not present in offline transparency projects. At the same time, there are a number of obstacles to achieving prolific transparency, including the very real danger that intended users do not have the capacities to understand, analyze and interpret the disclosed information. There are often substantial communication, trust and knowledge gaps that exist as a result of low interaction and a lack of infrastructure.

There is need by the government to develop learning networks to bridge these gaps. As technologically driven transparency continues to grow at rapid pace, these structures of multi-stakeholder (governmental or partnerships with private parties) collaboration must develop. These must be developed at every level and encourage people to harness the benefits of technology by hosting workshops, meetings and seminars to discuss how online tools can best serve the purpose of transparency. These mutual learning networks provide a vital space for continued discussion and partnership building. Stakeholder's timely access to vital information will enhance the confidence in the organization. This confidence can further be sustained and accelerated with adaptation of adequate technology. Technology is definitely a boon for those who have availability and accessibility to it. Bridging the infrastructure gap will surely enhance the transparency.

Conclusion

The development of mutual networks does not guarantee that technology-led transparency will be successful in the long-run. In short-run some of the bottlenecks impacting technology-led transparency projects are funding, low involvement and a lack of infrastructure. But it must be realized at the same time that corruption does not disappear when it is exposed. The realization of greater accountability in governance is long and complex. Online tools can definitely play a decisive role in this process, but can fail to generate the desired impact, if implemented without proper consideration and engagement of the relevant stakeholders and structures of governance.

Modern businesses are complex global operations. Transparency reduces opportunity for misuse of public money. Transparency and disclosure are now the key to do business in the new globalized scenario. The business organizations must ensure that all the parties concerned with whom they do business can rely on them regarding the conduct of the business. The business organizations must be committed towards fairness and high degree of professionalism. Hopefully, in the times to come, the pressure from investors, governments and society encourages business organizations to become more transparent.

REFERENCES

http://en.wikipedia.org
http://www.transparency.org
http://www.blackstone.com
http://www.sfc.hk

PART-3

Transparency, Disclosure and Social Justice

9

Transparency, Disclosure and Social Justice

D.N.S. Yadav

> "We, the people of India, having solemnly resolved to constitute India into a Sovereign, Socialist, Secular, Democratic, Republic, and to secure to all its citizens, Justice—social, economic and political; Liberty of thought, expression, belief, faith and worship; Equality of status and of opportunity…"
>
> —The Preamble of the Constitution of India

Introduction

The preamble of the Constitution of India makes it categorically clear that India is a democratic country committed to the ideals of justice and equality of opportunity to all people without any discrimination. Modern India faces a number of sensitive socio-economic problems which need to be addressed in a most urgent manner. Behind the shadow of socio-economic advancement India is busy in drawing the poverty line and counting those below poverty line. Unless the people are able to satisfy their hunger any talk of transparency and participation in government is meaningless for them. This should give sleepless nights to the persons at the top of the political system in the country, but unfortunately it is not so.

Transparency and Disclosure

It is well-known that power corrupts and absolute power corrupts absolutely. One can think about the fate of the common man when feeling prevails among the politicians and the bureaucrats that they are all powerful and are under no obligation whatsoever to disclose to the common man or to be transparent in their administrative and judicial functioning. The democratic set-up of governance visualizes that the government is accountable for the entire process of decision-making to the people who have elected them to rule.

The pillars of administrative accountability are 'transparency' and 'openness', which is possible only through the channel of sincere and honest disclosures. Such transparency has to cover all democratic institutions without exception whether legislature, executive or judiciary. We come across social exclusion the moment there is a lack of harmony in these three organs. It was never intended by the makers of the Constitution that these constitutional bodies should function in complete disharmony to each other. Such a disharmony is inevitable when there would be a tendency among them of non-disclosure and not to be transparent. Under the given situation of non-transparency and non-disclosure, in complete disregard to the spirit of the Constitution, the administration is bound to collapse in the way we are seeing these days.

It needs to be stressed that development to be real and inclusive has to be participatory and should inculcate the feeling of fairness, justice, ownership and accountability in the general masses. The racial, regional and gender based disparities may best be removed through a development agenda which is inclusive and is based on transparency and disclosure. The prevalent corruption is undoubtedly the result of opacity in various domains, processes and programmes run by the state and its instruments.

Social Justice and Equality

For understanding social justice in collective sense we need to understand justice, which is a concept of moral rightness based on ethics, rationality, law, natural law, religion and equity. The administration of law takes into account the inalienable and inborn rights of all the human beings and citizens. It implies equal protection of all the rights of the people and individuals without any sort of discrimination on the grounds of race, caste, gender, religion, national origin, colour, disability or age, or other characteristics being inclusive of social justice. Justice is connected to the concept of cardinal virtues. According to John Rawls "justice is the first virtue of social institution, as truth is of system of thought".

Social justice is synonymous with maximum happiness of the maximum number following Jeremy Bentham's principle of utility. In his book *A Fragment of Government*, Bentham says "it is the greatest happiness of the greatest number that is the measure of right and wrong". Governance should be transparent and inclusive so that it ensures maximum happiness of the maximum number. John Stuart Mill, who is the pioneer of utilitarianism, bases his theory in normative ethics holding that the proper cause of action is the one that maximizes utility, specifically maximizing happiness and reducing sufferings of the people. Anscombe took it to be a form of consequentialism. According to utilitarianism the moral worth of an action is determined only by its resulting outcome. However, it is debatable as to how much consideration should be given to actual consequences, foreseen consequences or intended consequences.

Bentham's book *An Introduction to the Principles of Morals and Legislation* is a masterpiece on governance. Bentham's work starts with principle of utility. As he observes: "Nature has placed mankind under the governance of two sovereign masters, pain and pleasure. It is for them alone to point out what we ought to do. By the principle of utility is meant that principle which approves or disapproves of every action whatsoever according to the tendency it appears to have to augment or diminish the happiness of the party whose intent is in question, or what is the same thing in other words to promote or oppose that happiness. I say of every action whatsoever, and therefore not only of every action of a private individual, but of every measure of government". Bentham introduces a method of calculating the value of pleasure and pain which is known as hedonist calculus. According to Bentham the value of a pleasure or pain can be measured according to its intensity, duration, certainty, uncertainty or remoteness. For administration of justice, Bentham makes it loud and clear that "the business of the government is to promote the happiness of the society, by punishing and rewarding ….in the proportion as an act tends to disturb that happiness, in proportion as the tendency of it is pernicious, will be the demand it creates for punishment". The Benthamite principles are applicable in modern democracies for achievement of collective welfare of the people.

The modern concepts of social justice are based on the teaching of St. Thomas Aquinas. Social justice as a secular concept has been established in the late twentieth century by the philosopher John Rawls. However, credit goes to Jesuit priest Lulgi Taparelli for coining the term "social justice". While adopting the term "social justice" Lulgi Taparelli wrote authoritatively in his journal *Civilta Cattolica* that engaging both capitalists and socialists approaches, undermine the unity of the society and neither the liberal capitalists nor the communists concerned themselves with public moral philosophy.

The concept of social justice is based upon the principles of equality and solidarity among its people. A just society would both understand and value human rights and recognize the dignity of every human being. The Constitution of the International Labour Organization (ILO) declares that "universal and lasting peace can be established only if it is based upon social justice". The Vienna Declaration and Programme of Action consider social justice as a purpose of the human rights education and protection of basic human rights by the world governments in a just, fair and reasonable manner.

In modern perspectives all societies have a basic structure of social, economic, and political institutions. The basic legitimacy of these institutions is based on the theories of social contract. All the societies need to examine the desirability and legitimacy of social arrangements from time to time since social development is an ever changing process. The government should concentrate on preservation of the good and eradication of the bad by means of well measured policy initiatives. John Rawls emphasizes that for better achievement of social justice governance should look for the agreement by the people who are subject to it by means of their participation in the governance. Although, it may not be easily practical but consent to such policy proposals would be for a larger public good to ensure the greater objectives of social justice parameters.

The concept of equality is to be understood in terms of social and political equality and reduction of economic disparity by means of affording the equality of opportunity to all. Social equality implies for all people within a society to have the same status in certain respects like equal rights to every person under the law, equal right to freedom of speech and expression, equal access to social goods and services, equal right to economic equity within the ambit of equality of opportunity. Social equality stands for unequal treatment under the law and absence of discrimination on the grounds of sex, race, age, caste, region, religion, income, language, health or disability and should go beyond the boundaries of class and caste considerations.

Since the French Revolution, equality has served as one of the leading ideals of body politic and in this respect at present probably it is one of the most debated issues of great social ideals. The precise notion of equality is to be seen in relation to justice and equality, the ideal measure of equality, the existence of equality and the value of equality. Equality is synonymous with egalitarianism, which could be identified as equalitarianism. It is a trend of thought that favours equality for particular category of or for all living entities. The equality doctrine maintains that all human are equal in fundamental worth or social status. When seen in terms of social justice it connotes as that all people should be treated as equal and have the same social, economical, cultural, political and other civil rights.

The practical concept of equality could be broadly categorized into social equality, political equality, economic equality, gender equality, racial equality. Equality of opportunity is the most potential term, where it is the prime responsibility of the governance to make available to all equality of opportunity under ideal conditions so as to ensure social and economic justice. Alexander Beckman suggests that, " ...equality does not mean an equal amount but an equal opportunity...do not make the mistake of identifying equality in liberty with the forced liberty of the convict camp. True anarchist equality implies freedom not the quantity. It does not mean that everyone must eat, drink, or wear the same thing, do the same work, or live in the same manner. Far from it the very reverse in fact ...the individual needs and tastes differ, as the appetite differs. It is equal opportunity to satisfy them that constitutes true equality. Far from levelling such equality, open the doors for greatest possible variety of activities and development. For human character is diverse".

Rule of Law

Oxford English Dictionary defines the Rule of Law as: "The authority and influences of law in society, especially when viewed as a constraint on individual and institutional behaviour, hence, the principle whereby all the members of a society including those in government are considered equally subject to publically disclosed legal codes and processes". Rule of law, thus implies that nobody is above law and every citizen is subject to the law of the land. Famous British jurist A.V. Dicey is the chief exponent of the rule of law, who popularized it during the Nineteenth century. He emphasized three aspects of the rule of law:

- No one can be punished or made to suffer except for a breach of law proved in an ordinary court.
- No one is above the law and everyone is equal before the law regardless of social, economic or political status.
- The rule of law includes the result of judicial decision determining the rights of the individuals.

Under the banner of the United Nations the rule of law has been defined as, "a principle of governance in which all persons, institutions and entities, public and private including the state itself, are accountable to laws that are publicly promulgated, equally enforced and independently adjudicated and which are consistent with international human rights norms and standards. It requires measures to ensure adherence to the principles of supremacy of law, equality before law, accountability to law, fairness in the application of law, separation of powers, participation in decision-making, legal certainty, avoidance of arbitrariness and procedural and legal transparency". Rule of law has been further defined by the General Council of International Bar Association (2009) in these words: "An independent impartial judiciary, the presumption of innocence, right to a fair and public trial without undue delay, a rational and proportionate approach to punishment, ...equality of all before the law, are all fundamental principles of Rule of Law. Accordingly arbitrary arrest, secret trials, indefinite detention without trial, cruel or degrading treatment or punishment, intimidation, corruption in the electoral process, are all unacceptable. The Rule of Law is the foundation of a civilized society. It establishes a transparent process accessible and equal to all. It ensures avoidance to principles that both liberate and protect".

In addition to the social dynamics of Rule of Law the most significant aspect of rule of law initiative is the study and analysis of the rule of law's impact on economic development. The rule of law movement cannot be fully successful in transitional and developing country like India unless the rule of law honestly addresses to the economic development of Indian society. Economic analysis of Constitutional law is a very important branch of rule of law to determine the constitutional economics by means of legal-institutional-constitutional rules that contain the choices and activities of economic and political agents in the society. It requires the study of the compatibility of economic and financial decisions within existing constitutional law framework.

Rule of Law in India guarantees and promotes fundamental rights and freedom of the citizens and respect for the principles of the democratic state based on rule of law. The popular habious corpus case, *ADM Jabalpur* vs. *Shivakant Shukla,* is one of the most important cases when it comes to the rule of law. This was in context with suspension of enforcement of Art. 14, 21 and 22 during the proclamation of emergency. It was held that the rule of law is that the government should be conducted within a framework of recognized rules and principles which restricted discretionary powers. The Supreme Court further observed in *Somraj* vs. *State of Haryana,* that the absence of arbitrary power is prime consideration of Rule of Law. There should be no application of discretion by the executive authorities without the rule of law. The principle implicit in rule of law is that the executive must act under the law and not by its own fiat and that is the cardinal principle of common law system and the same is followed in India. In *Keshvanand Bharati* vs. *State of Kerala,* the Supreme Court declared that the rule of law is one of the important aspects of the doctrine of basic structure. In *Maneka Gandhi* vs. *Union of India,* the Supreme Court held that Art. 14 strikes against arbitrariness and confines to the rule of law. *Minerva Mills Ltd.* vs. *Union of India* is also a masterpiece pronouncement by the Supreme Court on Rule of Law under Indian administrative set-up. Meaning thereby that for the purposes of ensuring social justice and equality at the grassroot level the executive has to follow the rules and regulations as made up by the nation's legal system, not only to ensure equality of opportunity and of equality of status to all, but also to avail equality of legal remedies as well, strictly in accordance with law.

Constitutional and Legislative Dimensions

The Constitutional Law of India is the fundamental law of the land which was put into force after India got Independence from British rule. It is the major legal policy document to ensure social, economical and political administration of the country in post-Independence era. The very Preamble of the Constitution enshrines within itself justice—social, economical and political...and equality of status and opportunity to all its citizens. In *Bachan Singh* vs. *State of Punjab,* the Supreme Court has enunciated that the Constitution upholds the dignity of man. The Preamble of the Constitution mentions the main objectives of the Constitution as has been pointed out in *Golak Nath* vs. *State of Punjab* that no authority created under the Constitution is supreme, it is the Constitution which is supreme.

The concept of separation of powers is inbuilt in the form of establishment of three constitutional bodies i.e. the legislature, the executive and the judiciary. The legislature is the main legislative body to perform the function of law making either in the central legislature i.e. the Parliament as far as the union list is concerned, or the State Legislative Assemblies with reference to the subjects mentioned in the State list. Concurrent list gets common application depending upon the need but in case of any contradiction the law made by the Parliament prevails. Legal rights are conferred and legal duties are imposed for the citizens, where the people can claim their rights in a just and reasonable manner subject to fulfilment of their duties as imposed under the law. The executive has the Constitutional authority to enforce the law without any bias or discrimination as made by the legislature. The Judiciary has the constitutional function to interpret the law according to the intention of the legislature and also to oversee proper law making or the implementation of the law and simultaneously to perform the function of judicial review as and when so required in the greater interest of justice. Where, the executive takes all care at the time of proper implementation of the objectives of social justice would be achieved, where the judiciary has to just keep a lawful watch for equal, just and fair enforcement of the law to its citizens.

The Universal Declaration of Human Rights (UDHR, 1948) made its great impact on Indian Constitution in the form of fundamental rights and other enactments as well in case of other statutory rights. Art. 14 read the entire philosophy of rule of law and the concept of social justice and equality in the form of fundamental right as: "The state shall not deny to any person equality before the law or the equal protection of laws within the territory of India". The executive and the judicial function is supposed to be well within the constitutional mandate in just and fair manner without the arbitrary application of law then only the administrator would be able to get the desired results of social justice. Art. 15 prohibits discrimination among individuals on the grounds of religion, race, caste, sex or place of birth. However, there is an exception to this provision, where class based discrimination appears in the form of reservation to scheduled castes/scheduled tribes, other backward classes in the matter of public employment. Art. 15(3) authorizes state to make special provisions for women and children. The justification behind this special protection through class and gender based discrimination is to provide these categories equality of opportunity since they have made to suffer perpetual societal exploitation at the hands of Indian society. Caste system has been a curse on Indian social system where the society had been divided into upper castes and lower castes. There had been no equality of status due to the caste barriers, which has been a big hurdle for social justice considerations.

Art. 17 abolishes untouchability in theory but practically this social taboo still mars the existing social system and the constitutional initiatives have proved to be futile. The Constitution of India identified the exploitative tendencies prevalent in the Indian society and made legal provisions in the form of right against exploitation, prohibiting of traffic in human beings and forced labour (Art. 23) and prohibition of employment of children in factories (Art. 24), but due to acute poverty conditions there are reported instances of trafficking in human beings and forced child labour. Protection of life and personal liberty (Art. 21) is the most significant fundamental right under all Constitutions world over. Similar is the right to fundamental freedoms (Art. 19) which have been conferred to all citizens without any discrimination.

On the front of educational justice great job has been done by means of introducing Art. 21-A, through the Constitution (Eighty-Sixth Amendment) Act, 2002, that, " the state shall provide free and compulsory education to all children of the age of six to fourteen years in such manner as the state may, by law, determine". It's a revolutionary measure towards social justice for the children of socially and economically weaker sections of the society, where twenty-five per cent of the seats in private schools shall be kept reserved for such children for the purpose of imparting education at the expense of the state. State of primary education in India is very pathetic in the sense there are well equipped private schools for socially and economically well to do sections of the society, whereas there are government schools with poor or no infrastructure facility for the children of the lower classes and weaker sections. Looking to these two extreme conditions on the opposite poles it would be rather day dreaming for the policy-makers to go for social justice. Under such circumstances even after six decades of independence it appears rather very difficult, if not impossible, to achieve the social justice landmarks. Education at large is the backbone of any social system and its further advancement.

The Directive Principles of State Policy (DPSP), are not enforceable by the courts as is the case with the Fundamental Rights, but these are very crucial for the purposes of formulating and legislating social and economic policy considerations of the nation. We see an inbuilt glimpse of social and economic justice impulse under the DPSP, which enjoin the government to:

- Establish a social order for the promotion of welfare of the people (Art. 38);
- Treat the citizens, men and women equally;
- Provide right to adequate means of livelihood (Art. 39-a);
- See that the ownership and control of material resources of the community are so distributed as best to subserve the common good (Art. 39-b);
- To see that the operation of the economic system does not result in the concentration of wealth and the means of production to the common detriment (Art. 39-c);
- Ensure equal pay for equal work for both men and women (Art. 39-d);
- Take steps so that the health and strength of workers, men and women, and tender age of children are not abused and that the citizen are not forced by economic necessity to enter avocations unsuited to their age or strength (Art. 39-e);
- See that the children are given opportunities and facilities to develop in a healthy manner and in conditions of freedom and dignity and that children and youth are protected against exploitation and moral and material abandonment (Art. 39-f).

Some of the important constitutional provisions introduced with the intention to incorporate transparency to settle down social justice parameters include the following:

- Organization of Village Panchayats (Art. 40) visualizes endowing them with such powers and authority as may be necessary to enable them to function as units of self-government.
- The state shall, within the limits of its economic capacity and development, take effective provision for securing the

right to work, to education and to public assistance in case of unemployment, old age, sickness and disablement, and in other cases of undeserved want (Art. 41).

- Make living wages for workers (Art. 42).
- Participation of workers in management of industries (Art. 43-a).
- Promotion of educational and economic interests of scheduled castes, scheduled tribes and other weaker sections of the society (Art. 46).
- It is the duty of the state to raise the level of nutrition and the standards of living and to improve public health (Art. 47).

The above provisions are the micro elements for social justice and the administration of the same would not be possible unless these micro elements are translated honestly in their true letter and spirit. Right to know is the fundamental right of citizens, which inculcates transparency and disclosure in the administrative decision-making, so that the people in a democratic set-up could know and keep themselves informed of the governing parameters in the administration of justice process of the nation. Keeping this fundamental in mind the Indian Parliament enacted, The Right to Information Act, 2005 with an avowed objective to ensure transparency and accountability through disclosures to its citizens. Parliament had to come out with this law to fight out rampant corruption prevalent in the Indian society and to fix accountability of the actors found responsible for wrongful and fraudulent governance.

Social Inclusion and Social Exclusion

The concept of distributive justice is essential for honest administration of social justice in India. Inclusive growth is the goal of social and economic development governance of the country is concerned. But, practically we find that only the chosen few, who are resourceful, are the beneficiaries of social or economic growth in the country. Large parts of the populations of the citizens are not able to enjoy the fruits of prosperity and the growth because they are poor and belong to the weaker section of the society. They are destined to be excluded, despite high profile claims of the people holding responsible positions in the governance.

Poverty is the most important causative factor of social exclusion. People having no money would be excluded from good food, adequate nutrition, proper schooling, proper health or medicinal facility, a proper house to live in, livelihood for the children, who would be ultimately forced to child labour just beneath the nose of the legal system. India has a long trail of social exclusion of dalits and backward classes based on caste discriminations. In spite of the legislative measures the socio-economic conditions of dalits and backwards is not much better. They are still the excluded lots in social, cultural and religious gatherings. This is not a healthy sign towards social harmony where the social bonds balance on a very sharp edge and any moment give rise to serious social unrest. Religious and gender based exclusions are very common in the existing Indian society and unless the transparent governance tackles the situation seriously this will have grave repercussion on the socio-religious-economic fabric of the nation.

Administration of Justice

What amounts to administration of justice in true sense is a very delicate issue? When a woman who has been raped the legal system of the country punishes the rapist in accordance with law of the land. Should we satisfy ourselves that by means of punishing the culprit justice has been administered to the raped woman? One may ask why there was at all a crime against women? Can't we respect and protect the dignity of the women? Why should she be treated as a commodity to be enjoyed with rather than her identity as an independent human being? If we consider that it is the responsibility of the judiciary only to administer justice, then we are absolutely wrong. The judiciary has no reply to the questions cited above. Why do we not honour the woman? The judiciary just can't reply it. It is the society as a whole which is squarely responsible for social inclusion and social exclusion. If a dalit is excluded and ignored by the society, then it is a social problem not a legal problem. Court would be helpless to do any justice in this regard that the dalit should be socially included. If the girl child is killed by the society in the womb of the mother or if she is killed afterwards, who is responsible for feticide or infanticide? When the society will learn to not to do injustice? We claim ourselves to be highly educated and highly civilized but still we have not learnt to be just and fair. It is in fact the mindset of the people which creates certain social situations which are not in consonance with the sound legal principles of the country. In these circumstances injustice is bound to happen.

Delay defeats the ends of justice. The Constitutional framework of India has established three tier court systems under the law. The courts are entrusted with judicial scrutiny in the light of evidence while performing the task of adjudication process. We come across the instances of undue delay and protracted trials in the Indian courts for years and years together. By the time the legal right of the plaintiff is adjudicated upon by the complicated legal system of the country, he passes away from this world in the hope of getting justice during his life time. Appreciation of evidences and interpretation of the law is the constitutional jurisdiction of the courts. But the collection of evidence is an executive function. There remains every possibility before the court that although there is evidence but it is not adequate as per judicial standards. The court is obliged to exonerate the person for want of sufficient evidence. It should not be left for the courts alone to carry the burden of administration of justice whether social or economical.

Judicial Activism *Vs.* Public Interest Litigations

The concept of public interest litigation has been linked with matters of public importance and has proved to be a big instrument in the hands of judiciary for purposes of administration of social justice. It was due to administrative inaction particularly on the issues of public interest that the higher judiciary stepped in which came to be known as judicial activism. Where the judiciary accepts the challenge of social justice and endeavours to settle the issue by means of establishing a harmony with the legal provisions and statutory interpretation it is said that judiciary has become active. The task of judiciary is to interpret the law in such a manner that ambiguity in the law if any is removed and the communication gap in the law are so explained that the intention of legislature is preserved and the law lives up to the expectations of the people at large.

Black's Law Dictionary defines judicial activism as a philosophy of judicial decision-making whereby the judges allow their personal views about the public policy, among other factors to guide their decision. Prof. Bradley Canon, a great political scientist, has posited six dimensions of judicial activism, *viz.*, majoritarianism, interpretive stability, interpretive fidelity, substance/democratizing process, specificity of policy, and availability of an alternate policy-making. David Strauss goes on to argue that the judicial activism is in fact overturning laws as unconstitutional, overturning judicial precedents and ruling against a preferred interpretation of the Constitution. Mr. K.G. Balakrishnan, former Chief Justice of India has said that, "In Indian context, there has been a raging debate on the proper scope and limits of judiciary specially of that role played by higher judiciary which consists of the Supreme Court at the centre and the High Courts in various states that form the Union of India. The terms of that debate have been broadly found with respect to the consideration of ensuring an effective 'separation of power' between the legislature, executive and judiciary as well as concerns about the efficacy and legitimacy of judicial intervention in the long run". As a role model of judicial activism Justice P.N. Bhagwati has made it explicitly clear that by means of judicial activism the Supreme Court has developed a new normative regime of rights and insisted that a state cannot act arbitrarily but must act reasonably and in larger public interest on pain of its action being invalidated by judicial intervention.

There are matters of public importance which could not be resolved merely by judicial intervention unless there is a fair degree of people's participation. Public service is full of rampant corruption all around and the ultimate sufferer is the society in the form of socio-economic offences which Edwin Sutherland terms as white collar crimes. The issues which are important from social justice angles are: starving people, problems relating to health and education, drinking water facility, protracted judicial administration, environmental pollution, child and forced labour, lack of proper transportation, collapse of rural small scale cottage industries, unemployment and urbanization due to serious unemployment situation, total lack of sensitivity and accountability in public administration, lack of adequate agricultural infra-structure, lack of proper policy initiatives for rural development, inhuman and exploitative social tendencies, offences against women and low caste, exploitation of labour and open violation of labour laws, proper administration of consumer justice, etc. Through PILs, the judicial activism has played a significant role to render social justice to the best of its capacity where the executive has completely failed to set the things right.

Public interest litigation has been taken up by higher judiciary as an exception to the rule of *locus standi*, for the sake of rendering social justice to the people who are poor, uneducated and because of lacking of resources they are not able to take the violation of their statutory and constitutional rights to the courts and their legal rights continues to be violated. For them there is no meaning of Art. 14, which has guaranteed a fundamental right to equality before law. The higher courts introduced this novel kind of social justice administration by means of exercising their writ jurisdiction by the Supreme Court of India under Art. 32 and the respective High Courts under Art. 226 of the Constitution of India. In India for the first time this concept came into application by the Supreme Court in *Mumbai Kamgar Case*, but in its real sense the PIL came to be recognized in *Judges Transfer Case* and was well developed in *Asian Games Case* and *Bandhua Mukti Morcha Case.* The Black's law dictionary defines public interest as something in which the public, the community at large has some socio-pecuniary interest, or some interest by which their legal rights or liabilities are affected. It does not mean anything so narrow as mere curiosity, or as the interest of the particular localities, which may be affected by the matters in question. Interest shared by the citizens generally in affairs of local, state or national governments. The higher judiciary even takes cognizance of administrative violations *suo motu* on its own, which is of public interest in nature and takes remedial measures by fixing accountability of the public authority in accordance with law. In the long run for the administration of social justice, judicial activism through PILs has proved to be an effective mechanism and would remain so for the sake of social justice as a last ray of hope.

Conclusion

To conclude, it is an undisputed fact that corruption in public life has become so cancerous that there is genuine and reasonable apprehension that the administration system would fail to deal with this incurable disease. The constitutional and legislative measures apart, the government exhibits lack of will power to control and regulate corruption in public life. Corruption percolates down from top to bottom. If one is corrupt at the top he would have no moral authority to stop corruption among his subordinates. The existing state of affairs is extremely dismal. People are out on streets in rage against corruption and we should not be surprised and should take it as a warning signal, to witness situations like civil war in Indian society in the times to come, unless prompt corrective measures are taken to root out the corruption. We need to muster moral courage to deal with the situation. We cannot legislate for morals. It only comes from within and not from without. People should realise that they are morally accountable for the poor masses of the Indian society.

It will be practically difficult for the Judiciary alone to render social justice unless all out honest, sincere and collective efforts are taken by all the three constitutional bodies as per the parameters of the Constitution of India. The Constitutional Law of India is all inclusive in the sense that it enshrines within itself the fundamental dimensions of social justice and equality as discussed above. But the million dollar question is that as to what has went wrong with the system that even after more than six decades of Independence, we are still groping in the dark and clamoring for Justice. It is the time for introspection as to what went wrong with us which led to precipitate the situation so low that we ourselves feel ashamed of it and to muster the moral courage to punish ourselves.

In democratic governance people's participation is an essential ingredient. Unless honest participation of maximum number of people is ensured in governance it will not be possible to realize the dream of transparency and disclosure. We have rightly gone for the local self governance at the local bodies and panchayat levels, but these bodies are so disorganized and marred by corruption that the entire purpose of participation through local self-governance is defeated. Basic infrastructure needs to be introduced with a regular training schedule for the members of the local bodies so that sensibility for the cause of social justice could be inculcated in them.

The modern society needs to examine the desirability and legitimacy of social arrangements from time to time. It is not necessary that one social or economic situation relevant to a particular point of time and social frame would continue to be the same in future as well. It would need a rigorous and honest social research by the team of social and economic experts dedicated for the socio-economic cause of the Indian masses. Social equality does not mean in true sense an equal amount but a just and fair equality of opportunity to all so that the deprived masses could at least muster the basic minimum for their survival with human dignity. The administrators of justice system while preparing the policy initiatives, should not mistake in identifying the element of equality with forced equality. Such an equality should be with due honour following the due process of law. We need to sincerely keep in mind that justice should not only be done but it should appear to have been done as well.

It is important to realise that the social dynamics would not be possible without taking in consonance with the economic dynamics of the nation. We need to regularly study and analyze the impact of rule of law on economic development of the society. Particularly to address the question how the rule of law would be helpful in removing economic imbalance in the existing social system? The study should be further directed to poverty alleviation initiatives so as to minimize inequality in income and to regulate concentration of wealth in a few hands only. Lastly, the impact of the rule of law and its movement cannot be fully successful in the transitional and developing country like India unless the rule of law is strictly adhered to and honestly addressed to the economic development of Indian society and the deprived masses.

REFERENCES

Bingham, Thomas (2010), *The Rule of Law*, Penguin Publication.

Bradley, C. Canon (1983), "Defining the Dimensions of Judicial Activism," *Judicature,* LXVI.

Brian, Barry (1989), *Theories of Justice*, California University Press.

David Schmidtz (2006), *Elements of Justice*, Columbia University Press.

Dicey, A.V. (1959), *An Introduction to the Study of the Constitution,* 10th Edition.

ILO, *The Preamble of International Labour Organization Constitution,* Geneva Stanford University (2002), *The Stanford Encyclopedia of Philosophy,* Stanford University Press, Stanford.

John Stuart Mill (1991), *Utilitarianism*, Oxford University Press.

Plato (1984), *The Republic*, Oxford University Press.

Rawls, John (1999), *A Theory of Justice*, Oxford University Press.

Sen, Amartya (2011), *The Idea of Justice*, Harvard University Press,

Stauss, David (1996), "Interpreting the Constitution," *University of Chicago Law Review.*

United Nations (1948), *Universal Declaration of Human Rights, 1948*, New York.

Vienna Declaration and Programme of Action, Part II.

Referred Judicial Pronouncements:

Bachan Singh *Vs* State of Punjab, AIR 1982 SC 1325.

Bandhua Mukti Morcha *Vs* Union of India, AIR 1984 SC 802.

Golak Nath *Vs* State of Punjab, AIR 1967 SC 1643.
Keshavanand Bharti *Vs* State of Kerala, AIR 1973 SC 1467.
Mumbai Kamgar Union Case, AIR 1976 SC 1455.
People's Union for Democratic Rights *Vs* Union of India, AIR 1982 SC 1473.
S.P. Gupta *Vs* Union of India, AIR 1982 SC 149.
Union of India *Vs* Naveen Jindal, AIR 2004 SC 1559.

10

Transparency, Disclosures and Governance

MNREGA and Social Audits in Madhya Pradesh

Yogesh Kumar and *D.C. Sah*

Social Accountability

Of late, ability of civil society to carry out social accountability initiatives has been strengthened dramatically with sizeable community participation and involvement. As Paul (2005) argues that growing concerns about issues of governance and accountability can be explained by growing dissatisfaction in accessing the rights and entitlement of poor citizens, apart from other causes. He identifies the following three factors responsible for increasing attention on governance deficit. First is the mounting dissatisfaction with the manner in which states have performed their functions. Ample evidence shows that in many cases, public investments have resulted in meager returns and low productivity. Some of the key contributing factors underlying this phenomenon are lack of transparency, inadequate rule of law, and corruption. Second is the failure to achieve significant poverty reduction and the consequent inequity and injustice millions of marginalized people face. The weak bargaining power and organizational capabilities of the poor have no doubt contributed to this outcome. Third is a growing realization that existing mechanisms for ensuring public

Note: Authors gratefully acknowledge support of Sandeep Khanwalkar, Vishal Nayak, Gyanendra Tiwari, Vinay Jha, Anamika Ajay, Ghufranul Hassan and Manoj Tiwari in operationalizing the social audits in Campaign mode and also for comments on an earlier draft. Usual disclaimers apply.

accountability have not been able to resolve governance and accountability problems.

Social accountability refers to the broad range of actions and mechanisms that citizens can use to hold the state to account, as well as the actions on the part of government, civil society, media, and other societal actors that promote or facilitate these efforts. According to World Bank (2006) social accountability mechanisms come into play in the following three critical areas:

(i) *Improved Governance:* Given the proven limitations of formal accountability mechanisms, including elections, to promote good governance and strengthen democratic processes, social accountability tools and approaches have emerged as potent strategies in monitoring government performance, demanding and enhancing accountability, and exposing government failures and misdeeds.

(ii) *Improved Public Policies and Services:* Whereas social accountability is often seen as a simple and direct process that takes place along the interface between the state and citizens, in actuality it is a complex process mediated by the character of the state's institutions and processes, as well as the social structure of the polity, including that of civil society. The World Bank (2003) has added significant depth and clarity to the debate on social accountability. It has redefined the arena by distinguishing accountability by political leaders and policy-makers from that of the state as provider of services. Emergent profiles of social accountability mechanisms offer insights whereby each of these accountability relationships can be made operational. By enhancing citizen information and voice, introducing incentives for "downward" accountability and creating mechanisms for participatory monitoring and citizen-state dialogue and negotiation, social accountability mechanisms can make important contributions to more informed policy design and improved public service delivery.

(iii) *Empowerment:* Social accountability initiatives can contribute to empowerment, particularly that of marginalized people. The World Bank (2001, 2002) recognizes accountability as an integral component of empowerment, and hence of poverty reduction and sustainable development. By providing critical information on rights and entitlements and introducing

> mechanisms that enhance citizens' voice and influence in relation to the government, social accountability initiatives serve to enhance both these key determinants of empowerment. Of particular importance is the potential of social accountability initiatives to empower those social groups that are systematically underrepresented in formal political institutions, such as women, youth, and poor people.

Social accountability mechanisms include a wide range of tools, methods, and strategies that involve ordinary citizens and civil society in the process of allocating, tracking, and monitoring the use of public resources. Social accountability mechanisms both complement and enhance conventional internal mechanisms of accountability, underscore citizens' rights to expect the government to act in the best interests of the people and to ensure that it does so, and use a range of both formal and informal rewards and sanctions. Social accountability encompasses an ever-widening spectrum of concepts and practices. These practices are initiated by a wide range of actors, for instance, communities, CSOs, government agencies, political leaders, the media, and donor and aid agencies; use diverse strategies, such as research, monitoring, participatory planning, civic education, evidence based advocacy, and coalition building. In a broad sense, social accountability initiatives straddle the functional areas, such as budgets, policy-making and planning, public goods and services, expenditures, and public oversight.

The WBI (2007) argues that citizen invoivement in preparing and analysing budgets is a rapidly expanding domain of social accountability. Participatory budget formulation is most common at the local level, but can also be found at higher levels. Increasing evidence points to the institutionalization of proactive public engagement and participation in the formulation of public policies and plans. Another category of social accountability practices seeks accountability with regard to the relevance, accessibility and quality of public goods and services. An important aspect of social accountability is citizens' ability to hold government accountable for how it handles public monies. Public expenditure tracking surveys are an example of an expenditure-related social accountability practice that can be applied at the national level, with the aim of monitoring the flow of financial or physical resources and identifying leakages or bottlenecks in the system. A final category of social accountability practices includes those that aim to improve public oversight and monitoring. Examples include the creation of independent citizen oversight committees or watchdog groups at the local or national level or forms of civic engagement that aim to enhance the effectiveness of existing oversight mechanisms.

MNREGA in Madhya Pradesh

The objective of this paper is to evaluate the strengths and limitations of social accountability work taking Social Audit of MNREGA as a case in Madhya Pradesh. The paper argues that the power of demand-side approaches in enhancing governance through the concepts of citizens' voice has serious limitations. In doing this, the paper (i) tries to understand the way MNREGA is implemented in Madhya Pradesh, (ii) seeks to provide evidence on the process in social accountability and its impact and present its limitations in empowering the marginalized labourers; and finally (iii) concludes that these processes can work wonders in bringing transparency in decision-making but are toothless in ensuring accountability.

The National Rural Employment Guarantee Act (NREGA) was notified on September, 2005.The salient objective of the Act is to enhance livelihood security in rural areas by providing at least 100 days of guaranteed wage employment in a financial year to every household whose adult members volunteer to do unskilled manual work. The basic aim of the Act is to provide: (a) strong social safety net for the vulnerable groups by providing a fall-back employment source, when other employment alternatives are scarce or inadequate; (b) growth engine for sustainable development of an agricultural economy; (c) empowerment of rural poor through the processes of a rights-based law; and (d) new ways of doing business, as a model of governance reform anchored on the principles of transparency and grassroots democracy.

MNREGA is a demand driven programme, predictably as a condition for productive asset accumulation. Covering 32 million job seekers, MNREGA in Madhya Pradesh provided employment to about 20 per cent of these per year in last 5 years. A total of 117 million person-day employment was generated by MNREGA in the state. Of this, about 43 per cent employment was provided to females and about 48 per cent to Scheduled Caste and Scheduled Tribes. Over the years the demand for employment in MNREGA is decreasing. In 2010-11, about 39 per cent of job card holders demanded work in MNREGA in Madhya Pradesh. This proportion reduced to 27 per cent in 2011-12. On an average, while 50 days employment was provided per household in 2010-11, the employment reduced to about 37 days in 2011-12. The schemes implemented in MNREGA are largely projects of water conservation (60%), road connectivity (17%) and land development (16%). However, only 11 per cent of all applicants completed 100 days of work in 2009-10, while in 2010-11, only 4 per cent of applicants received 100 days work. A number of reasons like use of machinery over labour, evaluation process and fudging of muster roll that result in reduced wages to genuine labourers.

Kumar and Sah (2012) have argued that not only MNREGA as an instrument of substantive justice has done little for marginalised groups; it could do precisely little for productive asset creation. They have further argued that emerging realities in rural Madhya Pradesh are indicating towards an absolute failure of MNREGA, both in creating employment and also in its role as facilitator of community and individual asset creation. The most vulnerable in society are too pre-occupied with migration-based livelihood struggles to take advantage of MNREGA. In the process, the not-so-vulnerable from the old hierarchies are being benefited (Kumar and Sah, 2012). Leakages of financial resources in the programme through fudging the musters tend to set wages even below the minimum wage rate. This makes working in the MNREGA unattractive for employment. This not only disturbs programme's self-targeting mechanism but also its relevance as a social protection mechanism. If MNREGA offers employment well below the subsistence level, either poor may not turn to work in the programmes resulting in a breakdown of the pro-poor targeting mechanism or, and more disturbingly, the social protection may be available to the citizens that really do not need such protection (Tomar, 2010; Kumar and Sah, 2011).

A study by Samarthan (2012) finds the following deficiencies in the programme:

(i) MNREGA falls far short of its objective of providing 100 days employment for eligible families because of weak procedures and poor management of the programme;

(ii) a number of non-eligible families have been given job cards which fuels corruption;

(iii) the measurement of MNREGA works is not transparent;

(iv) delay in payment to workers discredits the MNREGA programme;

(v) Vigilance and Monitoring Committees do not function properly; and

(vi) MNREGA budget and expenditure data are not accessible.

Social Audit as a Tool of Monitoring

The framers of MNREGA foresaw these complex issues that could affect the scheme and also realized the relevance of a citizen monitoring system like social audits to ensure accountability in the scheme. While from an institutional perspective social audits provided a better solution to tackling corruption in MNREGA, from a demand side perspective social audit mechanism realize the Constitutional vision of citizen centric governance. This is reflected in Section 17 of the Act which requires that:

- The Gram Sabha shall monitor the execution of works within the Gram Panchayat.
- The Gram Sabha shall conduct regular social audits of all the projects under the Scheme taken up within the Gram Panchayat.
- The Gram Panchayat shall make available all relevant documents including the muster rolls, bills, vouchers, measurement books, copies of sanction orders and other connected books of account and papers to the Gram Sabha for the purpose of conducting the social audit.

The social audits in Andhra Pradesh did prove that this accountability tool has capability of improving quality of implementation of MNREGA as well as the labour market (Pokharel *et al.*, 2008; Aakella and Kidambi, 2007). Study of Aakella and Kidambi (2007) on accountability in Andhra Pradesh reveals that social audit, like any other developmental reform, has to fulfil three conditions: administrative feasibility, political support and technical correctness. The Government of Andhra Pradesh is well-known in taking an initiative to ensure that social audits are conducted regularly and effectively. The rural development department of Andhra Pradesh for instance has created a separate office for social audit within the MNREGA directorate headed by a Director appointed from the state civil services. The office contains around 35 members from the government and NGOs as state resource persons. A district level resource group is also formed at every district to implement social audits in their districts.

Pokharel *et al.* (2008), examining the effect of social audits on the bargaining power of the MNREGS workers, argued that the awareness about MNREGS among the workers was 39 per cent before social audits which increased to 98 per cent one month post-social audit and remained so even after 6 months. It concluded by stating that 'Social Audit enhances citizens bargaining power with local officials and offers them excellent opportunities to address their grievances' (*Ibid*). Singh and Vatukuru (2010) while trying to understand the impact of social audits on the various aspects of MNREGS by comparing Andhra Pradesh and Karnataka argued that there is an overall increase in the quality of implementation of the programme in Andhra Pradesh when compared to Karnataka and this was attributed to the efforts in Andhra Pradesh to institutionalise a separate office for social audits. They have also found that social audits resulted in the increase of the size of the programme each year and this was attributed to high levels of awareness among people about the programme through social audit process which resulted in greater demand for work. The study suggested that the incremental approach adopted in Andhra Pradesh in which social audit were piloted in a few districts, lessons were learnt and then number of districts in which social audits are conducted were slowly increased was a major reason for the successful social audit processes in the state. Other factors of success of social audits are a trained manpower and a systematic process, co-option of lower bureaucracy, use of ICT and a devoted team at the state level. Thus the study reveals an out performance of Andhra Pradesh with respect to the implementation of social audits.

The above discussion reveals that a number of factors contribute together to an effective implementation of social audits. Evidences from Andhra Pradesh indicate that a successful social audit can have positive impact on the implementation of MNREGS which in turn will benefit the poor and marginalised. The effectiveness of a tool that is used to improve accountability in governance should be measured in terms of the process administered, the outcomes achieved and impact generated. Therefore, whether social audit is a useful citizen monitoring tool to improve programme accountability is dependent on the nature of the processes administered, the outcomes of the social audits and the impact it has had on the lives of the poor and marginalised.

Samarthan, a Non-Governmental Organisation (NGO), is working for improving implementation of MNREGA in Madhya Pradesh since last few years. Social Audit, along with labour budget and demand creation, budget tracking and organising labourers, was one of the important tools for bringing accountability and transparency in decision-making in MNREGA. In the next section an attempt is made to document the process and impact of social audits that were conducted, with the support of *Samarthan* in Madhya Pradesh first in intensive mode and then in campaign mode.

Experiences of Social Audit in Intensive Mode

The MNREGS provides scope for the Gram Sabha to monitor the implementation of the scheme. The works undertaken in the scheme are subject to social audit by the Gram Sabha. However, it has been observed that the Panchayats as well as the district and block administration are apprehensive of conducting social audit in the villages.

The Social Audit process conducted on 17th August 2011 in the village of Londhia, from a Panchayat of Sehore district, is discussed in this section. What has transpired in Londhia was also experienced in Rola and Kapuri villages too. The preparation of this event included: (i) meeting with labourers and beneficiaries on the issues related to MNREGA; (ii) support provided to the Vigilance and Monitoring Committee on document verification and consolidation; (iii) meeting with the Social Audit Committee on gaps in the present situation of person-days, measurement evaluation and delay in payment; and (iv) support to VMC on presentation of issues in the Gram Sabha.

The Gram Sabha on the 17th August 2011 began in the primary school of Londhia. The total strength of the Gram Sabha was around 50 members out of which 10 were women. The Secretary and Sarpanch were present while the Nodal officer was absent. A total of 6 Gram Panchayat members were present for this meeting. As per the rules of a Social Audit, a formal leader was chosen among the members to head the social audit. A member of Gram Sabha, a mate of the MNREGA and also a member of the VMC, was chosen to head the social audit. The issues put forward in the social audit were

(i) difference in stipulated and market price of materials: (ii) delay in payment by the local cooperative bank; (iii) unpaid wages; (iv) anomalies in payments made to skilled workers; (v) issues related to evaluation of work and the MNREGA engineer; (vi) utilization certificate not present at Panchayat level; and (vii) records unavailable for road constructed.

The Gram Sabha meeting lasted for a period of 3 hours. All the issues were recorded by the secretary and read aloud in front of the Sabha, along with the decisions taken. The Gram Sabha members decided that many of the issues raised above were to be discussed at the next especial Gram Sabha to be conducted within a month. The process of Londhia eventually culminated in a murky situation. It became clear that the Panchayat Secretary and Sarpanch are protected by higher echelons. No disciplinary action were initiated against the Secretary and Sarpanch despite complaints registered against them. As a result the villages are divided in two groups—one consisting of friends of Secretary and the other comprising victims of wrong decisions. As retaliation, the development work from Panchayats stopped in the village. The situation in Rola and Kapuri were no different after the August 2011 social audits in these villages.

The main points which emerged from the experience of Social Audit in these villages are highlighted below:

(i) Non-cooperation from Sarpanch and Secretary

- In Rola, Londhia and Kapuri Panchayats after the misuse of funds and fudging of muster-roll was identified the Sarpanch of these Panchayats started threatening the field workers and affected labourers and also vitiated the atmosphere against the involved CSOs.
- The Sarpanch of Rola, in connivance with the administration, did not allow legal procedures against him to take place.

(ii) Resistance from Administration

- The civil society organisation helping the labourers in social audits faced difficulties in receiving receipts of work-demand applications from blocks.
- Administration discouraged on-line applications filing.
- Administration shuttled any move for filing applications for

unemployment allowances.

- Media coverage was considered by block and district administration as anti-state activity.
- Utilisation Certificate of the MNREGA activity was denied.
- Despite sharing field experience regarding social audit with the senior government officials, CEO MNREGA, and Joint Secretary Ministry of Rural Development, response of the state was indifferent due to lack of political will to involve NGOs in Social audit.

(iii) Weak Support from the Policy-makers and Bureaucracy

- Issue of evaluation of tender based bidding cost of NGOs for the social audit was highlighted and mechanism of NGO involvement was suggested. There was a policy decision to withdraw engagement of NGOs from the social audit.
- Issues of social audit which demand attention of the senior administration was highlighted. Social audit could not become a priority for the administration.

The evidences indicate that Social Audits in Madhya Pradesh have turned out to be a non-event. Social Audit Committees exist on papers in most of the Panchayats. Members of the social audit committee are unaware about their inclusion in the committee and about their roles. Sarpanch and Panchayat secretary are not interested in opening-up the decisions for scrutiny in Social Audits. Even when Social Audit is able to bring issues of large scale fudging of muster rolls, work evaluation process and less payment, delayed payments, individual work remaining incomplete but shown completed in MIS, no one is accountable for these. This is because of the nexuses between Panchayat and higher levels officials. As long as prosecution of erring Panchayat officials is within the ambit of administration, prosecution against them is hard to initiate. This helps in avoiding accountability in development decision-making.

With hand-holding support in 10 intervening Gram Panchayats in Sehore and Panna in 2010 and 2011, the Social Audits have: (i) brought transparency in decision-making but accountability is still a far cry; (ii) disturbed the social harmony of the village society; (iii) divided the community in groups, the erring Panchayat Officials and their supporters and the affected beneficiaries and their friends, and

(iv) resulted in stopping all development work in intervening Panchayats. This raises an important question, 'what is the use of such a tool of transparency and accountability when it becomes detrimental to development. At present, Social Audit Cell of state MNREGA Council is in the process of institutionalising Social Audit in Madhya Pradesh. Only time will tell if such initiatives will die prematurely, because of internal contradictions.

Evidences from Social Audits in Campaign Mode

For Social Audit which was slated for 15th to 21st August 2012, *Samarthan* tried to up-scale Social Audits from 10 intervening Panchayats of Sehore and Panna, to about 890 Panchayats in 13 blocks in 10 Districts of Madhya Pradesh (Panna, Satna, Rewa, Badwani, Jhabua, Dhar, Sehore, Jabalpur, Seoni and Damoh). The strategy with which the up-scaling was attempted was to identify and train two youths from each of the 890 Panchayats on Social Audit. These youths were educated young persons who were Panch or Ex-Sarpanch from the Panchayat, or were family members of MNREGA workers. They were equipped with MIS reports relating to total work done in their Panchayats, expenditure on wages and labour and a list of workers who had worked in MNREGA in last one year, and employment provided and total wages paid to them. The youths met the identified labourers and validated the MIS findings on employment provided and wage paid. If there were discrepancies in the MIS and actual payments made to labourers, the youths met the members of Social Audit Committee constituted by state on August 2011 and appraised them about this discrepancy. The labourers met the committee members and requested the members to bring this discrepancy in 15th August Social Audit.

The main points which emerged from the experience of Social Audit in campaign mode in these villages are highlighted below:

(i) Data from all the 890 locations could not be analysed but it is clear that MIS Reports on wage payment are highly manipulated, which results in leakages and low wage payments to genuine labourers. The manipulation is relatively more rampant on work executed by line departments compared to work executed by Panchayats.

(ii) As the conduct of social audit is mandated by the MNREGA and also a detailed set of rules have been created to conduct these processes in every village, one would expect that due to this mandate, social audits would be conducted in all the villages of the country. The State government almost always reports that social audits are conducted regularly by all the Gram Sabhas. For example, according to the statistics provided on the MNREGS website, over 99 per cent of the Gram Panchayats in Madhya Pradesh conducted social audits in the year 2012-2013. However, the evidences collected from the Gram Sabha of Madhya Pradesh reveal a different picture. In reality, it was found that around 29 per cent of the sampled villages failed to conduct social audits as prescribed by law.

(iii) The data reveal that on an average only 10 per cent of the people in the selected villages attended the mandatory Gram Sabha. The level of public involvement is far below what one would desire. Around 8 per cent of the total sampled villages could not hold Gram Sabhas because an adequate number of people (10 per cent of the total registered voters in the village) were not present at the venue to complete the quorum. On the other hand, there were 10 villages where between 25-40 per cent of the people attended the meetings. One could observe that the percentage of people who attended Gram Sabha varied widely from one village to the other. Another observation was that out of the villages in which Gram Sabhas were conducted, only 22 per cent of the people present were women. In 46 per cent of the Gram Sabha, only less than 10 women attended the meeting. However, there were also villages that provided hope. Around 11 villages where Gram Sabhas were held, 45-55 per cent of the participants were women. However, it was also observed that in many villages where the Sarpanch or Secretary feared that their corrupt acts will be discussed at the meeting, the attendance registry (which should ideally be filled by villagers who attend Gram Sabha) was found to be filled much before the Gram Sabha was held. In such cases, Gram Sabhas are only held in paper and not in reality.

(iv) The discussions at the Gram Sabha reveal two broad types of issues—one related to corruption and the other related to inefficiency (see Table 10.1). Fudging of muster rolls, using fake documents to embezzle money, confiscating job cards

Table 10.1: Issues Discussed in Social Audits in Campaign Mode (*Percentage of Total Social Audits*)

Issues Discussed	*Badwani*	*Damoh*	*Dhar*	*Jabalpur*	*Jhabua*	*Panna*	*Rewa*	*Satna*	*Sehore*	*Seoni*	*All*
Work Did not Start	56.0	80.0	34.6	54.2	28.3	88.0	40.4	47.7	62.3	78.6	56.9
Delay in payment	44.0	60.0	26.9	33.3	30.4	86.7	29.2	30.2	21.7	82.1	41.7
Low Wages	20.0	53.3	7.7	33.3	2.2	85.3	31.5	27.3	15.1	57.1	33.5
Expenditure and Bills	44.0	40.0	11.5	33.3	34.8	81.3	13.5	15.9	13.2	28.6	30.5
Quality of Construction	12.0	40.0	11.5	41.7	6.5	82.7	21.3	36.4	10.4	46.4	30.5
Facilities at Worksite	20.0	33.3	3.8	41.7	4.3	72.0	15.7	22.7	8.5	53.6	26.2
Old Age Labourers	16.0	46.7	3.8	37.5	0.0	77.3	28.1	56.8	8.5	64.3	32.6
Muster Rolls	12.0	20.0	7.7	33.3	2.2	73.3	11.2	18.6	13.2	53.6	25.0
Timely Work	20.0	73.3	15.4	58.3	6.5	74.7	25.8	22.7	14.2	57.1	32.8
Job Card Related	8.0	60.0	3.8	20.8	0.0	73.3	9.0	25.0	8.5	53.6	24.1
Use of Machine	16.0	26.7	7.7	4.2	2.2	65.3	6.7	27.3	6.6	60.7	21.5
Women Issues	8.0	40.0	0.0	50.0	0.0	80.0	19.1	18.2	11.3	53.6	27.6
On Farm Investment	68.0	46.7	19.2	45.8	15.2	76.0	18.0	20.5	38.7	46.4	38.3
Completion Certificate	8.0	20.0	0.0	20.8	0.0	72.0	7.9	2.3	6.6	14.3	17.4
Records presented	8.0	73.3	19.2	45.8	2.2	62.7	9.0	54.5	8.5	17.9	25.7
Total Audits	100 (25)	100 (15)	100 (26)	100 (24)	100 (46)	100 (75)	100 (89)	100 (44)	100 (106)	100 (28)	100 (478)

Note: Figures in brackets are number of social audits conducted.

from the workers denying them right to work and abuse of power by the implementing agencies for the benefit of a few are examples of rampant corruption in the system. Delay in payment, issues related to measurement of work and incompletion of work are issues that highlight the inefficient implementation of the works. Social audit processes, therefore, show that the quality of implementation of MNREGA in Madhya Pradesh is poor and that despite large amounts of money being spent on the programme, the problems related to the programme delivery have limited its role in improving the quality of lives of rural poor.

(v) It was noted that while the Sarpanch/Up-Sarpanch presided the meeting in 91.4 per cent of the villages where Gram Sabha were held, but the nodal officers were present only in 41.3 per cent of the villages. The absence of nodal officers meant that an impartial reporting of the Gram Sabha proceeding would be not documented and presented at the District Level Programme Coordinator who is responsible to take action on the issues raised at the Gram Sabha level. Another important responsibility of the Panchayat officials who preside over at the Gram Sabha meeting is to present the documents related to the implementation of the works under MNREGA to enable evidence based discussions rather than turning the nature of the discussion into a blame game.

(vi) It was found that out of the 478 villages, where social audits were conducted, in less than 26 per cent of the villages, documents were presented which affected the nature of the discussions in many cases. Most of the misappropriations occur through fudging of these documents and the non-presentation of these documents at the meeting indicates.

(vii) A precondition to a successful Gram Sabha discussion is administrative support. There is only very little that the Gram Sabha can achieve in the absence of representatives from the implementing agency at Panchayat level and also representatives from the district level offices (nodal officers). It was observed that the levels of administrative will to facilitate and conduct social audits were very low. As the proceedings of the social audits were not recorded, actions against erring officers are difficult to initiate.

Despite a lack of administrative support, the discussions at the Gram Sabha definitely showed a positive sign towards empowerment of the Gram Sabha as a key local self-governing institution. Many issues were raised by the Gram Sabha members regarding the implementation of MNREGA works in their villages. One of the key outcomes expected from social audit processes is to monitor the implementation of the programme, raise issues if any and increase answerability from the implementing agencies. Through social audits, villagers were empowered with information and the platform to claim their rights and entitlements. A number of issues were raised regarding the fudging of muster rolls like making ghost entries, fake entries of details of households that do not qualify to benefit from MNREGA, entering wrong details of work done to embezzle money in the name of wage payment. Issues related to the abuse of power by the Sarpanch and Secretaries were raised during the Gram Sabha. In a few cases the Sarpanch/Secretary were found to confiscate the job cards from the labourers denying them the right to access work, many cases were raised regarding delay in payment. The use of contractors to hire cheap labour from other places was found to be practised in some villages. In a few villages, the Gram Sabha alleged that the Panchayat officials produce fake bills and vouchers for disbursement of money for works which would have not even been started in reality.

To sum up, the entire discussion on the quality of social audit processes reveals numerous inadequacies in the implementation of the social audits. The poor quality of social audits is due to lack of commitment and efficiency from the programme authorities and also lack of participation from citizens. However, experiences from some villages provide a brighter picture. These villages demonstrate that despite the numerous challenges, the social audit processes have empowered citizens with information which has in turn resulted in the empowerment of Gram Sabha as an institution. These experiences though few in number demonstrate that social audits act as an important tool for citizen empowerment that helps them demand better services and greater accountability from the institutions. In about 55 per cent villages out of 895, Social Audit was conducted with evidences of discrepancies being placed in Gram Sabha. In Panchayats where Social Audit did take place, the discussion lasted from 1 to 5 hours. In these Panchayats, discussions were either on delayed payment or payment of less wages than fixed by state, fudging in muster roll or expenditure in MNREGA, incomplete work shown as complete, work not being provided despite demand for the same made by the labourers. In all these Panchayats, the aggrieved labourers demanded action against the erring Secretary and Sarpanch. As only in 26 per cent Panchayats nodal officers were present, the discussions were recorded as minutes of Gram Sabha only in a minuscule of Panchayats. But this campaign clearly proved that if equipped with proper documents (evidences from MIS reports and their validation in villages) the MNREGA labourers are capable to fight injustice they have faced in MNREGA. This process certainly forced transparency in operations in MNREGA. Through these information from MIS the MNREGA labourers are forcing the administration to call special Social Audits on MNREGA. This is the first step towards social transformation.

Advocacy at Block, District and State Level

The findings of social audits was shared with District Collector and CEO district Panchayat of all 10 districts. These findings were also shared with media and Chairperson of District Planning Committees in these districts. In Sehore and Panna, the aggrieved labourers have also registered their complaints in *Jansunwai*.

Samarthan has supported state MNREGA Council in framing by-laws of social audit committee. On 1st March 2013, a society was formed for effective implementation of social audit provisions. *Samarthan* is one of the members in the society. Issues emerged from the social audit process were fed to the social audit cell for necessary action. A state level public hearing was also organised on 22nd January and 30 selected cases from 10 districts were presented and discussed. Public hearing was attended by parliamentarian, Social Audit Director, media activists, advisor, right to food campaign and select group of CSOs. As a follow up of this hearing, 27 cases were lodged under Public Grievance Redresses Cell of MNREGA for further action. These evidences were also submitted to Grievance Redressal Cell of MNREGA. The verification and investigation for resolving the cases is on. The cases have been sent to Block level CEOs of the district for verification. The MNREGA Council can take disciplinary action against the erring Sarpanch and Secretaries only after receiving the report from the Blocks.

Challenges Identified

During the week of August 15-22, 2012, *Samarthan* helped the youth volunteers to organise over 800 village level meetings on social audit. The trained youth volunteers conducted social audit in about 500 villages. The campaign unfolded in three stages, namely, preparatory, facilitation and post-implementation follow-up with Panchayats and MNREGA administration. The following challenges were identified in the social audit process.

First, the MNREGA administration and the Panchayat officials are resisting Social Audits in Panchayats. However, with an increased awareness among the labourers, the Panchayats are under pressure. Social audit campaign has led to some transparency. But the district administration and Panchayats are increasingly becoming wary of these initiatives and trying to thwart these efforts. Threat calls from the Sarpanchs, MLAs, Janpad CEOs and Panchayat Secretaries to youth volunteers and NGOs have become common.

Second, neither Gram Sabha members nor the members of Social Audit Committee are aware of the provision of Social Audit. Hence, the community pressure for accountability and transparency is dormant. In other words, awareness is an issue that obstructs the social audit process. Villagers are not aware about the objectives, process and mechanism of social audit in majority of the villages. It was also observed that villagers are not aware that there is a sub-committee formed at village level named as Social Audit Committee which does physical verification of sample of works and submit its report after verifying the documents. Like the Gram Sabha members, the PRI members and the Secretary also lack the understanding on social audit.

Third, the necessary documents for social audit have to come from the Panchayats. But the Panchayat Secretary and the Janpad CEO are not ready to share information necessary for social audits.

Lastly, the designated Nodal Officers for social audits do not participate in Social Audits; as a result, the proceedings of the Social Audits are not recorded, for further actions.

The Way Ahead

Invariably misappropriation of funds at the Panchayat level has links with higher echelons. As a result action against the involved officials is hard to initiate. All those who were instrumental in asserting the social audits, felt resentful because of the bad blood it creates, which damages the tranquillity and development of the village. This raises the question of utility and implications of social audits as a transparency tool in prevailing socio-political environment.

Despite the guidelines of Ministry of Finance, Government of India that the C&AG shall be responsible for exercising control and supervision over the proper maintenance of accounts and their audit for all the three tiers of Panchayati Raj Institutions, Social Audits are unrealisable proposition in Madhya Pradesh. This is because Social Audit has no legitimacy, at present. Consequently, at different echelons of PRIs, there is neither a need for social audit nor any fear of its implications. There is, therefore, a need to link personnel from C&AG office with social audit, to give the process some legitimacy.

Awareness about social audit is a big concern and steps need to be taken for creating awareness for conducting social audit. At village level, minimum one notice board in one hamlet could be placed and managed by Social Audit Committee At cluster of villages, active labour groups can be formed, with dual role of—(i) information dissemination about MNREGA, changes in the Act and its rules, and mechanisms of the social; audit; and (ii) facilitation of social audit.

Regular capacity-building training for the members of Social Audit Committee is a must for successful social audit to take place. A core group can be formed at a cluster of 10 Gram Panchayats where capacity-building process can be coordinated by one agency. Training of young labourers and panchayat functionaries will help in conducting social audit in a campaign mode by the State. By developing a cadre of social auditors through e-learning will also help the process of social audit.

Media Advocacy on grievances of labourers would also bring anomalies to the notice of the MNREGA administration. The grievances of the labourers would get a voice in the form of news articles. The effective liaison with local media and communication strategy of sharing report and field realities with media would result in larger dissemination of the problem, once the issues are highlighted in media and the local administration may become proactive in redressing these issues. Establishing proper links with local officials, media members, Panchayat functionaries and proactive labours will lead to desired advocacy outcomes.

A block level support group is required to strengthen the implementation process by interacting and appraising the local implementing agencies including block level MNREGA administration. This group, comprising of media personnel, youth volunteers, CSO members, college teachers and retired government officials, could function as pressure point relating to anomalies emerging from social audits. The findings of social audit may also be fed to state MNREGA council for appropriate actions.

REFERENCES

Aakella, Karuna V and Sowmya Kidambi (2007), 'Social Audits in Andhra Pradesh: A Process in Evolution', *Economic and Political Weekly*, November.

Kumar, Yogesh and D.C. Sah (2012), 'Caste Hierarchies and Substantive Discrimination through MNREGA', *Man and Development*, Vol. 34 (4).

MNREGA Net (2011), 'Introduction', in MNREGA Net (eds.), *The National Rural Employment Guarantee Act: Design, Processes and Impact*, MNREGA Net Services, UNDP and Government of India, New Delhi.

Navnit, B. (2011), 'Ensuring Transparency and Accountability in MNREGA', MNREGA Net (eds.), *The National Rural Employment Guarantee Act: Design, Processes and Impact*, MNREGA Net Services, UNDP and Government of India, New Delhi.

Paul, S. (2005), *Auditing for Social Change'*, Public Affairs Centre, Bangalore (mimeo).

Pokharel, Atul, Yamini Aiyar and, Salimah Samji (2008), *'Social Audits: From Ignorance to Awareness—The AP Experience'*, World Bank, Intellicap, SPIU—Government of Andhra Pradesh, February, Hyderabad.

Samarthan (2010), *Impact Assessment of MNREGA in Madhya Pradesh*, Study submitted to Poverty Monitoring and Policy Support Unit, State Planning Commission, Madhya Pradesh, Samarthan, Bhopal.

Shah, M., P. Ambustha and P. S.Vijay Shankar (2011), 'A Charter of Reforms for MNREGA', in MNREGA Net (eds.), *The National Rural Employment Guarantee Act: Design, Processes and Impact*, MNREGA Net Services, UNDP and Government of India, New Delhi.

Shah, M. (2004), 'The National Rural Employment Guarantee Act: A Historic Opportunity', *Economic and Political Weekly*, 11 December.

Singh, Ritesh and Vinay Vatukuru (2010), *Enhancing Accountability in Public Service Delivery through Social Audits: A Case Study of Andhra Pradesh*, Working Paper, Accountability Initiative.

Tomar, Shubhra S. (2011), *Livelihood Struggles and Seasonal Migration in Madhya Pradesh*, Doctoral Thesis, Vikram University, Ujjain (mimeo).

WBI (2007), *'Empowering the Marginalised'*, World Bank Institute Working Paper, Public Affairs Foundation, Bangalore and WBI, Washington DC.

World Bank (2001), *World Development Report 2000/2001: Attacking Poverty,* Oxford University Press, New York.

——(2002), *Empowerment and Poverty Reduction: A Sourcebook.* Washington, DC. http://www.worldbank.org/poverty/strategies.

——(2003), *World Development Report 2004: Making Services Work for Poor People,* Oxford University Press, New York.

——(2006), *Social Accountability Source Book,* World Bank, Washington, DC.

11

Transparency, Disclosure and Governance

A Case of Transformation of Caste Scrutiny and Validation Process in Maharashtra

Rohan Joshi

Introduction

This paper presents an in-depth case study of Caste Scrutiny and Validation Process in Department of Social Justice and Special Assistance, Government of Maharashtra. This case study is used as a basis for discussion of transparency and governance and for developing a possible strategy for bringing transparency and good governance in government processes. Four terms, namely, Transparency, Accountability, Disclosure and Good Governance, are often used together or even interchangeably in current development discourse. This paper attempts to provide functional definitions of these concepts and examines, with the use of the case study, correlations between the four.

The methodology used for the case study is of qualitative research. Interviews, participant observations and analysis of secondary data made for the purpose of this case study show that the concept of good governance has certainly moved beyond theoretical discourse to practice as visible in the form of some notable best practices. Similarly, various aspects of governance have been studied in depth by academicians as well as practitioners. However, a concrete strategy or an operational roadmap for good governance is rarely documented. An effort to document such a strategy for good governance is made through this paper.

Information, statistical data presented in this section, unless otherwise mentioned, was gathered by the author during his work with Dr. Babasaheb Ambedkar Research and Training Institute, Pune between January 2013 to May 2013 through various interactions with applicants, officers working with CSCs and participant observations during interactions with applicants

Understanding Transparency, Disclosure and Governance

One of the most commonly understood meanings of the word Governance is "the process of decision-making and the process by which decisions are implemented" (ESCAP, 2013). Governance is normally described as involving government. However, government is just one of the actors in governance. Depending on the level of government that is under discussion such as State Government, Local Government, there could be several other actors such as civil society and the private sector, media, etc. involved in the process of governance.

Transparency means that decisions taken and their enforcement are done in a manner that follows rules and regulations. It also means sharing information and acting in an open manner. Transparency assumes that free, timely and adequate access to information is provided through various media and information that is shared is latest, relevant, accurate and adequate. Transparency is fundamental in keeping checks on corruption; hence it is widely recognised as a core principle of good governance. Transparency is also considered essential for controlling corruption in public life.

United Nations, Economic and Social Commission for Asia and Pacific (UN, ESCAP, 2013) defines accountability as follows:

> "Accountability is a key requirement of good governance. Not only governmental institutions but also the private sector and civil society organizations must be accountable to the public and to their institutional stakeholders. Who is accountable to whom varies depending on whether decisions or actions taken are internal or external to an organization or institution. In general an organization or an institution is accountable to those who will be affected by its decisions or actions. Accountability cannot be enforced without transparency and the rule of law."

Disclosure largely refers to sharing of information that indicates government activities and processes. The main objective of governments providing information to its citizens is not only to promote openness, transparency and accountability in administration, but also to ensure participation of people in all matters related to governance (Parigi, Geeta and Kailasam, 2004).

From the definitions presented above it is adequately clear that Good Governance encompasses transparency, accountability and disclosure. But the concept of good governance is wider. There are other factors that are also essential for good governance, such as, consensus orientation, responsiveness, participation, rule of law, efficiency, strategic vision and consensus orientation (*see* Fig. 11.1).

	Equitable and Inclusive	
Transparency	Accountability	Disclosure
Responsiveness	Good Governance	Consensus Orientation
Participation	Rule of Law	Efficiency
	Strategic Vision	

Fig. 11.1: Factors Essential for Good Governance

Source: UN, ESCAP, 2013.

Bringing Transparency in Governance: Caste Scrutiny and Validation Process in Maharashtra

India has a long history of exclusion of different social groups, *viz.*, a number of castes, tribes and religious minorities, from various aspects of social activities which include education and certain types of jobs, etc. Post Independence, various constitutional safeguards as well as policy support on the lines of affirmative action, have been extended to these communities from the view of recovering the development backlog, bringing the hitherto excluded social groups in the centre of social and economic activity of the country. Caste based reservation in India are one such tool of affirmative action that ensures representation of persons belonging to these communities in education, welfare schemes, government jobs, etc. which in effect ensures overall participation and positive representation of historically excluded communities in the mainstream society (Elango, 2012). The

Articles 15, 16, 335, 338, 340, 341 and 342 of the Constitution of India make special provisions for advancement, in any respect, of persons belonging to the Scheduled Castes (SCs), Scheduled Tribes (STs) and Other Backward Classes (OBCs).

In order to secure the benefits provided under these sections of the Constitution it is obligatory that every person who claims to be a member of Scheduled Caste or Scheduled Tribes produces a Caste Certificate signed by a competent authority as sufficient proof in support of a candidate's claim to make him/her eligible for various relaxations and concessions. (Mukherjee, 1999). In certain cases re-validation or authorization of a caste certificate of a person is necessary. This validation is done through caste scrutiny and validation process. Validity Certificate (issued after the validation process) is an important document for a person belonging to scheduled castes, scheduled tribes or other backward communities since it validates eligibility of person/s belonging to any of these communities to get access to reservation benefits. As mentioned above, generally a caste certificate serves as sufficient proof of SC, ST or OBC status of a person. However, in the following cases a caste validity certificate in addition to caste certificate is required:

- For reservations in educational institutes
- To benefit from various State Sponsored Welfare schemes
- For reservations in government service
- For reservations in legislatures
- To obtain relaxation in the upper age limit for certain jobs

Failure on the part of a person who claims to belong to SC, ST or OBC category in producing a caste validity certificate issued by competent authority leads to termination of any benefits available to the persons belonging to these categories.

In Maharashtra, the process of caste scrutiny and validation of persons belonging to Scheduled Castes (SCs), Other Backward Castes (OBCs), Special Backward Castes (SBCs) and *Vimukta Jati* and Nomadic Tribes (VJNT) is handled by Caste Scrutiny Committees (CSCs) working under the Department of Social Justice and Special Assistance of Government of Maharashtra. As per directions of the Hon. Supreme Court of India "all the State Governments shall constitute a Committee of three officers, namely, (1) an Additional or Joint Secretary or any officer higher in rank of the Director of the department concerned, (2) the Director, Social Welfare/Tribal Welfare/ Backward Class Welfare, as the case may be and (3) in case of Scheduled Castes another officer who has intimate knowledge in the verification and issuance of the social status certificates. In the case of the Scheduled Tribes, the Research Officer who has intimate knowledge in identifying the tribes, tribal communities, parts of or groups of tribes or tribal communities" (Judgement on 28 April 1997 in *Kum. Madhuri Patil and Another* Vs. *Add. Commissioner, Tribal Development, Thane and Others*).

While the main function of these committees is to verify the caste claim of an applicant and issue a caste validity certificate, additionally, the CSCs are empowered to take legal action against bogus claimants. Currently fifteen CSCs located in various parts of the state, each consisting of officers appointed by the State Government, handle thousands of caste validation claims every year. The majority of these applications are from students pursuing higher education, government officers and persons contesting elections of State or Local bodies.

What Existed Before Transformation?

With the significant rise in literacy levels among SC, OBC communities, growing political consciousness and participation in electoral politics, and increased awareness of the benefits of reservation in government jobs for persons belonging to these communities, overall demand for caste validity certificates has increased in recent times. While this should be seen as a mark of the partial success of caste based reservation policy of India, the reservation benefits have also lured persons from various non-scheduled castes claim themselves as belonging to SC and OBC communities. The challenge ahead of CSCs is not only to validate thousands of applications received every year but also to identify false claims and restrict persons from non-scheduled communities from receiving benefits meant strictly for scheduled castes.

Significant growth in number of applications for caste validation certificates led to accumulation of applications with Caste Scrutiny Committees (CSCs). CSCs were not equipped with adequate number of competent human resources or infrastructure such as space, furniture and other office equipment to handle the increased number of claims (Caste Validity Scrutiny Committee Research Project, Sept 2012, BARTI). Additionally each committee was located at different geographical location and worked in isolation, hence the transfer of cases from one committee to another, when required, did not happen. As a result, thousands of applications received by each CSC remained unprocessed for periods ranging from a few months to several years, while ideally each application should only take about a fortnight to process. Applicants who had to travel from their villages, towns or places of work to the CSC offices to check status of their applications often returned with no definite knowledge of the actual status of application. Some also faced a rude shock, after waiting for several years, in the form of denial of their claim without any further explanation from CSC. In the absence of caste validity certificates, many students and government employees had to forgo their Constitutional right of reservations in education and government jobs.

While many applicants either chose to wait or actually sacrificed their benefits, many also resorted to illegal shortcuts such as offering bribes to members of CSCs to process their applications faster. Many "agents" emerged in the system who ensured quick delivery of caste validity certificates, which are meant to be issued free of cost, for illegal fees ranging from Rs. 5000 to Rs. 25 lakh per certificate depending on urgency and purpose. Predictably, in no time this illegal shortcut actually became the only way of procuring caste validity certificates. The emergence of agents also added significantly to the growth in the number of bogus applications and the receipt of Caste Validity Certificates by persons not belonging to scheduled castes simply by paying large sums to agents. Moreover, cases were reported in which counterfeit Caste Validation Certificates were created by agents and sold to applicants at very high cost.

Number of complaints from persons who could not or chose not to pay the cost of caste validation certificates kept on increasing. Notably, the persons who could not pay the cost of certificates were typically from economically vulnerable backgrounds and in many cases belonged to socio-economically marginalized communities within Scheduled Castes. Many leading vernacular newspapers and periodicals in Maharashtra published the plight of these applicants. Some applicants whose applications were not processes for several years during their complaints to the Department of Social Justice and Special Assistance, also claimed of illicit network between agents and local politicians and officers in bureaucracy. Similarly, political parties, typically those working closely with scheduled castes in

Maharashtra politicized the issue and brought it up for discussion during multiple assembly sessions. Some applicants who were left waiting for their caste validation certificates resorted to legal action and filed public interest litigations. Taking cognizance of the same, Mumbai High Court issued directives for complete reform of the caste validation process in Maharashtra. However, besides the addition of some Caste Scrutiny Committee and appointments of a small number of human resources in some of the CSCs the situation remained largely unchanged (*Atrocity News*, October 2012).

The Process of Transformation

In August 2012 Dr. Babasaheb Ambedkar Research and Training Institute (BARTI), an autonomous institute under the Department of Social Justice and Special Assistance, Government of Maharashtra, took charge of coordination of caste validation process in Maharashtra. Newly appointed Director General of BARTI volunteered to take up the coordination of the caste validation process which hitherto lacked any central coordination. Director General of BARTI along with his officers spent hours every day facing students, in-service government officers from various scheduled caste communities, often coming in agitated and feeling helpless, to complain against the delays and corruption in the caste validation process.

An overhaul of the existing caste verification system, done by BARTI through a fact finding research of Caste Scrutiny Committee located at Pune (BARTI, 2012) and numerous discussions with applicants, chairpersons as well as junior staff members of the CSCs and other government officers, brought four key issues to the surface:

1. Pending Applications with all 15 CSCs
2. Below par performance of CSCs
3. Lack of access to information to applicants on the functioning of CSCs
4. Emergence of sub-systems, illegal practices causing further deterioration of CSCs.

An overarching issue here was that of thousands of pending caste validation applications which were lying with each of the 15 CSCs over the years. BARTI decided to focus on the issue of pending applications first while also solving for others along the way. The key milestones in this problem solving process are described below:

Solving Pending Applications: An overview of pending applications with each of the CSCs showed that nearly 1.86 lakh applications were pending while hundreds of new applications were coming in every day (*Sakal Times*, December 2012). Unless this backlog was covered it was impossible to process new applications. Hence, BARTI decided to target the backlogs first and announced through leading newspapers across the state that all pending applications will be solved within a period of three months from the date of announcement. Series of Caste Validity Distribution Camps were organized throughout the state where all caste validity certificates that were ready for distribution with the CSCs were distributed to the applicants.

A leading newspaper in Pune reports this process as follows:

> "A team of over 70 associates of the Dr Babasaheb Ambedkar Research and Training Institute, (BARTI) has succeeded in clearing over 15,500 caste validity certificates in a record four weeks time. The clearance of many of these certificates was pending for the last 15 years. The certificates were distributed through 21 counters specially opened up at the Yerwada office of BARTI for two days on October 2 and 3. Applicants, to their surprise, found the entire process took them less than a few minutes."
>
> (*Sakal Times*, 4th October 2012).

Strengthening CSCs: As a first step of streamlining the work of CSCs, all CSCs were provided with basic furniture and office equipments such as computers, printers, stationary, etc. Simultaneously, to assist the regular employees of CSCs, BARTI engaged approximately 70 retired government officers, IT professionals, early tenure MBAs, Research Assistants on contract basis. These officers were posted at different CSCs based on requirement of human resources. The biggest challenge here was recruitment of Chairman of CSC, which has to be a government employee of the rank of Additional District Collector. BARTI approached the Department of Social Justice and Special Assistance for immediate recruitment of Chairmen and got several appointments done in a short period of time. CSCs where absenteeism or disciplinary issues of Chairmen and other committee members were reported, strict control measures were taken in the form of the installation of Biometric Attendance Machines, CCTV cameras etc.

Computerization of Caste Validity Application Process: Data on the status of all pending and processed applications was collected from CSCs and the lists were published on a dedicated website. To support the applicants who were not savvy with the use of internet, a helpline was started which worked 16 hours a day and provided support to applicants in knowing the status of their applications. Additionally important Government Rules, Orders, List of Scheduled Castes in Maharashtra were published online for the reference of applicants. Additionally, with the help of a leading Software Company in Pune, entire application process for caste validity was made available online. Within a very short period of time the software for online applications was developed and made functional. Simultaneously, the use of online application system was promoted through newspapers.

Checks on Malpractices: To check the malpractices such as the issue of forged caste validity certifices High Security Paper was introduced with the help of the Government Photozinco Press. Similarly, regular meetings were conducted with CSC officers with a view of aligning them on importance of improving the caste validity process. The officers who showed willingness during these meetings to bring change in their mindsets were rewarded while those who continued underperforming or being fraudulent faced disciplinary actions.

Sustainability Measures: While clearing backlogs of caste validity applications was the priority and the backlogs at each CSC were recovered through caste validity distribution camps, it was essential to take sustainability measures. It would not have been possible for BARTI to continuously run the process of caste validity on mission mode with injected human resources and infrastructure. It was important to take certain measure that would ensure, one, that the pace of caste validity distribution is maintained in a longer run and two, no CSCs return to their original situation, as described earlier in this section, once the backlogs are cleared. One of the key steps in this direction was promotion of online applications and setting up a practice of clearing any new application within a fortnight. Secondly, research and documentation of false caste claims was done to make CSC's decision on false caste claims easy. Generally, identifying false caste claims can take time since it often involves sociological, anthropological study of the claimant. A list of doubtful castes was published on website and distributed across the CSCs. Doubtful castes are those castes which are scheduled but do not have reservation benefits as other SCs or are not scheduled at all but persons belonging to these often try to claim themselves as SCs.

Main Lessons

The case presented above is one of the success stories of bringing good governance in Government processes. BARTI started with solving a problem at a time in caste validation process that eventually led to a complete transformation of the caste validation process in Maharashtra. It was hence described by some newspapers as emergence of a new model of governance in Maharashtra (*Atrocity News*, October 2012).

When we look at the steps BARTI took to correct the problems in caste validation process, we find that at each stage transparency was brought into the system. It substantiates the point that transparency is fundamental to bring good governance. Providing timely and free access to information is essential for bringing transparency.

Another important factor of good governance that emerges here is that to practice good governance in systems such as this, it is important that the best interests of various disadvantaged groups are taken into account and that the needs of the most vulnerable in society are kept in mind during decision-making and implementation. Any system of governance is incomplete if it is not responsive to the present and future needs of society.

REFERENCES

Atrocity News (2012), *Another Model of Governance: Now Clean Caste Validity Certificates*, October, Pune.

BARTI (2012), *Caste Validity Scrutiny Committee Research Project*, Dr. Babasaheb Ambedkar Research and Training Institute, Pune.

Etzionim, Amitai (2005), "Is Transparency is the Best Disinfectant", *The Journal of Political Philosophy*, George Washington University.

Johnston, Michael (2001), *Good Governance: Rule of Law, Transparency and Accountability*, Department of Political Science, Colgate University.

Rogers, James D. (2007), "Accountability, Transparency and Governance in Sierra Leon," Keynote address at the Second Audit Risk and Governance Africa Conference, Zanzibar, Tanzania, 17-20 July.

Sakal Times (October 2012), *Some Pending for over 15 years, 15,500 caste certificates cleared,* October, Pune.

Sakal Times (2012), *Now Caste Verification to Go Online,* December, Pune.

Saladin, Al Jurf (undated), *Good Governance and Transparency: Their Impact of Government.*

United Nations (2013), *What is Good Governance,* ESCAP, Bangkok.

World Health Organization (undated), *Measuring Transparency to Improve Good Governance in Public Pharmacuetical Sector,* Syrian Arab Republic.

12

Transparency and Governance

Issues and Challenges for Food Security

Gurulingappa G. Koppa

Introduction

Food is the most basic of all human needs and collective food security governance has been with us since the dawn of human society. Failure to perform it effectively has inevitably engendered social unrest. The riots in capital cities around the world in late 2007 are reminiscent of the hungry crowds that threatened the life of Roman Emperor Claudius in AD 51 and the bread riots that helped to spark off the French Revolution in 1789. History and common sense tell us that a functioning food system is an indispensable pillar of a stable economy and a society capable of reproducing itself.

First priority was given to eradicate hunger and malnutrition in the Millennium Development Goal (MDG) in 2000. Steady progress was made for several years mainly owing to success achieved in emerging economies. However, the global food security crisis in 2007-2008 pushed an additional 100 million people worldwide into poverty and hunger. Moreover, the crisis highlighted the intrinsic fragility of all countries, notably because of the global inter-connectedness and dependency on trade. The volatility of the prices of staple food brought the specific vulnerability of low-income, net-food importing counties and of their populations to the fore. Three quarters of the billion of hungry people live in rural areas of agriculture-based developing economies, which are and will be most affected by demographic growth and environmental challenges in the future.

Food governance is an increasingly difficult task in a globalised world. On the one hand, it involves multiple layers of decision-making. The capacity of single households to ensure an adequate supply of food for its members is affected by developments from local to global levels. Increasingly, the nation states are losing control over the factors that determine the food security of their populations. The range of imponderables has widened from acts of God, like the droughts or locusts that appear in the earliest narratives of the human race or coups by political or military powers to the impalpable workings of globalised economic forces.

This paper presents a framework and a set of strategies for establishing open, democratic and transparent governance processes that lay the foundation for the policies with the overall goal of building a sustainable, healthy and just food system. According to UNDP (2007): "Food security exists when all people, at all times, have physical, social and economic access to sufficient, safe and nutritious food that meets their dietary needs and food preferences for an active and healthy life. The four pillars of food security are availability, access, utilization and stability."

The Context

In the midst of globalization, food security governance has become increasingly complex. For most of the 20th century, it was mainly focused on issues of agricultural production. Today access and ecological concerns are understood to be equally relevant. Governance needs to consider not only how food is produced but also how it is processed, distributed, and consumed. Food governance has become a complex web of often overlapping or contradictory formal policies and regulations, complicated by unwritten rules and practices that are not subject to political oversight.

The governance of food security is a much-contested terrain. It is no coincidence that agriculture has been the stumbling block of the Doha Round of the WTO negotiations. Decisions that affect the food security of the population of a country will involve and alert many social forces: the state, businesses, and civil society. The outcome of negotiations is affected by the power relations among these groups and by the degree to which states manage to mediate in the common interest. Power relations are often very lopsided and government mediation is frequently insufficient.

Getting a better handle on the global governance of food is by no means an easy task. However, now is the time to make effort in that direction. Over the past three years, a series of interrelated crises has unmasked the systemic flaws in the current world food system and highlighted its tendency to reward a small club of privileged economic actors and their political allies. These very crises have opened up the political opportunity to reform the world governance of food security fundamentally. Let us look at some of the evidence that is accumulating in favour of a substantial and substantive change.

Global food output has expanded over the past fifty years, keeping up with population growth despite neo-Malthusian predictions from some quarters. Although, the productivist discourse is still very much with us, it is increasingly evident that the problem is not so much a technical one of producing more food as a political one of ensuring that food is available to those who need it. Moreover, we have a better idea of who are most in need. Majority of the hungry are poor rural food producers. This finding has dispelled the myth that there is a divide between the interests of producers and consumers. Thus, fighting hunger in the developing world has to begin with supporting small holder food producers' capacity to feed their own families.

At the same time, burgeoning problems of obesity and unsafe food are sensitising public opinion and policy-makers to the fact that there are problems with the food system in the North as well as in the South. Globally, more people suffer from over-weight and obesity than from hunger. Diabetes type II kills some 3.8 million people a year (Lan *et al.*, 2009). Mad cow disease in the UK, Salmonella in US eggs and dioxin-affected Belgian chickens are just some of the recent examples of the food risks engendered by insufficiently and inappropriately regulated industrial food production and processing in the North.

The food crisis does not travel unaccompanied. Climate change and the energy crisis have shown that a food system based on the intensive use of petrol products and chemicals is not sustainable. According to recent UNEP publications, the conventional agriculture model that is strongly subsidised by both the European Common Agricultural Policy and the US Farm Bill accounts for 14 per cent of the total annual greenhouse gas emissions. This is mostly due to the use of nitrogen fertilisers derived from rarefying petrol. Yet, UNEP maintains, the agricultural sector could be largely carbon neutral by 2030 and produce enough food for a growing population if localised agro-ecologic systems proven to reduce emissions were widely adopted. In addition, the entire globalised distribution process of the world food system is dependent on being able to discount the energy and petrol cost of whisking food around the world. The rapine popularly termed "land grabbing" is converting large areas to the production of crops that are processed into agri-fuels or food and exported to rich countries. In the process, local producers and pastoralists are frequently expelled.

During 2008, many observers predicted that the food price peaks would simply melt away after enjoying their moment of stardom and cede the headlines to the next crisis. Now, on the contrary, it has become evident that price volatility is likely to be with us for the near future. Prices of major commodities soared in the last months of 2010, and the FAO Food Price Index for January 2011 was the highest (in both real and nominal terms) since the index began in 1990. The World Bank has predicted at least five more years of volatility. The role that financial speculation on food commodities has played regarding food price volatility has shown that current regulatory mechanisms are unsatisfactory if not non-existence. The effects of volatility will continue to constitute a source of social unrest throughout the world, as the food riots in Mozambique in September 2010 demonstrated. During the financial crisis, governments have transgressed against traditional policy precepts in order to save banks and financial institutions. There is every reason to hope that such exceptions to neo-liberal governance may also come into play for food — if only the stakes are high enough. Unaffordable food helped set off the popular revolts in the Maghreb.

To such developments, no government can be indifferent, as President Sarkozy underlined during the French Presidency of the G-20 and G-8 in 2011. The window of opportunity is open.

Framework for Governance for Food Security

Framework that gives direction to the planning and development of a process should be grounded in a vision for a sustainable, healthy, and just food system that provides adequate, healthy, acceptable, and safe food for all. We need food system that respects ecosystems as well as the people, animals, and organisms that depend on them. The framework is the big picture—it is the way that we envision what we are working towards.

In pursuit of the vision of a sustainable, healthy and just food enabling policy environment requires institutions and organizing structures that facilitate public participation in shaping policies, norms, values and rules. Moreover, a democratic society must be able to guarantee the meaningful and active involvement of all individuals, groups, and institutions in decision-making processes. In other words, people must have a say in how their food is produced and where it comes from, and they must have an active role in realizing the principles of food sovereignty.

There is real momentum on governance analysis and several initiatives are underway in different organizations such as the World Bank, ODI and European Union. While there are some clear common features, including a focus on the political context/intelligence, on actors and institutions and on processes underpinning decision-making, differences in approaches remain. Some governments support normative based approaches (grounded in the international human rights framework), while others favour more positive approaches (i.e. work with existing reform space to reach an improved food security outcome). Still some others put emphasis on political economy analysis, that is realistic and incremental approaches in fostering governance or "feasible" change rather than the change associated with a good or democratic governance agenda.

Governance is seen as crucial for development processes and for achieving sustainable development results. In recent years, several international organizations have focused on governance and political economy analysis, including the World Bank, the European Union and the ODI. Within FAO, the concept of governance is increasingly applied at sector level (e.g. land governance, fisheries governance, forest governance, governance of plant genetic resources). At the same time, efforts have been made to promote human rights based approach to food security in FAO work. The FAO Voluntary Guidelines to Support the Progressive Realization of the Right to Food see good governance as an "essential factor for the realization of all human rights including the progressive realization of the right to adequate food."

Governing food systems to reduce hunger and malnutrition at country level is becoming ever more difficult, as food security increasingly depends on many exogenous factors and major global trends such as energy, climate change, protracted crisis, international investments, bio-fuels production, trade and finance.

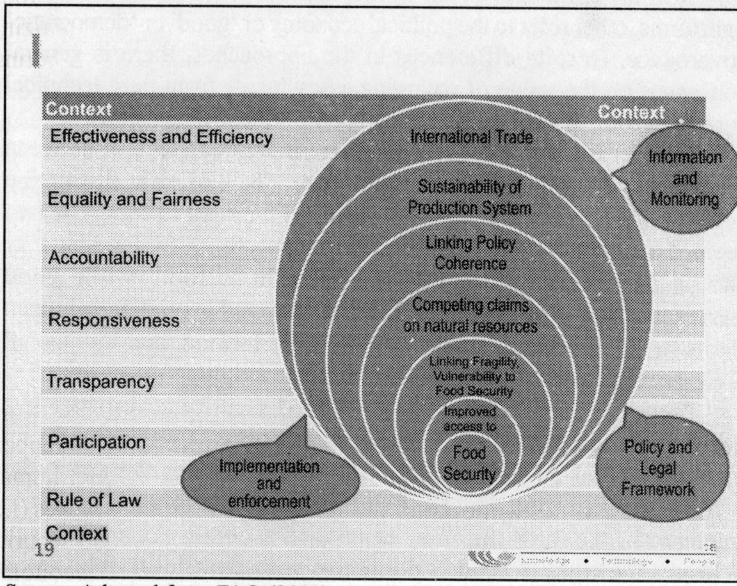

Source: Adapted from FAO (2011).

Fig. 12.1: Conceptual Framework for Food Security Framework

How relevant is global strategic framework from individual country perspective like India? The authority for food security is spread out among a number of international organizations, each with its own objectives and policy preferences, and distinct functions; this makes the system of governance highly fragmented, with objectives that may often overlap and contradict one another. Global governance can sometimes result in pushing countries to take decisions that in the long-term may not be conducive to a better food security for their population e.g. decisions related to agri-business, speculation or land investments.

There is a need to put more emphasis on governance concerns when providing technical assistance to governmental and non-governmental counterparts, e.g. on the nature of the policy formulation process, mechanisms for citizens' participation, mandates, responsibilities and composition of the institutional setting for food security coordination, transparency about the work and access to information, mechanisms and procedures for addressing grievances, manage disputes and enforce decisions. Depending on the development paradigm an individual or an agency adopts some frame in human right terms, other refer to the political economy or 'good' or 'democratic' governance. Despite differences in the approaches, there is general consensus on the value of enlarging assessments from pure technical considerations to also include social and political dimensions.

While it is acknowledged that there is interconnection between human rights and good governance, there a lack of clear distinction between human rights based approach and the right to food.The two seemed to be used interchangeably. Good governance for food security should be put into relation with the right to food, while good governance as a general concept must be analyzed in relation to human rights based approach, i.e. beyond the right to food, and include all civil, political, social, economic and cultural rights.

There has been a debate whether food security governance is a development objective or it describes a process. Considered as an objective, good governance for food security shares the same aim with the right to food. But the two concepts differ when it comes to frameworks, i.e. how they may be applied at country/regional level. Whereas the right to food is normative with clear legal obligations established through international law, good governance takes a more 'positive' approach as an action-guiding tool.

According to FAO (2011), it is appropriate to talk about 'governance for food security' rather than 'food security governance'. As food security is an outcome and not a sector, referring to 'food security governance' may be confusing. In the same line of reasoning, there was a general agreement that good governance for food security should be seen as a means for achieving a desired goal and not as a development objective in itself. In order for good governance to lead to better food security, the governance of sectors that contribute to this goal should be improved ('land tenure governance' or 'forestry management and governance' to give two examples). At a global level, however, the term 'food security governance' may still be used as it refers to the institutions that comprise the governance regime for food security at global level. According to FAO: "Governance for food and nutrition security relates to formal and informal rules and processes through which public and private actors articulate their interests, and decisions for achieving food and nutrition security (at local, national, regional and global level) are made, implemented and sustained."

Speaking in FAO terminology, Governments adhere to a development goal that is either expressed in human rights terms (realizing the human right to food) or in conventional development terms (achieving food and nutrition security for all). To reach this development objective, governments should strive for enhanced access to food through transfers, safety nets and other social programmes on the one hand, and investment in development, in particular in support of agriculture and rural development, on the other. Good governance for food security constitutes the enabling environment that allows the two tracks to become effective.

It is acknowledged that some countries prioritize normative goals such as right to food, while others even if signatories to the relevant international human rights treaties are more comfortable with the concept of good governance for food security. Good governance for food security is perceived as more appropriate as it goes beyond Government to include how other actors such as traditional/customary authorities, private and professional sectors, and civil society articulate their interests and affect the adoption and implementation of food and nutrition security measures. The question is how to reconcile the need/requests to work with both normative goals and governance approach to food security. As one possible way forward, FAO considered to acknowledge that governance can play an important role in determining the nature of the way towards the right to food goal. This relationship with good governance as an "essential factor for the realization of all human rights including the progressive realization of the right to adequate food" is also supported by the Right to Food Guidelines (Guideline 1.3).

Seven dimensions proposed in the working analytical framework (Fig. 12.1) may or may not be relevant to governance for food security in a given country.This will entirely depend on its specific historical, economic, cultural and legal context. The proposed principles should be put in perspective and qualified by reality: the right combination and dosage of principles that fit the specific country should be determined on the basis of a holistic analysis and its specific context. The challenge is finding the right balance.

As mentioned earlier huge socket of 1 billion is food insecure worldwide with more in times of crises. There is thus a growing belief that this represents a failure of governance and that the 'standard' technical response to food insecurity may not be enough. Governance, and the way in which politics and institutions interact will in practice have a critical impact, for example, on how resources are managed and allocated, how services are delivered or on planning and policy.

This means that a common analytical framework for understanding the context and dealing with it in support of food security is necessary.

When looking at the governance for food security, one should not look through the lens of a future ideal state of governance. It is the current reality of governance for food security that should be analyzed and understood. Such an analysis would be a good basis on which to develop a realistic picture of what domestic actors and international organizations and donors can do to enhance governance for food security.

In this sense, there could be more focus on the context and on actors and stakeholders in governance for food security—who are they, what is their degree of ability to help or have an impact on a given aspect of food security policy or programme, what are their interests and incentives for maintaining the situation as it is or for changing it, are there alliances within and between the stakeholder groupings, etc.

The question is whether the suggested framework is appropriate in both development and emergency situations, and how its flexibility could be ensured. Seven dimensions are all considered possibly relevant, although in differing dosage and combinations. It is suggested to replace efficiency and effectiveness with professionalism, quality and evidence-based decision; to replace the principle of equality and fairness with gender equity and to add empowerment.

REFERENCES

De Schutter, Oliver (2009), "Governing World Food Security: A New Role for the Committee on World Food Security" in Right to Food and Nutrition Watch, *Who Controls the Governance of the World Food System?*

FAO (1970), *Report of the Second World Food Congress*, FAO, Rome.

——(2002), *World Agriculture: Towards 2015/2030*, FAO, Rome.

——(2006), *Trade Reforms and Food Security: Country Case Studies and Synthesis*, FAO, Rome.

——(2009), *Declaration of the World Summit on Food Security*, 16-18 November 2010. WSFS2009/2, FAO, Rome.

——(2011a), *Food Price Index*, 03/02/2011, www.fao.org/worldfoodsituation/FoodPricesIndex/en.

——(2011b), *Save and Grow: A Policymaker's Guide To The Sustainable Intensification of Smallholder Crop Production*, FAO, Rome.

——(2011c), *Good Food Security Governance: The Crucial Promise to the twin Approach*, FAO, Rome.

Third World Network (2006), *Globalization, Liberalization and Protectionism: Impacts on Poor Rural Producers in Developing Countries*, IFAD, Rome.

World Bank (2007a), *World Bank Assistance to Agriculture in Sub-Saharan Africa: An IEG Review*, World Bank, Washington, D.C.

—— (2007b), *Agriculture for Development: World Development Report 2008*, World Bank, Washington, D.C.

—— (2010), *New World: New World Bank Group: Post-Crisis Directions*, Paper prepared for the April 25, 2010 Development Committee Meeting, World Bank, Washington D.C.

13

Disaster Management

Role of Transparency and Disclosure

Nirmita Mehrotra

Introduction

The complex nature of disasters has led to recognition that risk reduction through increased resilience will require a strategy that is inter-disciplinary. True inter-disciplinarity only occurs where a number of separate disciplines surrender their own concepts and goals, and collectively move themselves by reference to a common set of strategic concepts and goals.

According to strict Latin root, *resilire,* to leap back or rebound, the idea of resilience refers to the ability of an entity or system to 'recover from position elastically' following a disturbance or disruption of some kind. The first and more traditional definition, so called 'engineering resilience' concentrates on the stability of a system near an equilibrium or steady state, where resistance to disturbance and speed of return to the pre-existing equilibrium are used to define the ideas of resilience (Holling, 1973; Simie and Martin, 2010). The second definition, ecological resilience, focuses on whether disturbances and shocks cause a system to move into another regime of behaviour. The third concept socio-ecological resilience, characterizes interplay of disturbances, reorganizations, sustaining and developing. It is based on adaptive capacity, transformability and learning innovations. Comfort (1999) argued that response of socio-technical system to risk is equivalent to level of adaptation, and various types of responses may occur depending on the technical structure, the flexibility and cultural openness to use a technology.

In context of emergency management, the term resilience was established through the Hyogo framework of Action 2005-2015 by United Nations as a result of World Conference on Disaster Reduction in 2005. The framework focused on the prioritization of risk reduction, identifying risks and enhancing early warning systems, building a culture of safety and resilience, reducing underlying risk factors, and strengthening disaster preparedness and response capabilities (UNISDR, 2005).

Tierney (2003) described resilience as "physical and social systems to withstand forces and demands generated by disaster events to actively cope with such events and to actively cope with such events through employing effective response and recovery strategies". Tierney argued on the four components of resilience as robustness, redundancy, resourcefulness and rapidity within four domains of technical, social, organizational and economic as Mcmanus (2007) model of 4R, which were Reduction, Readiness, Response and Recovery, used concept of resilience as functions of vulnerability management and adaptive capacities.

Phillips Berkes (2003) defined system attributes of resilience as—(i) the amount of disturbance a system can absorb and still remain within the same state or domain of attraction, (ii) the degree to which the system is capable of self-organization, and (iii) the degree to which the system can build and increase the capacity for learning and adaptation.

Comfort defined level of adaptations based on defined attributes as—(i) non-adaptive responses where adaptation is inadequate for existing level of risk, (ii) emergent adaptations where adaptation is insufficient but incipient, (iii) adaptive operations where management is adequate but with restrictions and lastly (iv) auto-adaption where adaptation is innovating, creative, spontaneous, outstanding and optimal. Under this definition institutional resilience would imply the capacity of the institutional framework to absorb shocks with adaptation, flexibility and long-term goals. Chen, Gausi and Sage (1975) stated that successful implementation of technology for societal problems should consider three levels namely symptoms, institutions and value. Firstly, it is through symptoms, we try to treat problems, secondly through institutions to implement technology and thirdly by value elements and systems (Sage, 1977).

Fig. 14.1: Disaster Management in a Socio-Technical System

Coaffee (2004) argues that there are three key dimensions that differentiate resilience from traditional notions of disaster planning and recovery. First, the emphasis is on hazard mitigation and preparedness rather than post-disaster management. Second, there has been a widening of the emergency planning agenda to embrace security challenges in addition to natural hazards and technological 'accidents'; this is despite the fact that the latter categories have a far greater collective impact. The third dimension concerns the role of institutional resilience to protect key infrastructural systems. Resilience of urban system categorized in four components to cover different functional variations:

- *Economic Resilience:* Role of economic resilience in reducing monetary losses in disasters is achieved through the adoption of mitigation strategies that aim to lessen probability of failure (Rose, 2006), other parts include property losses, business disruption post event.
- *Institutional Resilience:* Which includes elements that measure how organizations structure, capacity, leadership, training and experiences (Tierney and Bruneau, 2007)
- *Infrastructural Resilience:* Tightly coupled and interconnected infrastructure (Perrow, 1999), the less resilience it exhibits. A

high degree of interdependence reduce resilience since a disruption in one sector cascades into impacts on other sectors (Chang *et al.,* 2007; McDaniels *et al.*, 2007).

- *Community Competence:* Another form of resilience and highlights those attributes of places that promote population wellness, quality of life and emotional health (Norris *et al.*, 2008)

Carpenter defined pattern of resilience as adaptive strategies that are self-organized, sustained with minimal outside support and associated with outcomes that uphold key social institutions with a positive benefit for cooperation and risk mitigation. Carpenter continues that patterns of resilience are oriented towards protecting and enhancing institutions with a positive effect on cooperation and risk mitigation and gave example of Amara, Iran, Sungusungu in Tanzania where tribes are primary institutions embodying law, justice, order and many other. The processes of enhancing stability in fragile states are themselves change processes; depending on community's resource, social and institutional capital.

Baud and Hordjik (2009) in their paper 'dealing with risks in Urban Governance: what can we learn from Resilience thinking' focused on features of adaptive governance as flexible institutions, knowledge system that integrate different set of knowledge, the capacities of learning by experiment, creativity and self-organizations.

Urban Governance

UN-HABITAT defines good urban governance as the exercise of political, economic, social and administrative authority in the management of an urban entity. It is the sum of the many ways individuals and institutions, public and private, plan and manage the common affairs of the city. It includes formal institutions as well as informal arrangements and the social capital of citizens. It is characterized by transparent decision-making, sound financial management, public accountability, decentralized and equitable resource allocation, and probity. Transparency and accountability are essential to stakeholder since it creates an environment of trust and openness, which results in collaboration and partnerships in addressing urban challenges.

The private sector may benefit from transparency and accountability by:

1. Participating as stakeholder for consultations on city resources utilization and other important issues.
2. Perform regular and independently executed programmes to test public officials' integrity response.
3. Foster the introduction of a business management model to the public sector that will remove administrative and procedural incentives for corruption.
4. Assist the public sector in adopting enforceable standards of accountability and service delivery, such as ISO that will transcend the terms of public office bearers.

The supportive role of the private sector towards good urban governance can be realized at four levels: National, Sector, City and Neighbourhood levels. Transparency may be defined as the disclosure of government information and its use by the public. Transparency, under this definition, requires a public that can access, understand, and use the information it receives. *Transparency comprises not only the disclosure of government information*, but also the access comprehension, and use of this information by the public.

Transparency International, a global civil society organization that seeks to fight government corruption, defines transparency as "a principle that allows those affected by administrative decisions, business transactions or charitable work to know not only the basic facts and figures but also the mechanisms and processes." Directive aims to implement the initiative's core values through four strategies:

1. Publish government information online.
2. Improve the quality of government information.
3. Create and institutionalize a culture of open government.
4. Create an enabling policy framework for open government.

Resilience and Role of Institutions

Disaster risks are actually driven by a number of unresolved, underlying causes such as vulnerable rural livelihoods, poverty, poor urban governance, lack of good governance, declining ecosystem services, and power inequality, which eventually lead to an uneven distribution of risk both socially and spatially, thereby "increasing the risks faced by the poor and further amplifying poverty" (UNISDR 2009). Cutter (2008) stated institutional or organizational resilience based on component features an structure of organization, respond behaviour as organization structure, capacity leadership, communication technology and emergency assets.

Birkmann (2006) quoted Cannon *et al.* as reference for assuming that institutions are organizations. Despite efforts to partly distinguish organizational and institutional aspects of vulnerabilities, including the acceptance that understanding both organizations and institutions is as important as physical vulnerabilities. Birkman stated that organizational and institutional vulnerabilities to be as important as physical vulnerabilities and divided their analysis into three spheres as economic, social and environmental vulnerability. Though initially he cites institutional aspects such as good governance, warning and legislation as institutional aspect, but later concludes through institutional analysis that all domains of vulnerability such as physical, social, economic and environmental vulnerabilities are indeed outcome of institutions. Four noble laureates, North (1993), Simon (1978), Ostrom (2009) and Willanson (2009), asserted on the basis of ample evidence that economic vulnerabilities are the outcomes of institutions. Findings on the role of institution on environmental outcomes have consistently shown that physical vulnerabilities such as building structures are shaped by institutions rather than income alone.

In aftermath of Gujarat Earthquake, the persistent case of deliberate vulnerabilities pointed lack of states capacity to monitor and regulate housing construction. There have been perennial problems caused by low quality building material, deliberate non-compliance with building codes, regulations and safety norms, which has transformed the regions seismic hazard into disaster of catastrophic proportion. For example — the main earthquake affected parts of Ahmedabad was its affluent areas. The failure of its up market and recently constructed luxury apartment to withstand tremors indicated that delinquency played significant role alongside vulnerabilities born of poverty, aging housing stock and unregulated buildings. Pointedly the root cause of enormous disaster in Gujarat was found to be lacuna in Institutional Framework:

1. Lack of organizing capacity within municipalities.
2. Lack of coordination among different departments
3. Failure in incorporation of scientific, administrative and technological advances in Public Sector.
4. Conscious negligence to appease powerful builder lobby.

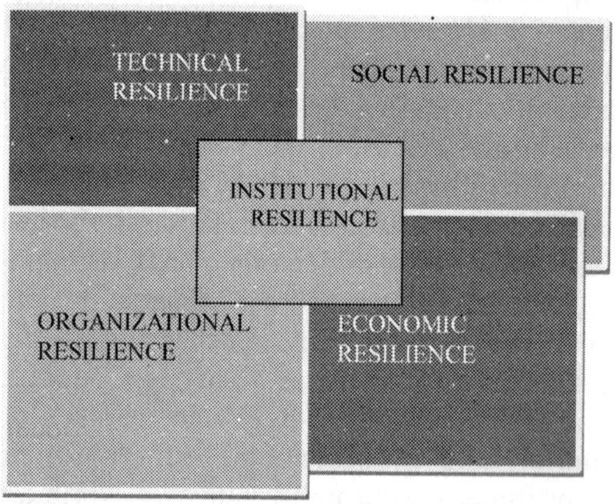

Source: Author

Fig. 14.2: Institutional Resilience Affecting All Other Domain of Resilience

Jones Lindsey *et al.* (2010) in the Overseas Development Institute formulated a framework for governance of adaptive capacity. They stated that the adaptive capacity relates to system's ability to foster innovation and experimentation as part of learning process, to cope with and respond to changing circumstances. This innovation is not only about high tech large scale innovations, but also micro level initiatives, as many of the actions taken to adapt to changing shocks and trends will be done spontaneously at the local level. Key elements of Adaptive governance in this context are informed decision-making, governance that is flexible, collaborative, learning based and better able to cope with changing circumstances. Adaptive Governance has to recognize both the technical capacity of institutions and power relations behind decision-making. Jones (2010) continues that the decisions made are less about technical features and more about whose interest count, whose voice is heard. The institutional rules and behaviour norms that govern how individuals react in the face of shock and changing trends will also play in adaptive capacity (Dulal *et al.* 2010).

Self-Organization by Local Actors

Buad and Hordijik (2009) look at the urban governance models where feature like flexible institutions, integrative knowledge system, capacities of learning by experiment creativity and self-organization. Transparency and Disclosure can play a significant role in creating flexible institutional structures, where decision-making can be decentralized at different levels with an outcome oriented planning. They argued on a debate on kind of governance away from traditional top down models and command and control state led approach to a multi actor network approach. In relating resilience thinking to urban governance, it recognizes more actors, more space for ideas and participation from actors outside government, more flexible patterns of planning and management. It emphasizes the necessity of including the strength of the horizontal networks between local governments, and those of civil society organizations or private companies. The resilience model emphasizes vertical linkages between different scale levels. If vertical networks, linking civil society and private sector are taken into account, they will provide a comprehensive set of networks which can contribute to more effective governance. Takeda and Helms (2006) stated failure of bureaucracy in management of disasters due to three reasons:

1. Decisions are made in closed group, which takes time and does not recognize unorganized, outside information.
2. Institutional structure and officials suffers from role fixation, are reach to 'no reaction' status' to a new situation, till the instructions role down from the top.
3. System has a slow response time to take swift decision. Refusal to recognize outside information and resources and refusal to admit failure in disaster management, has resulted in increased death, agony and denial of basic human rights during response and relief work.

Even in most marginalized urban neighbourhood, local actors do have certain capacity to respond to environmental hazards (Pelling, 2003), and this is the central concern for building adaptive capacity.

Though self-organization in socio-technical system like urban system have been considered as black box approach, the recent research of Shalizi mathematical models and Parunack (2001) suggested coupling of sub-systems to reduce disorder. In this concept civil society association where local actors are indulged in collective action play significant role in creating order especially as evident in events of disaster response and recovery. Examples from Japan, Indonesia and India are used here to emphasize the role of local actors in events of chaos and local municipal bodies were instrumental in generating opportunities for collective action from residents groups.

ISA Baud and Nainan (2008) represented a case of Mumbai, where Advance Locality Management (ALM) groups from the residents of neighbourhood, with original mandate of monitoring and improving visible basic services at neighbourhood level, were instrumental in holding the local government for accountability. Though ward committees of elected representatives, representing low income and vulnerable groups of society, dependent on political connections and authority, ALM representing middle class residents dealt directly with executive wing of local government to raise their point and ensure delivery of required services. ALM's have been formed of cooperative societies and welfare organizations to manage staff deficits due to restrictive staffing policies since 1995 particularly for conservancy departments dealing with solid waste management. They extended themselves in beautification of streets and other specific concerns of their areas including water management, together with solid waste collection from house to house and segregation. The movement of partnership from local city government for collaborative works with non-governmental actors (CBOs) encourage inter organizational networks. There is urgent need of these networks to be made a part of disaster management and resilience building.

In 1994, an outbreak of plague epidemics in the city of Surat, India threatened to spread around the world after infecting around 300,000 people and killing 52 persons. About 60 per cent of the population fled the city and the industry suffered an estimated loss of Rs. 12 billion. Outbreak of plague was basically due to flooding of Tapi river a month before and when few deteriorating dead bodies of animals blocked drains. There emerged a model of community participation in the direct leadership of the Surat Municipal Corporation (SMC). In face of the unprecedented crisis a seven-point action plan launched for restoring normalcy at the earliest in collaboration with the non-governmental agencies, civil society, and the private sector working together. This model of urban management initiated changes at local level turned the city into second cleanliest city without any external financial or technical support.

The Gujarat Earthquake of 2001 introduced local community as vital component of a successful disaster mitigation processes. 'Patanka Navjivan Yojana' a model programme involving fifteen agencies from India and abroad pooled together, to embark on issues of investment for people's knowledge building, improving livelihood options, empowering individuals so that they can take care of their own needs, strengthening local institutions and partnering with local governments as key factors for successful mitigation. The concept of decentralised planning is based on a combination of top-down and grass root approach with local representation through civic engagements.

Japan is known for its vulnerability to disasters. For example, Japan is ranked fourth in the world in the evaluation of physical exposure to tropical cyclones (UNDP, 2004). Furthermore, since Japan is located on the boundary between an oceanic plate and a continental plate, Japan is geographically more vulnerable to damage by earthquakes and volcanoes than other countries. In particular, the coastal areas, where populations, assets, and city function have accumulated, are vulnerable to tsunamis, since Japan is surrounded by the sea and has complicated coast lines (Cabinet Office, 2008a). For example, the Hokkaido-Nanseioki earthquake struck Okushiri Island, Hokkaido in 1993 and wide-ranging damage was reported including the collapse of houses, destruction of buildings by fire, aquatic submersion of houses by tsunamis, damage to fishery harbors by castaways, and more. At the Great Hanshin-Awaji (Kobe) Earthquake Disaster in 1995, the number of buildings which collapsed or were heavily damaged was around 250,000 and the number of people captured in the buildings was around 35,000. After the earthquake happened, telephones didn't work and there was a heavy traffic on the road, 27,000 people were rescued by neighbours and 80 per cent of them were alive. However, 8,000 people were rescued by Army, Police or Fire Fighters and less than 50 per cent of them were alive. This fact gives us a lesson that the activity of local community is the key to mitigate earthquake disaster.

Based on lesson from the 1995 Great Hanshin-Awaji Earthquake Disaster, the number of community-based organization increased rapidly in Japan. In 2003, there were more than 100,000 organizations covering more than 60 per cent of families in the whole country. For example, the city of Kobe has 416 community-based organizations covering 81.8 per cent of member families. Each organization has a structure consisting of a headquarter and team leaders. Following the Kobe earthquake of 1995, the Japanese government has promoted the Voluntary Disaster Preparedness Organization (VDPO) to build communities that are more sustainable and resilient to natural disasters, particularly for the community's capacity to respond. The Japanese government, in collaboration with local governments, has promoted establishing the Voluntary Disaster Preparedness Organization (VDPO) to improve community-based disaster preparedness. Each prefectural government promoted establishment of VPDO in order to reduce the vulnerability of damages.

Similarly, in Indonesia, multiple organizations emerged as agents and have exercised agency beyond the state where and when the state government was unable to effectively respond. Few organizations emerged as an agent in driving and shaping governance and institutional change in disaster management at multiple levels on the other hand, a organization named KOKAMI, has emerged as an agent in exercising community disaster preparedness. The underlying conditions of their authority and legitimacy include a mix of knowledge base, consent and trust from the state, and an extensive network at multiple levels and across scales including support from the broad-based community and a diverse array of partners.

Another recent example amplifying effects between different types of governance systems can be found in the case of Hurricane Katrina in New Orleans in 2005. A large part of the storm's devastating impact did not result from a lack of scientific information or failed meteorological predictions (*Science*, 2005) but rather from the combination of a rigid federal emergency management system (Greber, 2007; Schneider, 2005) and an ill-prepared and disorganized fragile local governance system (Burns and Thomas, 2006; Kiefer and Montjoy, 2006). The failure of disaster management resulted in massive political distrust and called for political resignations and reorganization of the disaster management apparatus (Waugh, 2006).

In events of disasters, horizontal and vertical restructuring facilitate self-organization of the communities in both the bottom up and top down governance. Phenomenon of self-organization is deduced from illustrative examples of Voluntary Disaster Preparedness Organization (VDPO) in Japan and 'Kudambashree' by Government of Kerala (India) and other success stories of Patanka Navjivan Yojana, where government promoted resilience of the community by devolution of finance and convergence of other schemes operating at grassroot level to Neighbourhood Groups (NHG) and Community Development Society (CDS) under Municipalities. The Alleppey municipality CDS won the "We, the Peoples: 50 Communities award", initiated in commemoration of the Fiftieth Anniversary of the United Nations in 1995.

The coordination of Non-Governmental Organisations (NGOs) among themselves and with government agencies has been improving over the years and NGOs have made significant contributions in most of the recent disasters. The NGOs that responded to the Orissa Super Cyclone of 1999 came together under the banner of the Orissa Disaster Mitigation Mission (ODMM) for coordination purposes. After the Gujarat Earthquake of 2001, a network of NGOs under the banner of Kutch Nav Nirman Abhiyan helped to establish a network of information kiosks called SETUs for two way information exchange between communities and the Government in the earthquake affected areas. After the Indian Ocean Tsunami in December 2004, in Nagapattinam in Tamil Nadu, more than 500 NGOs responding to the Tsunami came together as the NGO Coordination and Resource Centre (NCRC) to collect, collate, and share information. In Bihar during Kosi Floods, Sphere India supported the setting up of the inter-agency working groups at the state and district levels. Besides the formal arrangements, informal community based systems also exist in many areas, such as the civil society flood early warning systems that operate through community groups in the villages covering the flood prone areas from upstream Assam to even the downstream villages in Bangladesh. Most of these have been isolated experiences of synergetic partnership between civil society organisations with government institutions, facilitated to a large extent by the senior administrators at the field level.

Network Governance

Naim Kapucu (2005) stated the significance of inter-organization network in response to co-ordinations based on September 11, 2001 terrorist attack on World Trade Centre. He also used a theoretical framework drawn from dynamic network theory and complex adaptive system theory to bring forth on the issues of productive collaboration among the public, private and non-profit organizations for increased efficiency in disaster response. In recent years, such inter organizational collaboration has become a prominent aspect of the functioning of many different types of organizations. The number and significance of collaborative forms of organizing, including inter-organizational teams, partnerships, alliances, and networks, have increased tremendously. In complex and turbulent environments, organizations frequently develop formal or informal relationships in order to work together to pursue shared goals, address common concerns, and/or attain mutually beneficial ends. Kapucu (2005) used the term 'network' to describe multiple-organizational relations involving multiple nodes of interactions. A network is group of individuals or organizations who, on a voluntary basis, exchange information and undertake joint activities and who organize themselves in such a way that their individual autonomy remains intact.

Kapucu used the term network to describe multiple-organizational relations involving multiple nodes of interactions. A network is a group of individuals or organizations who, on a voluntary basis, exchange information and undertake joint activities and who organize themselves in such a way that their individual autonomy remains intact. In this definition important points are that the relationship must be voluntary, that these are mutual or reciprocal activities, and that belonging to the network does not affect autonomy and independence of the members. There are instances where changing governance structures and technical changes may actually reduce uncertainty (Comfort, 1999; Weick, 2001). Comfort (1999) recognized that disaster represent occasion in which the boundaries between organizational and collective behaviour are blurred.

Information Sharing, Collaboration and Resilience

Kapucu (2005) addressed issues of inter-organization coordination among organizations as evolved in response to extreme event and stated the increase in interaction as they share information and resources. As organizations from different sectors share information and resources, victims are served better as a result of collaboration. The interactions of organizations in a large system can generate greater complexity then the organizations themselves. Resilient social systems are characterized by reduced failure, measured in terms of lives lost, damage, and negative social and economic impacts, and reduced time to recovery — that is, more rapid restoration of the social systems and institutions to their normal, pre-disaster levels of functioning. Aaron Wildawsky (1971) describes resilience as "the capacity to cope with unexpected dangers after they have become manifest, learning to bounce back." Organizations can contribute to resilience in a society by incorporation other emergency response organizations and by integrating volunteers into emergency operations as appropriate.

Extreme events are occurrences that are notable, rare, unique, and profound, in terms of their impacts, effects, or outcomes. When extreme events occur at the interface between natural, social and human systems, they are often called "disasters" (Red Cross, 2001). Quarantelli and Dynes (1977) define disaster as the disruption to society after the "event". Everybody is affected in extreme events and individuals and single organizations cannot prevent the harm caused by the event. In extreme events standard procedures cannot be followed and they require dynamic system to adapt to unanticipated and rapidly changing conditions.

The September 11, 2001 terrorist attack is an example of an extreme event with significant impact upon humanity. Extreme events trigger greater density of communication and interaction among organizations that stimulates collective action. A critical aspect of this process is the formation of new and or stronger networks among multi-sector organizations. Inter-organizational networks in emergencies can play an important role in facilitating the flow of information across organizational boundaries. In this context, local actors and agents from non-governmental organization play significant roles. Continuum of roles from local actors can ensure Disaster Resilience as follows:

1. Clear delineation of roles and responsibilities of NGO during each phase of disaster.
2. NGO's leverage routine practice in Disaster Planning and dual benefits in emergency preparedness and daily operations.
3. Guidance on resource allocation both financial and non-financial
4. Improvisation in information exchange among NGO's, between NGO's, Governmental agencies and community residents.

5. Local actors have belongingness with the place and community, familiar with existing hazards, type of emergency needs and community in their neighbourhood, which require immediate support. They also help prioritization of immediate needs of the community and its specific members for example the people with disability, chronic illness or pregnant ladies.
6. Local actors represent the community's issues and concerns. They are the community network and sensors, through which government can sense impact of their policies, benefits gained by the projects and welfare schemes and participation of communities in decision-making and enforcement.

Emergence of Self-Organizing Networks

The original "principle of the self-organizing dynamic system" was formulated by the cybernetician Ashby in 1947. It states that any deterministic dynamic will automatically evolve towards a state of equilibrium. The concept of self-organization is becoming increasingly popular in various branches of science and technology. Although there is no generally accepted definition (Gershenson and Heylighen, 2003), a self-organizing system may be characterized by global, coordinated activity arising spontaneously from local interactions between the system's components or "agents". Self-organization establishes a relation between the behaviour of the individual components and the structure and functionality of the system as a whole. Simple interactions at the local level give rise to complex patterns at the global level. This phenomenon is called *emergence*.

Self-organization emerges from interactions between elements of systems and in a way, forms the very core of governance processes. Control over and guidance of these processes is distributed over the full set of actors and over different process systems, a fact which has provided the basis for network approaches to policy-making. Gershenson and Heylighen (2003) also explores the growing role played by network in a system and how it could be useful in capacity building and emergency response during disaster. This is particularly significant when the hierarchical power of government in society is waning to be effective in terms of governance of multi-modal risk and vulnerability. Sorensen and Torfing defined key elements of the network governance (as reported in Bortel and Mullins, 2009) as follows:

1. A relatively stable horizontal articulation of interdependent but operationally autonomous actors;
2. Actors interact through negotiations;
3. Negotiations take place within regulative, normative, cognitive and imaginary framework;
4. The framework is self-regulatory within limits set by external agencies.
5. The framework contributes to the production of public purpose.

Increasing organizational and technological inter-connectedness may create more possibilities of multi-organizational partnerships for the surge of an extreme event. The WTC disaster illustrates how in disaster settings high levels of cooperation and collaboration among organizational and community actors can co-exist. Communities responding to disasters are seen as coping collectively with shared pain, loss, and disruption and as temporarily suspending ongoing conflicts and disagreements in the interest of meeting urgent needs and beginning the recovery process. Trustworthiness and social capital can, especially, play an important role in extreme events within which there is no clear policy or guidelines available to the participant organizations and individuals.

Comfort (2004) argues that process of self-organization in context of disaster environment generate interaction among organizations and their operating environment in newly evolving complex system, offer insight into general problem of initiating change. He also argued that self organization is potentially important in explaining process of change. Self-adaptation and self-management literature took its roots from biology inspired solutions like ants colony, termites building functionally complex mounds, flocking of birds and immune system of mammals including human beings. Colonies of social insects possess what has been classified as Swarm Intelligence. A broad definition of the term implies a sophisticated collective behaviour borne out of primitive interactions among members of the group to solve problems beyond the capability of individual members. Such colonies are characterized by:

1. *Self-Organization:* Decentralised and unsupervised coordination of activities.
2. *Adaptiveness:* Response to dynamically varying environment.
3. *Robustness:* Accomplishing the group's objectives even if some members are unsuccessful.

Self-organization emerges from interactions between elements of systems and in a way, forms the very core of governance processes. While actions of governments may appear as something different than self-organization, they are in fact just an additional dimension of self-organization. Control over and guidance of these processes is distributed over the full set of actors and over different process systems, a fact which has provided the basis for network approaches to policy-making. Governance involves the coordination of activities within a society concerning its collective problems. Such governance can be the result of self-organization, or be the result of external control. External control involves some form of rule setting, monitoring, and sanctioning which is exercised by a system outside the system that is being controlled. This leads to the distinction of two systems: the societal system, and the external control system. The external control system can emerge in two ways. First, actors in society can self-organize into structures which include monitoring and sanctioning, which develop into distinct systems, resulting in an external control system. The other possibility is that actors have coercive means which enable them to establish control over a society like the *Khap Panchayat* which decide the conduct within their spheres of influence.

Conclusion

Transparency and disclosure can play a significant role in inducing flexible institutional structures, where decision-making can be actually decentralized at different levels with an outcome oriented planning. Information revolutions through means of mass communication like Twitter and Facebook has capacity to generate collective actions, which could be positively utilized to enhance Institutional resilience through collaborative and network of formal, informal organization. Transparency and Disclosure can equip organization with a management system to support learning and facilitate continuous growth and development, as well as flexibility when managing diversity. Transparency and Disclosure has untapped potential as a means of Institutional learning and sharing of learning on a wider platforms for building networks of collective actions, rather than confining it as an accountability monitoring instrument for checking integrity of each other.

REFERENCES

Coaffee, J. (2008), "Risk, Resilience and Environmentally Sustainable Cities," *Energy Policy,* 36.

Comfort, L.K. (1994), "Self Organization in Complex System: Integrating Theory and Practice in Dynamic System," JPART.

Comfort, L.K. (1999), *Shared Risk: Complex Systems in Seismic Reponse,* Elsevier Science, Oxford.

Cutter, S. *et al.* (2008), "A Place Based Model of Understanding Community Resilience," in *Global Environment Change,* Elsevier Science, Oxford.

Duit, A. and V. Galaz V (2008), "Governance and Complexity—Emerging Issues for Governance Theory,"*Governance: An International Journal of Policy, Administration, and Institutions*, 21 (3).

Godschalk, D. (2003), "Urban Hazard Mitigation: Creating Resilient Cities," *Natural Hazard Review,* 4 (3).

Kapucu, Naim (2011), "Disaster and Emergency Management Systems in Urban Areas," *Cities.*

McEntire, D.A. (2005), "Why Vulnerability Matters: Exploring the Merit of an Inclusive Disaster Reduction Concept", *Disaster Prevention and Management*, 14 (2).

McEntire, D.A. (2008), "Rising Disasters and Their Reversal: An Identification of Vulnerability and Ways to Reduce It", in Pinkowski, J. (Ed.), *Disaster Management Handbook,* CRC Press, Boca Raton, FL.

Mehrotra, N. (2010), "Disaster Management: Need of Revival in Policy Framework," *Institute of Town Planners India Journal,* 7 (2).

Ostrom, E. (2005), *Understanding Institutional Diversity,* Princeton University Press, Princeton.

Paavola, J. (2007) "Institutions and Environmental Governance: A Reconceptualization," *Ecological Economics.* 63:93-103.

Pahl-Wostl, C. (2009), "A Conceptual Framework for Analyzing Adaptive Capacity and Multi-Level Learning Processes in Resource Governance Regimes," *Global Environmental Change.*

Parvin, Gulsan Ara and Rajib Shaw (2011), "Climate Disaster Resilience of Dhaka City Corporation: An Empirical Assessment at Zone Level," *Risk, Hazards and Crisis in Public Policy,* 2(2).

Pelling, M. (2003), *Vulnerability of Cities,* Earthscan.

Senge, P. (1990), *The Fifth Discipline: The Art and Practice of Learning Organization,* Double Currency Book. New York.

Tierney, K. and M. Bruneau (2007), "Conceptualizing and Measuring Resilience: A Key to Disaster Loss Reduction," *TR News.*

UNISDR (2012), "Resources for 'Making Cities Resilient'" *http://www.unisdr.org/campaign/resilientcities*

Weick, Karl E. (2001), *Making Sense of the Organization*, Blackwell Business, Oxford, Massachusset.

14
Transparency and Disclosure in Consumer Issues

Sheetal Kapoor

Introduction

Consumer affairs today encompass all aspects of consumer welfare. Consumer is considered an inevitable part of the socio-economic-political system, where the exchange initiated and transaction realised between two parties, namely buyers and sellers has an impact on a third party i.e., society. The inherent profit motive in mass production and sales also offers the opportunity to many manufacturers and dealers to exploit consumers. Problems of defective goods, deficiency in service, spurious and duplicate brands, misleading advertisements are rampant and often the gullible consumer falls prey to it. Thus, the need for consumer satisfaction and consumer protection is now well recognized.

We are all consumers as we buy different commodities and services) from the market for our own consumption. We are dependent on the market to fulfil our basic needs. From purchasing a small item such as bread and butter to big ticket items such as automobiles, refrigerator and air conditioners. Consumers today want value for money, a product or service that would meet reasonable expectations, is safe in use and there is full disclosure of the product specification. These expectations are termed as 'Consumer Rights'.

Government of India has taken initiative to pass progressive legislation to safeguard the interests of the consumers. The most important milestone in Consumer Movement in the country has been the enactment of the Consumer Protection Act, 1986. The Act has set in motion a revolution in the field of consumer rights that perhaps cannot be paralleled anywhere else in the World. The Act applies to all goods and services unless specially exempted by the Central Government, in all sectors whether private, public or co-operative. The Act enshrines all the consumer rights which are internationally accepted. As per the Act, the consumer protection councils have been established at Central, State and District levels to promote and protect the consumer rights. The government by now has enacted 24 pro-consumer Acts to control buyer-seller relations at the market place.

Unfair Trade Practices

The term Unfair Trade Practice (UTP) broadly refers to any fraudulent, deceptive or dishonest trade practice; or business misrepresentation of the products or services that are being sold which is prohibited by a statute or recognised as actionable under law by a judgement of the court. In Consumer Protection Act, 1986 an Unfair trade practice means a trade practice which, for the purpose of promoting the sale, use or supply of any goods or for the provision of any service, adopts any unfair method or unfair or deceptive practice including any of the following practices:

- The practice of making any statement in an oral or written form falsely representing that the goods are of a particular standard, quality, quantity, grade, composition, style or model.
- Falsely representing that the services are of a particular standard, quality or grade.
- Falsely representing any re-built, second-hand, renovated, reconditioned or old goods as new goods.
- Representing that the goods or services have sponsorship, approval, performance, characteristics, accessories, uses or benefits which such goods or services do not have.
- Representing that the seller or the supplier has a sponsorship or approval or affiliation which such seller or supplier does not have.
- Making a false or misleading representation concerning the need for, or the usefulness of, any goods or services.
- Giving to the public any warranty or guarantee of the

performance, efficacy or length of life of a product or of any goods that is not based on an adequate or proper test thereof.

- Making to the public a representation in a form that purports to be a warranty or guarantee of a product or of any goods or services; or a promise to replace, maintain or repair an article or any part thereof or to repeat or continue a service until it has achieved a specified result, if such purported warranty or guarantee or promise is materially misleading or if there is no reasonable prospect that such warranty, guarantee or promise will be carried out.
- Materially misleading the public concerning the price at which a product or like products or goods or services, have been or 'are, ordinarily sold or provided' and, for this purpose, a representation as to price shall be deemed to refer to the price at which the product or goods or services has or have been sold by sellers or provided by suppliers generally in the relevant market unless it is clearly specified to be the price at which the product has been sold or services have been provided by the person by whom or on whose behalf the representation is made.
- Giving false or misleading facts disparaging the goods, services or trade of another person.
- Permitting the publication of any advertisement whether in any newspaper or otherwise, for the sale or supply at a bargain price, of goods or services that are not intended to be offered for sale or supply at the bargain price, or for a period that is, and in quantities that are, reasonable, having regard to the nature of the market in which the business is carried on, the nature and size of business, and the nature of the advertisement.
- Permitting:
  (a) the offering of gifts, prizes or other items with the intention of not providing them as offered or creating impression that something is being given or offered free of charge when it is fully or partly covered by the amount charged in the transaction as a whole;
  (b) the conduct of any contest, lottery, game of chance or skill, for the purpose of promoting, directly or indirectly, the sale, use or supply of any product or any business interest;
  (c) withholding from the participants of any scheme offering

gifts, prizes or other items free of charge, on its closure the information about final results of the scheme.

- Permitting the sale or supply of goods intended to be used, or are of a kind likely to be used, by consumers, knowing or having reason to believe that the goods do not comply with the standards prescribed by competent authority relating to performance, composition, contents, design, constructions, finishing or packaging as are necessary to prevent or reduce the risk of injury to the person using the goods;
- Permitting the hoarding or destruction of goods, or refusal to sell the goods or to make them available for sale or to provide any service, if such hoarding or destruction or refusal raises or tends to raise or is intended to raise, the cost of those or other similar goods or services.
- Manufacture of spurious goods or offering such goods for sale or adopts deceptive practices in the provision of services.

Some examples of the use of unfair practices adopted by businessmen or institutions are given below:

Use of false testimonials to convince buyers, quoting misleading prices, disparaging a rival product in a misleading manner are some examples of misleading advertisements. A fairness cream is advertised with the claim that its user will get a fair complexion within a week. The television commercial of 'Fair and Lovely' cream where a father commented 'Kash Mera Beta Hota' because the daughter was dark skinned and was not getting good job was banned after the issue was raised in Parliament.

It is being seen that many times students apply in many professional colleges for better future. Sometimes, after paying fees in a particular college if you want to withdraw it because you have got admission in some other course then the previous college refuses to give back your money. In such cases since the student has not availed any service the first institution has to reimburse the entire amount. But private institutes are reluctant to return the fees to the students after deducting the registration fees or a token amount. Many times schools and colleges are involved in making tall claims that they have very qualified teachers or they give a particular degree which is affiliated to a particular University and later on deceive the students.

In the case of *Bhupesh Khurana vs Vishwa Buddha Parishad* an action suit was filed by twelve students who had joined the BDS course offered by the Buddhist Mission Dental College run by Vishwa Buddha Parishad. The students' complaint was that the college, in its advertisement and prospectus inviting applications for the course, had given the impression that it was affiliated to Magadh University, Bodh Gaya and recognized by the Dental Council of India and was fully equipped to give the degree of Bachelor of Dental Science. However, after joining the college and attending classes, the students found to their dismay that the annual examinations were not being held because the college was neither affiliated to Magadh University, Bodh Gaya and nor recognized by the Dental Council of India. As a result the students lost two precious academic years, but also spent money on fees, hostel charges, etc. holding the college to be deficient the National Commission directed it to refund the admission expenses of all the twelve students along with interest of 12 per cent (*Bhupesh Khurana vs Vishwa Buddha Parishad*, 1994 NC).

Many times packages are used by manufacturers as a camouflage to deceive consumers, especially as regards the quantity of the product contained in the packet. For example, a consumer should only pay for the sweets and not for the box. Unless the package is transparent, the buyer cannot judge the contents by appearance. If quality and ingredients information on the package label is absent, the buyer has to purchase almost blindly. Under the Packaged Commodities Rules, all packages must carry the retail price inclusive of all taxes. But many times, this price is either obliterated or is overwritten by another price. Many manufacturers carry a brand name of some reputed manufacturer. The brand name may be an exact imitation with some slight change in spellings or logo. Technically this practice is known as product cloning and is very rampant during festival season. There is no feasible way to check the weight and volume of the contents unless the buyer opens the package to ascertain the weight. During festivals many of the items are being bought for gifting purposes.

Pharmaceutical companies spend huge amounts of money in missionary selling because if the doctor recommends their medicine the profits of the company would rise. Many cases of the violation of the Drugs and Cosmetics Act and Drugs and Magic Remedies (Objectionable Advertisements) Act have been registered. A separate Department of Pharmaceuticals was set up by the Government of India in July 2008 with the vision "to enable Indian pharmaceuticals industry to play a leading role in the global market and to ensure abundant availability, at reasonable prices within the country, of good quality pharmaceuticals of mass consumption." The National Pharmaceutical Pricing Authority (NPPA) was set up much earlier in 1997. A recent study by the Ministry of Corporate Affairs in Government of India itself has found that several leading pharmaceutical companies are resorting to mark up of 1100 per cent and more. The 'Draft National Pharmaceuticals Pricing Policy-2011 is a good tool in the hands of the Government to deal with this area of immediate concern but unfortunately this policy document only tried to legitimize high prices of drugs. Finally, after lot of struggle by organizations the criteria of fixing the ceiling price of 348 medicines under National List of Essential Medicines (NLEM) by adopting the simple average price of all the brands having market share of 1 per cent or more was approved by the Government. Though the policy was notified on 7th December, 2012, the new prices of 348 medicines, included in the list are not mentioned.

These days we find that when we go to the market to buy groceries or medicines the marketers charge us at the MRP and do not pass on the discounts to the consumers. Surprisingly, the MRP has become Minimum Retail Price. However, few retailers give marginal cut in the MRP. The MRP is fixed by the manufacturers. The difference between ex-factory price and the MRP is normally very high. The government suffered losses in computing excise duty on the ex-factory price. Therefore, the government amended the Central Excise Act 1976 empowering it to levy excise duty on MRP, rather than on the manufacturing price or ex-factory price for goods falling under the purview of Standard and Weight Measures Act or any other law. Very few retailers give discounts to consumers on MRP and the consumer continues to be at the mercy of the retailers who sell the products at MRP without any discounts.

Minimum Retail Price (MRP) is fixed by the manufacturers and is inclusive of a number of items such as taxes, freight transport charges, commission payable to dealers, all charges towards advertisement, delivery, packing, forwarding and the like. While inclusion of some of the items such as taxes, freight and delivery and packing charges in the sale price is understandable, the addition of commission payable to dealers, and advertisement charges, etc. which are not fixed by the government but the manufacturer according to their sales promotion policy, is always out of proportion and exorbitant. This results in escalation of the sale price to the detriment of the consumer. As a matter of fact MRP printed on the packaged commodities is often used by the manufacturers for profiteering, such as giving impression that MRP is fixed by the government. In some cases MRP is followed by 'local taxes extra' which is totally illegal. In today's scenario it is usually found that the prices of consumer goods traded in the markets are settled arbitrarily by the manufacturers. In different markets within one city different products have different rates of taxes. It becomes very difficult for consumers to check whether retailers are actually charging the correct amount of local taxes on the products they sell. Therefore, the confusion in respect of price of the goods is natural for the consumer and the manufacturers gain huge profit as the actual manufacturing cost is very low. The manufacturers arbitrarily fix the price and the consumers are compelled to purchase goods at higher costs.

Under the Weights and Measures (Packaged Commodities) Rules, all packed goods should carry certain essential information on the contents of the package, such as its weight or volume, the name and address of the manufacturer, the date of manufacture, and in case of food packages, the best before date and, quantity, the Maximum Retail Price (MRP), expiry date. The need of the hour is to disclose the First Point Price and the nature of taxes paid. The prices charged by restaurants and movie halls for the mineral water bottle or cold drink are exorbitant.

The Medical Council of India (MCI) was set-up to regulate medical profession. MCI and State Medical Councils are empowered to take disciplinary action when prescribed Code of Ethics is not observed by the doctors. They are empowered to debar doctors from practicing medicine. Even then thousands of cases are being filed due to unethical medical practices. According to Pre-Natal and Diagnostic Techniques Regulation and Prevention Act, Pre-natal sex determination tests, are banned but without flouting and engaging in unfair trade practices the shameful decline in child sex-ratio would not have flourished.

In the above paragraphs we have given some examples of how the consumer is exploited by the traders unless he takes precautions. Awareness at the time of purchase of goods and services and knowledge of the law can give consumers power in the market place and help in reducing the losses caused by ignorance.

Problems Faced by Rural Consumers

Many rural consumers are illiterate and are easily vulnerable to the unscrupulous and unethical marketing practices of the greedy marketers (Kapoor, 2007). A few examples of this are given below.

For any branded product there are a multitude of 'local variants' which are cheaper and therefore, more attractive to the villagers. Sub-standard and spurious products are being passed on to the rural consumers under the brand name which are deceptively similar to the popular brand names. For example, use of 'Calgote' for Colgate. This violates the provisions of the Trade and Merchandise Marks Act.

The Drugs and Cosmetics Act forbids the making of any tall claims or magical effect about any drug. Severe penalty is provided for an offence under the Act. However, the rural consumer is gullible to quacks, fake ayurvedic drugs and cosmetics.

Since, the rural consumers lack product and price information and possess less bargaining power and buying insight they are being deceived by the traders. On the pack of the products the 'MRP' the maximum retail price is printed but many rural consumers do not check that. As provided by the Consumer Protection Act no dealer can charge more than the MRP of an item although they can reduce the price to any extent.

The prohibition of drugs and magic remedies is often openly flouted in the rural areas where the quacks and unscrupulous traders play with the lives of people with impunity.

Certain products which are advertised in the rural areas or through the local media are not available with the vendors and sometimes the in-transit time may even be more than 15 days, so that the villagers have to go for some other substandard brand.

The consumers are often exploited due to ignorance and lack of unity among them. As per CUTS Report on State of Indian Consumer, 2012 (Cuts, 2012) in India even after 25 years of passing of the Consumer Protection Act only 20 per cent consumers know about the Act and only 42 per cent consumers have heard about consumer rights. In a survey done by Centre for Consumer Studies, in the rural areas 40.2 per cent were overcharged, 14 per cent are victims of adulteration, 12 per cent complained about poor quality of products, 7.5 per cent complained about deficiency in services and 7.4 per cent complained about lesser weights (Misra and Pathania, 2012).

Consumer Protection Act, 1986

On April 9, 1985 the General Assembly of the United Nations passed a Resolution adopting a set of guidelines for consumer protection and authorized Secretary General United Nations to persuade the member countries especially the developing ones to adopt policies and laws for better protection of the interests of the consumers. India being one of the signatory to the Resolution enacted the Consumer Protection Act, 1986 to fulfil its obligation. The Parliament enacted the legislation in December 1986, which came into force on April 15, 1987. The main objectives of the Act are to provide for better protection of the interests of the consumers and for that purpose to make provision for the establishment of consumer councils and other authorities for the settlement of consumers' disputes. The Consumer Protection Act (CPA), 1986 is a benevolent piece of social welfare legislation providing for simple, speedy and less expensive remedy for the redressal of consumer grievances in relation to defective goods and deficient services.

The Act provides effective, people oriented, broad based and efficient remedy to consumers against unfair dealings and exploitation (Taxmann Allied Services, 2008). The Act applies to all goods and services whether by private, public or co-operative body unless it is especially exempted by the Central Government by a notification in the Official Gazette. CPA is an improvement over the other existing laws for consumer protection as it is compensatory in nature, where as remedies under other laws are basically punitive or preventive in nature and are designed to provide relief only in specific situations. The remedy under CPA is in addition to and not in derogation of provisions of any other law for the time being in force. The Act gives statutory recognition to six consumer rights, which are right to safety, right to information, right to choose, right to be heard, right to seek redressal and right to consumer education (Singh, 1996). The Act postulates establishment of advisory and adjudicatory bodies to safeguard the interests of consumers. The Advisory structure is in the form of Consumer Protection Councils at Centre, State and District levels. These Councils are constituted on Public-Private Partnership (PPP) basis. The purpose of these bodies is to review the consumer related policies of the government and suggest measures for further improvements.

The Act also provides for quasi-judicial adjudicatory machinery at three levels i.e. District, State and National levels called District Forum, State Consumer Disputes Redressal Commission and National Consumer Disputes Redressal Commission. At present there are 621

District Forums, 35 State Commissions and an apex body the National Commission. The District Forum is presided by a person who is or qualified to be District Judge. Besides President there are two other members, one member is woman. The State Commission is presided over by a sitting or retired High Court Judge and the National Commission by a sitting or retired Supreme Court Judge. The pecuniary jurisdiction for these bodies has been prescribed under the Act. The District Forum can adjudicate on matters, where the value of claim is up to rupee twenty lakh, the State Commission where value of claim is more than twenty lakh but upto rupee one crore and the National Commission where the claim is over one crore. These adjudicatory bodies are quasi-judicial bodies and are regulated according to the principles of natural justice. They are required to decide complaint within a period of three month from the date of notice where no testing is required and within a period of five month where testing is required.

The Act ensures the following Rights of Consumer:

- Right of protection from marketing of the goods and services which are hazardous to life and property;
- Right to be informed about the quality, quantity, purity, standard and price of the good or services, so that consumers are protected from the unfair trade practices;
- Right to have access to variety of the goods and services at competitive prices;
- Right to be heard and to be assured that consumers' interest will receive due consideration;
- Right to stop unfair trade practices, restrictive trade practices and exploitation of consumers;
- Right to consumer education; and
- Right of speedy and simple redressal to consumer disputes.

Under Section 12 of the Consumer Protection Act, a complaint, in relation to any good sold or delivered or any service provided, may be filed by:

- The consumer to whom such goods are sold or delivered or agreed to be sold or delivered or such services provided or agreed to be provided;

- Any recognized consumer association, whether the consumer to whom the goods sold or delivered or agreed to be sold or delivered or services provided or agreed to be provided is a member of such association or not;
- One or more consumers, where there are numerous consumers having the same interests; and
- The central or the state government.

The act applies to all goods and services in private, public or co-operative sector. The act is concerned to protect the consumer against:

- an unfair trade practice or restrictive trade practice adopted by any trader or service provider;
- the goods bought by him or agreed to be bought by him suffer from one or more defects;
- the services hired or availed of or agreed to be hired or availed of by him suffer from deficiency in any respect;
- a trader or service provider has charged a price in excess of the price fixed under the law, displayed on the goods or agreed between the parties
- goods and services which are hazardous to life and safety are being offered for sale to the public.

The following fee structure for the cases filed in the District Forums has been prescribed by the Ministry of Consumer Affairs, Food and Public Distribution by Rule 9A of the Consumer Protection (Amendment) Rules, 2004:

Value of goods or services	*Amount of fee payable*
(1) Upto Rs. One lakh	Rs. 100
(2) Rs. One lakh and above but less than Rs. Five lakh	Rs. 200
(3) Rs. Five lakh and above but less than Rs.10 lakh	Rs. 400
(4) Rs. Ten lakh and above but not exceeding Rs.20 lakh	Rs. 500

As Table 14.1 depicts, 80,014 cases were registered since inception up to 6-3-2013 with the National Commission, out of which 86.55 per cent cases were disposed of, while 13.95 per cent were still pending with the National Commission. In case of State Commission 6,00,097 cases were registered since inception up to March 2013 and 84.13 per cent cases were disposed off. A staggering number of 32.42,324 cases were registered throughout the District Consumer Forums in the country and was better as 92.35 per cent cases were disposed.

Table 14.1: Total Number of Consumer Complaints Filed/Disposed by Consumer Forums Upto 06.03.2013

Name of Agency	*Cases filed Since Inception*	*Cases Disposed of Since Inception*	*Cases Pending*	*% of Total Disposal*
National Commission	80014	69253	10761	86.55%
State Commissions	600097	504834	95263	84.13%
District Forums	3242324	2994256	248068	92.35%
Total	3922435	3568343	354092	90.97%

Source: ncdrc.nic.in

A state-wise analysis indicates significant variations in the number of cases registered and cases disposed by the National and State and Consumer Forums. The total number of cases registered up to March 2013 with various State Commissions was highest for Uttar Pradesh followed by Maharashtra, Rajasthan, Gujarat, Haryana and Delhi (Table 14.2). It signifies that consumer awareness is associated with consumer movement as in case with Rajasthan, Kerala, Himachal Pradesh, Uttarakhand and Delhi literacy rates are higher. Per cent cases disposed by the State Consumer Forums also depict regional variations. States with lower disposal percentage are Nagaland (24%), Uttar Pradesh (57.55%), Manipur (69.06%), Bihar (70.24%) and Maharashtra (72.39%).

Table 14.3 shows the statement of cases filed/disposed in various District Forums since inception upto 6-3-2013. Performance of District Forums was better across the states except for Mizoram (with 81.33 per cent of disposal of cases), Daman & Diu (with 88.89%), Uttar Pradesh (with 86.74%). We find that 92.35 per cent of cases have been disposed off, which is a positive sign.

Justice Delayed is Justice Denied

Unlike the civil courts, the consumer courts are quasi-judicial authorities that have to follow simple, summary procedure for quick

Table 14.2: Cases Filed/Disposed off/Pending in the National Commission and State Commissions Upto 06.03.2013

Name of States	*Cases filed since Inception*	*Cases Disposed Off Since Inception*	*Cases Pending*	*% of Disposal*	*As on*
National Commission	**80014**	**69253**	**10761**	**86.55**	**28.02.2013**
Andhra Pradesh	28675	27469	1206	95.79	31.12.2012
A & N Islands	42	38	4	90.48	31.01.2008
Arunachal Pradesh	63	61	2	96.83	30.11.2012
Assam	2577	1867	710	72.45	31.12.2012
Bihar	15333	10770	4563	70.24	30.09.2012
Chandigarh	12204	12035	169	98.62	31.12.2012
Chhattisgarh	8612	8016	596	93.08	31.01.2013
Daman & Diu	25	20	5	80.00	31.03.2011
Delhi	34653	32857	1796	94.82	31.01.2013
Goa	2321	2252	69	97.03	31.01.2013
Gujarat	44989	36905	8084	82.03	31.01.2013
Haryana	42841	42718	123	99.71	31.01.2013
Himachal Pradesh	7871	7629	242	96.93	31.01.2013
Jammu & Kashmir	6652	6061	591	91.12	31.12.2012
Jharkhand	5101	4601	500	90.20	31.12.2012
Karnataka	44505	39485	5020	88.72	31.01.2013
Kerala	25502	24307	1195	95.31	31.12.2012
Lakshadweep	17	16	1	94.12	31.12.2012
Madhya Pradesh	41886	36958	4928	88.23	31.01.2013
Maharashtra	57109	41344	15765	72.39	30.06.2012
Manipur	139	96	43	69.06	30.09.2008
Meghalaya	262	175	87	66.79	31.10.2012
Mizoram	200	196	4	98.00	31.01.2013
Nagaland	25	6	19	24.00	31.12.2011
Odisha	21883	15667	6216	71.59	31.12.2012
Puducherry	959	944	15	98.44	31.12.2012
Punjab	29596	23575	6021	79.66	31.12.2012
Rajasthan	51308	46999	4309	91.60	31.12.2012
Sikkim	42	41	1	97.62	31.12.2012
Tamil Nadu	24223	22125	2098	91.34	31.12.2012
Tripura	1421	1397	24	98.31	31.01.2013
Uttar Pradesh	67119	38625	28494	57.55	31.12.2012
Uttarakhand	4641	3856	785	83.09	31.12.2012
West Bengal	17301	15723	1578	90.88	31.12.2012
Total	600097	504834	95263	84.13	

Source: ncdrc.nic.in

disposal of complaints. The Presidents and Members of the District Forum constitute the backbone of the Forum. They play a major role in enhancing the faith of the consumers in the redressal mechanism.

Table 14.3: Statement of Cases filed/disposed of/pending in District Fora Upto 06.03.2013

Name of States	*Cases Filed Since Inception*	*Cases Disposed off Since Inception*	*Cases Pending*	*% of Disposal*	*As on*
Andhra Pradesh	192331	186441	5890	96.94	31.12.2012
A & N Islands	330	301	29	91.21	31.03.2006
Arunachal Pradesh	404	338	66	83.66	30.11.2012
Assam	13704	11976	1728	87.39	31.08.2010
Bihar	84369	73573	10796	87.20	30.09.2012
Chandigarh	46795	45614	1181	97.48	31.12.2012
Chhattisgarh	37292	34129	3163	91.52	31.01.2013
Daman & Diu	162	144	18	88.89	31.03.2011
Delhi	239215	228875	10340	95.68	30.09.2011
Goa	6387	5840	547	91.44	31.01.2013
Gujarat	173597	161750	11847	93.18	31.01.2013
Haryana	220997	203297	17700	91.99	31.01.2013
Himachal Pradesh	57043	53672	3371	94.09	31.01.2013
Jammu & Kashmir	20792	18855	1937	90.68	31.12.2007
Jharkhand	33985	30720	3265	90.39	31.12.2012
Karnataka	155588	150723	4865	96.87	31.01.2013
Kerala	180640	172869	7771	95.70	31.12.2012
Lakshadweep	75	65	10	86.67	31.12.2012
Madhya Pradesh	184906	169904	15002	91.89	31.01.2013
Maharashtra	255993	236744	19249	92.48	30.06.2012
Manipur	1037	1012	25	97.59	30.09.2008
Meghalaya	847	750	97	88.55	31.10.2012
Mizoram	3466	2819	647	81.33	31.12.2010
Nagaland	290	266	24	91.72	31.12.2011
Odisha	92978	86305	6673	92.82	31.12.2012
Puducherry	2907	2714	193	93.36	31.12.2012
Punjab	154458	148813	5645	96.35	31.12.2012
Rajasthan	289436	261290	28146	90.28	31.12.2012
Sikkim	296	280	16	94.59	31.12.2012
Tamil Nadu	102719	97061	5658	94.49	31.12.2012
Tripura	2751	2538	213	92.26	31.10.2012
Uttar Pradesh	565666	490670	74996	86.74	31.12.2012
Uttarakhand	34759	32598	2161	93.78	31.12.2012
West Bengal	86109	81310	4799	94.43	31.12.2012
Total	3242324	2994256	248068	92.35	

Source: ncdrc.nic.in

Table 14.4 shows that 632 district forums have been established but only 608 are functional. Delays in appointments affect the speedy adjudication of consumer complaints.

Table 14.4: State Commissions/District Forums as on 06.03.2013

States	*Whether SC Functional or Non-Functional*	*No. of District Fora*	*Functional*	*Non-functional*	*As on*
Andhra Pradesh	Yes	29	29	0	31.12.2012
A & N Islands	Yes	1	1	0	31.3.2006
Arunachal Pradesh	Yes	16	13	3	30.09.2012
Assam	Yes	23	21	2	31.12.2012
Bihar	Yes	38	38	0	30.09.2012
Chandigarh	Yes	2	2	0	31.12.2012
Chhattisgarh	Yes	16	16	0	31.12.2012
Daman & Diu	Yes	2	2	0	31.03.2011
Dadra & Nagar Haveli	Yes	1	1	0	31.03.2011
Delhi	Yes	10	10	0	31.12.2012
Goa	Yes	2	2	0	31.12.2012
Gujarat	Yes	30	30	0	31.12.2012
Haryana	Yes	21	19	2	31.12.2012
Himachal Pradesh	Yes	12	12	0	31.12.2012
Jammu & Kashmir	Yes	2	2	0	31.03.2009
Jharkhand	Yes	22	18	4	31.12.2012
Karnataka	Yes	30	30	0	31.12.2012
Kerala	Yes	14	14	0	31.12.2010
Lakshadweep	Yes	1	1	0	31.12.2012
Madhya Pradesh	Yes	48	48	0	31.12.2012
Maharashtra	Yes	40	40	0	30.06.2011
Manipur	Yes	9	9	0	31.12.2008
Meghalaya	Yes	7	7	0	31.10.2012
Mizoram	Yes	8	8	0	31.12.2010
Nagaland	Yes	8	8	0	31.12.2011
Odisha	Yes	31	31	0	31.12.2012
Puducherry	Yes	1	1	0	31.12.2012
Punjab	Yes	20	20	0	31.12.2012
Rajasthan	Yes	37	37	0	31.12.2012
Sikkim	Yes	4	4	0	31.12.2012
Tamil Nadu	Yes	30	22	8	31.12.2012
Tripura	Yes	4	4	0	31.12.2012
Uttar Pradesh	Yes	79	75	4	31.12.2012
Uttarakhand	Yes	13	12	1	31.12.2012
West Bengal	Yes	21	21	0	31.12.2012
Total		632	608	24	

Source: ncdrc.nic.in

Table 14.5 shows that as on 6-3-2013 there were three vacancies of the President and 22 vacancies of members of the State Commission lying vacant. In case of District Forums there were 100 posts of

Table 14.5: State Commissions and District Forums as on 06.03.2013

States	*State Commission*		*District Forum*		*As on*
	President	*Member*	*President*	*Member*	
National Commission	**0**	**2**			**31.01.2013**
Andhra Pradesh	1	0	8	6	31.12.2012
A & N Islands	0	0	0	0	31.3.2006
Arunachal Pradesh	0	0	0	14	30.11.2012
Assam	0	1	1	9	31.12.2012
Bihar	0	1	0	18	30.09.2012
Chandigarh	0	0	0	0	31.12.2012
Chhattisgarh	0	2	1	10	31.12.2012
Daman & Diu	0	0	0	2	31.03.2011
Delhi	0	1	0	1	31.01.2013
Goa	0	0	0	0	31.01.2013
Gujarat	0	0	4	1	31.01.2013
Haryana	0	1	7	9	31.01.2013
Himachal Pradesh	0	0	0	3	31.01.2013
Jammu & Kashmir	0	0	0	0	31.12.2011
Jharkhand	0	0	3	12	31.12.2012
Karnataka	0	2	6	27	31.01.2013
Kerala	0	1	0	1	30.05.2012
Lakshadweep	1	1	0	1	31.12.2012
Madhya Pradesh	0	1	1	11	31.01.2013
Maharashtra	0	2	33	54	30.06.2012
Manipur	0	0	0	1	31.12.2008
Meghalaya	1	0	0	1	31.10.2012
Mizoram	0	0	0	0	08.03.2010
Nagaland	0	0	0	0	31.12.2011
Odisha	0	1	7	9	31.12.2012
Puducherry	0	0	1	0	31.12.2012
Punjab	0	1	3	2	31.01.2013
Rajasthan	0	0	7	3	31.12.2012
Sikkim	0	0	0	4	31.12.2012
Tamil Nadu	0	1	7	33	31.12.2012
Tripura	0	0	0	0	31.01.2013
Uttar Pradesh	0	6	11	10	31.12.2012
Uttarakhand	0	0	0	7	31.12.2012
West Bengal	0	0	0	0	31.12.2012
Total	3	22	100	249	

Source: ncdrc.nic.in

Presidents and 249 members of the District Forum lying vacant. For law to be effective there should be no posts in the District Forums and State Commission lying vacant otherwise consumers would loose faith in the system.

In order to ensure expeditious disposal of complaints, Section

13 (3A) of the Consumer Protection Act provides for disposal of cases within 90 days where no analysis or lab testing of the products is required. Where testing of products is required the disposal of case can be done in 150 days. In reality cases run for many years and this clause is often breached. Adjournments according to the CPA amendment in 2002 should be allowed in exceptional circumstances and if given the court should record the reasons for it in writing and justify it.

Judgements Having Adverse Effect on Consumer's Courts

It would be pertinent to refer to some important court judgements' which have affected the working of the Consumers Courts.

On 1st September, 2009 Hon'ble Supreme Court gave the judgement that Consumer Courts have no jurisdiction to try telecom disputes. Any dispute of the consumer against his service provider related to inflated bills, value added services and others cannot be taken to consumer courts. The Supreme Court in its judgement has said that from now on such disputes would be resolved through arbitration provided under Section 7B of the Indian Telegraph Act, 1885. As the Telegraph Act is a special law, its provisions would prevail over a general law, such as the Consumer Protection Act, 1986.

With the landmark judgement on 13th November, 1995 by the Supreme Court in Indian Medical Association vs V P Shantha case it was said that though medical practitioners belong to the medical profession, and are subject to the disciplinary control of the Medical Council of India and/or State Medical Councils constituted under the provisions of the Indian Medical Council Act but this would not exclude the services rendered by them from the ambit of the Consumer Protection Act. But in 2005 in Jacob Mathew's case the Supreme Court said that every error of judgements is not a case of medical negligence. Doctors can adopt one of the several accepted courses of treatment.

The MRTP Act had the powers of taking *suo motu* action in case of misleading advertisements whereas the Consumer Protection Act does not have such powers. Only if a consumer or industry complains to the Consumer Courts or to ASCI action can be taken. By the time the action is taken by these bodies to either withdraw or modify the offending advertisement the advertisement has already conveyed the false message. Therefore, it is time to make some amendment in the Act and to give powers to the consumer courts for *suo motu* action so that they can take up cases of false advertisements on their own.

Suggestions to Make the System More Consumer Friendly

Some suggestions are given below to improve the effectiveness of the Consumer Protection Act:

- Inability of the companies to sort the complaints internally forces the consumers to go to Consumer Courts. There should be an audit by an independent agency regarding consumer complaints and the data should be freely available on the websites of companies.
- Since 2007 the consumer courts have been overburdened with cases and the buyer-seller contract is tilted in favour of the seller. Therefore, the backlog cases should be quickly handled even if it involves putting night courts, an extra bench, etc.
- Consumer Courts are functioning with staff deputed from other departments who do not have any experience in judicial practices. It is necessary to provide intensive training to the members of the Consumer Forums before putting them on the job. The present practice is to provide training after assuming charge as member.
- All members of consumer fora should shed civil court personality and demeanor. Their judgements should be pro-consumer and the compensation given to the consumer should be adequate.
- There should be proper coordination among the President and members of the Fora, so that the cases are decided in time without any adjournments.
- The President of the National Commission should be empowered to take up *suo motu* action in consideration of the damages affecting a sizable number of population, e.g. misleading advertisements.
- Ombudsmen have been created in various sectors such as, insurance, banking and electricity. There is a need to create more Ombudsmen for free and fast redressal of consumer complaints in sectors such as advertising, real estate, tourism.

- Voluntary Consumer Organisations should be encouraged to come forward in settling consumer disputes. Many VCOs are involved in comparative testing of various products and services but may consumers do not know about it.
- More mediation centres such as National Consumer Helpline, Core Centres should be opened for dissemination of information to the consumers.
- It is time to amend the Consumer Protection Act, 1986 for quick and speedy redressal of consumer cases.

The government by now has enacted 24 Pro-consumer Acts to control buyer-seller relations at the market place. Some government departments, such as, telecommunications and electricity organize *Lok Adalats* from time to time so that the grievances of consumers relating to their departments can be handled. This is a practical method to handle consumer grievances and seek a solution. Some departments, such as, railways have made their services efficient and guide the consumers through information. In the banking sector Ombudsmen are there for speedy redressal of consumer grievances relating to deposit accounts, dishonour of cheques, credit cards, debit cards, ATM's etc.

A separate Department of Consumer Affairs has been created for promoting and protecting the welfare of consumers. To meet the objective the Department is undertaking various measures involving all concerned to strengthen the consumer movement in the country. Some of the steps recently taken by the Ministry of Consumer Affairs, Food and Public Distribution, are given below:

- The Government of India has launched a massive multi-media promotional campaign '*Jago Grahak Jago*' to focus consumer attention on everyday consumer problems.
- A scheme has been taken over to set up Consumer Clubs at schools and colleges. It would try to educate students about their rights as a consumer and to mobilize youngsters to strengthen the consumer movement in the country.
- The National Consumer Helpline, a project started by the Ministry on March 15th, 2005, attends consumer grievances from all over India. It has a toll-free number 1800-11-4000 which can be dialed from BSNL/MTNL lines, between Monday and Saturday from 9:30 am to 5.30 pm. It provides

information and advice about alternate dispute resolution methods in a wide range of products and services. NCH is located at the Department of Commerce, Delhi School of Economics, University of Delhi.

- Another, technology based site CORE scheme has been taken up to counsel the aggrieved consumers. The Consumer Online Resource Empowerment Centre provides online counselling and a complaint redressal mechanism to consumers from across India. Consumers can access its website www.core.nic.in for a comprehensive database on consumer issues.
- Centre for Consumer Studies at Indian Institute of Public Administration (IIPA) has been engaged in imparting training to various institutions such as, administrators, academicians, etc. It also sponsors research projects in the area of consumer protection and consumer welfare.

Thus, many new schemes have been started by the government to empower the Indian consumers. Nowadays, no company wants to be seen as an entity for unjust business practices. Consumers must be vigilant and should not hesitate to vindicate their rights in consumer fora. The strategy of "caveat emptor" i.e. the buyer needs to be beware of products has now shifted to "caveat venditor" i.e. the vendor or the marketer needs to be aware of the needs of the consumer. The marketer can only survive unless the consumer purchases his products. Ethical consumption has become a reality for consumers, as well as businesses around the world. Every single purchase decision has an affect on the environment, consumer health and the workers who manufacture the products. Companies have to understand that the key to building long lasting relationship with consumers is the creation of superior customer value and satisfaction. Even the marketer, producer or the service provider is a consumer of some other goods and services. Thus, what is required is a vibrant consumer movement, that is much closer to the people and is pro-poor, pro-women and pro-rural. Only alert consumers can protect themselves and the society.

REFERENCES

Bhupesh Khurana vs. *Vishwa Buddha Parishad* 1994 (NC).

Cuts (2012), *State of Indian Consumer Report, 2012*, Cuts-international.org

Government of India (1986), *The Consumer Protection Act, 1986*, New Delhi.

Kapoor, Sheetal (2007), *Consumer and the Market*, Monograph, Centre for Consumer Studies, IIPA, New Delhi.

Misra, Suresh and Mamta Pathania (2012), "Changing Profile of Rural Consumers in India—Need for Education and Awareness," *Consumer Protection in India: Issues and Concerns*, IIPA, New Delhi.

Singh, Gurjeet (1996), *The Law of Consumer Protection in India: Justice Within Reach*, Deep and Deep Publications, New Delhi.

Taxmann Allied Services (2008), *Consumer Protection Law Manual with Practice Manual: India,* Taxmann Allied Services Private Limited, New Delhi.

The Consumer Protection Act, 1986.

PART-4

Transparency, Disclosure and Human Rights and Justice Delivery System

15

Transparency, Disclosure and Human Rights

Shri Ram Arun

Privacy versus Transparency?

Privacy and transparency are tools of public good essential for the proper functioning of a democratic society, and both are defences against abuses of power. Yet there are inevitably times when they come into conflict. For example, many records held by public bodies inevitably identify or contain personal information about their employees. It may well be in the public interest for there to be transparency about the salaries or salary brackets attached to certain roles, the level of seniority of officials responsible for making certain decisions, or which officials attended certain meetings with third parties. The traditional expression of the relationship between privacy and transparency as a balancing act between the rights of the individual and the interests of the community is a false dichotomy that has led to a great deal of confusion in the operation of RTI laws. There is in fact a significant overlap in the contents of the two regimes, as former UK Information Commissioner Richard Thomas has noted: "Both involve the growing discipline of information rights — or rather the information duties and obligations on those who are holding either personal or official information. Both are heavily concerned with transparency and access. Both have a wide horizontal impact affecting virtually every aspect of public, commercial and private life."

Concepts of Human Rights and World Religions

Broadly speaking the Human Rights can be categorised as: (1) rights and freedoms to which all humans are entitled, (2) economic development, (3) social progress, and (4) achieving world peace. This concept is enshrined in almost all the religions of the world. All religions are based on the principles of compassion for everyone. It is noteworthy that all religious leaders preach openly in congregations, disclose the tenets and teachings of their religion and are mostly transparent through Holy Books. However, there are certain abrasions as self-proclaimed groups think that they are the sole custodians of their faith and commit atrocities on the followers of other faiths and at times on their own co-religionists.

Hindu philosophy and scriptures say that the whole universe is one family (**वसुधैव कुटुम्बकम्**) and let everyone be happy, all remain disease free, all to have compassion for each other and let there be no sorrow for any (**सर्वे भवन्तु सुखिनाः, सर्वे सन्तु निरामयाः, सर्वे भद्राणि पश्यन्तु, मा कश्चित् दुःख भाग भवेत्।**). However, Hinduism has certain social weaknesses like caste system, prejudices towards deprived sections of society, discrimination against women. Certain trends of radicalism like riots, attacks and explosions, etc. towards non-Hindus are scars on Hinduism.

Buddhist philosophy is enshrined in '*Panchsheela*', i.e. (1) non-violence, (2) no theft, (3) no illicit sex, (4) no lies, and (5) non-intoxication. Lord Buddha advised the well tamed people to control themselves. Only the well tamed people, the heedful people, know the way to stop contentions, quarrels and disputes and how to live in harmony, in friendliness and in peace. It is pity that three Nobel Laureates for World Peace, who are Budhists had to suffer humiliation and infringement of their own Human Rights at the hands of their respective Governments. They are His Holiness Dalai Lama, who is in exile in India since 1959, Ms Aung San Suu Kyi of Myanmar who was imprisoned and Liu Xiaobo, a lawyer of China under imprisonment.

Jainism is also based on non-violence and forgiveness. Christianity says: hate the sin and not the sinner, Lord forgive them who do not know as to what they are doing and love thy neighbour.

The central concept of Islam is the notion of absolute equality of humanity. Islam has laid down universal fundamental rights for humanity which are to be observed and respected in all circumstances in the following words "it is not permissible to oppress women, children, old people, the sick or the wounded; women's honour and chastity must be respected; the hungry must be fed, the naked be clothed and the wounded or diseased be treated medically irrespective of whether they belong to the Islamic community or are from amongst its enemies." The Islamic state may not interfere with the personal rights of non-Muslims, who have full freedom of conscience and belief and are at liberty to perform their religious rites and ceremonies in their own way.

Some extremist Islamic groups, however, violate these tenets of Islam. The objective of Jamaat-e-Islami is "Iqamat-e-Deen" or "Nizam-e-Mustafa," i.e. the establishment of a pure Islamic state, governed by Sharia law. The Jamaat opposes Westernization, ideologies such as capitalism, socialism and secularism, and practices such as bank interest and liberal social mores. The Taliban created a new form of Islamic redicalism that causes Human Rights violations. According to Human Rights Watch, the Taliban's bombings and other attacks are in violation of human rights. The Islamic Human Rights Commission (IHRC) is a non-profit organization which expresses views on issues involving Islam and human rights.

World Religions for World Peace

His holiness Dalai Lama says that:

> "The principles are in accordance with the ethical teachings of all world religions. I maintain that every major religion of the world—Buddhism, Christianity, Confucianism, Hinduism, Islam, Jainism, Judaism, Sikhism, Taoism, Zoroastrianism—has similar ideals of love, the same goal of benefiting humanity through spiritual practice, and the same effect of making their followers into better human beings. All religions teach moral precepts for perfecting the functions of mind, body, and speech. All teach us not to lie or steal or take others' lives, and so on. The common goal of all moral precepts laid down by the great teachers of humanity is unselfishness. The great teachers wanted to lead their followers away from the paths of negative deeds caused by ignorance and to introduce them to paths of goodness. We practitioners of different faiths can work together for world peace when we view different religions as essentially instruments to develop a good heart—love and respect for others, a true sense of community. The most important thing is to look at the purpose of religion and not at the details of

theology or metaphysics, which can lead to mere intellectualism. I believe that all the major religions of the world can contribute to world peace and work together for the benefit of humanity if we put aside subtle metaphysical differences, which are really the internal business of each religion."

Magna Carta: The Beginning of Human Rights

King John of England issued a charter known as *Magna Carta* on 15 June 1215 to proclaim certain rights pertaining to freedom, respect of certain legal procedures, and accepted that his will could be bound by the law. It explicitly protected certain rights of the King's subjects, whether free or fettered, and implicitly supported what became the writ of *habeas corpus*, allowing appeal against unlawful imprisonment.

Modern Concept of Human Rights

The modern concept of human rights developed in the aftermath of the Second World War, in part as a response to the Holocaust, culminating in the signing of the *Universal Declaration of Human Rights* by the United Nations General Assembly in 1948. It recognized that all human beings are born free and equal in dignity and rights. They are endowed with reason and conscience and should act towards one another in a spirit of brotherhood *Article 1 of the* United Nations Universal Declaration of Human Rights.

The Universal Declaration of Human Rights (UDHR) was adopted on 10 December 1948. The date has since served to mark Human Rights Day worldwide. The High Commissioner for Human Rights, as the main UN rights official, and her Office play a major role in coordinating efforts for the yearly observance of Human Rights Day. The day commemorates the work of human rights organizations and those who defend the human rights worldwide.

All over the world many people—among them some are renowned and some are anonymous—whether in groups, organization or alone are working towards the campaign of Human Rights in order to end discrimination. Many governmental and non-governmental organizations are also actively participating in various activities of Human Rights Day so that people everywhere in the world learn about their Human Rights.

The United Nation's General Assembly proclaims the Universal Declaration of Human Rights as a common standard of achievement for all peoples and all nations, to the end that every individual and every organ of society, keeping this Declaration constantly in mind, shall strive by teaching and education to promote respect for these rights and freedoms and by progressive measures, national and international, to secure their universal and effective recognition and observance, both among the peoples of Member States themselves and among the peoples of territories under their jurisdiction.

The Human Rights Day promotes and spread awareness about the following articles under UDHR (Universal Declaration of Human Rights):

- All human beings are born free and equal in dignity and rights.
- Everyone is entitled to all the rights and freedoms set forth in this Declaration, without distinction of any kind, such as race, colour, sex, language, religion, political or other opinion, national or social origin, property, birth or other status.
- Everyone has the right to life, liberty and security of person.
- No one shall be held in slavery or servitude; slavery and the slave trade shall be prohibited in all their forms.
- No one shall be subjected to torture or to cruel, inhuman or degrading treatment or punishment.
- Everyone has the right to recognition everywhere as a person before the law.
- All are equal before the law and are entitled without any discrimination to equal protection of the law.
- Everyone has the right to an effective remedy by the competent national tribunals for acts violating the fundamental rights granted him by the constitution or by law.
- No one shall be subjected to arbitrary arrest, detention or exile.
- Everyone is entitled in full equality to a fair and public hearing by an independent and impartial tribunal, in the determination of his rights and obligations and of any criminal charge against him.
- Everyone has the right to freedom of movement and residence within the borders of each State.

- Everyone has the right to leave any country, including his own, and to return to his country.
- Everyone has the right to a nationality. No one shall be arbitrarily deprived of his nationality nor denied the right to change his nationality.

Scope of Human Rights

The scope of Human Rights is very large and includes the following:

1. International human rights law refers to the body of International Law designed to promote and protect human rights at the international, regional and domestic levels.
2. International Human Rights law is primarily made up of International Treaties and Customary International law.
3. Other international human rights instruments in the form of Declarations, Guidelines and International principles contribute to the implementation, understanding and development of international human rights law.
4. International Human Rights Law can be enforced on Domestic, Regional or International Level. States that ratify human rights treaties commit themselves to respecting those rights and ensuring that their domestic law is compatible with their international legislation.
5. Customary peremptory norms of International Law that relate to human rights are considered binding on all nations, although the status of such norms is commonly disputed. When Domestic Law fails to provide a remedy for human rights abused parties may be able to resort to regional or international mechanisms for enforcing human rights.
6. International Humanitarian Law, regulates armed conflicts and Refugee Law. War crimes, crimes against humanity and genocide may be regulated by international human rights law but each have a substantial body of independent international law.
7. The International Criminal Court (ICC) has jurisdiction over the crime of genocide, war crimes and crimes against humanity.
8. The enforcement of International Human Rights Law is the responsibility of the Nation State, and it is the primary responsibility of the State to make human rights a reality.

The Evolution of Human Rights

The First-generation human rights are covered by the Universal Declaration of Human Rights 1948. They deal essentially with liberty and participation in political life and include, among other things, freedom of speech, the right to a fair trial, freedom of religion, and voting rights.

Second-generation human rights are related to equality and began to be recognized by governments after First World War. They are fundamentally social, economic and cultural in nature. Secondary rights would include a right to be employed, rights to housing and health care, as well as social security and unemployment benefits. They were also covered by the Universal Declaration of Human Rights, and further embodied in Articles 22 to 27 of the Universal Declaration, and the International Covenant on Economic, Social, and Cultural Rights,

Third-generation human rights are those rights that go beyond the mere civil and social, as expressed in many progressive documents of international law. The term "third-generation human rights"remains largely unofficial, and thus houses an extremely broad spectrum of rights, including:

- Group and collective rights
- Right to self-determination
- Right to economic and social development
- Right to a healthy environment
- Right to natural resources
- Right to communicate and communication rights
- Right to participation in cultural heritage
- Rights to intergenerational equity and sustainability

International/National Organizations/Offices for Safeguarding Human Rights

The following agencies are responsible for safeguarding Human Rights

1. High Commissioner on National Minorities of the Organization for Security and Co-operation in Europe.
2. The Directorate-General for the Environment of the European Commission has as its mission 'protecting, preserving and

improving the environment for present and future generations, and promoting sustainable development'.

3. United Nations Commission on Human Rights.
4. United Nations Human Rights Council (UNHRC).
5. International Institute for Peace Justice and Human Rights.
6. Human Rights Watch (HRW).
7. People's Union for Civil Liberty (PUCL).
8. National Human Rights Commission.
9. State's Human Rights Commissions.

Human Rights in India

Following measures have been taken in India to ensure protection of Human Rights of Indian citizens in general and certain groups like women, children, scheduled castes and scheduled tribes in particular:

- **1950:** The Constitution of India establishes a sovereign democratic republic with universal adult franchise. Part 3 of the Constitution contains a Bill of Fundamental Rights enforceable by the Supreme Court and the High Courts. It also provides for reservations for disadvantaged sections in education, employment and political representation.
- **1952:** Criminal Tribes Acts were repealed and such categories were "denotified". A new Act 'Habitual Offenders Act 1952' was enacted.
- **1955:** Reform of family law concerning Hindus gives more rights to Hindu women.
- **1973:** Supreme Court of India ruled in Kesavananda Bharati case that the basic structure of the Constitution (including many fundamental rights) is unalterable by a constitutional amendment.
- **1975-77:** State of Emergency in India—extensive rights violations take place.
- **1978:** SC rules in Menaka Gandhi vs. Union of India that the right to life under Article 21 of the Constitution cannot be suspended even in an emergency.
- **1978:** Jammu and Kashmir Public Safety Act, 1978 passed.
- **1984:** Operation Blue Star and the subsequent 1984 Anti-Sikh riots resulting in killings of thousands of Sikhs at various places in India.

- **1985-86:** The Shah Bano case, where the Supreme Court recognised the Muslim woman's right to maintenance upon divorce and that sparked protests from Muslim clergy. To nullify the decision of the Supreme Court, the Rajiv Gandhi Government enacted The Muslim Women (Protection of Rights on Divorce) Act 1986.
- **1988:** Prevention of Corruption Act passed.
- **1989:** Scheduled Caste and Scheduled Tribe (Prevention of Atrocities) Act, 1989 passed.
- **1989:** Kashmiri insurgency sees ethnic cleansing of Kashmiri Pandits, desecrating Hindu temples, killing of Hindus and Sikhs, and abductions of foreign tourists and government functionaries.
- **1992:** A constitutional amendment establishes Local Self-Government (Panchayati Raj) as a third-tier of governance at the village level, with one-third of the seats reserved for women. Reservations were provided for scheduled castes and Scheduled tribes as well.
- **1992:** Babri Masjid demolished by Hindu mobs, resulting in unprecedented riots across the country.
- **1993:** The Protection of Human Rights Act passed,
- **1993:** National Human Rights Commission was established under the Protection of Human Rights Act.
- **2001:** Supreme Court passes extensive orders to implement the right to food.
- **2002:** Violence in Gujarat emanating from killings of Hindu Kar Sevaks at Godhra and then, targeting of Muslim minority at other places where large number of them were killed and subjected to miseries.
- **2005:** A powerful Right to Information Act was passed to give citizen's access to information held by public authorities.
- **2005:** National Rural Employment Guarantee Act (NREGA) guarantees universal right to employment.
- **2006:** Supreme Court orders police reforms in response to the poor human rights record of Indian police.
- **2009:** Delhi High Court declares that Section 377 of the Indian Penal Code, which outlaws a range of unspecified "unnatural" sex acts, is unconstitutional when applied to homosexual acts between private consenting individuals, effectively decriminalising homosexual relationships in India.

- **2013:** Following the nationwide public outrage over the issue of gang rape and murder of Nirbhaya in Delhi and subsequently other such incidents, the Parliament had to pass the 'Criminal Law Amendment Act 2013' relating to protection of women and children from sexual offences. This Criminal Law (Amendment) Act, 2013 was passed to amend the Indian Penal Code, 1860, the Code of Criminal Procedure, 1973, the Indian Evidence Act, 1872 and the Protection of Children from Sexual Offences Act, 2012. It amends sections 100, 228A, 354, 370, 370A, 375, 376, 376A, 376B, 376C, 376D and 509 of Indian Penal Code, 1860. It also inserts new sections 166A, 166B, 326A, 326B, 354A, 354B, 354C and 354D in Indian Penal Code, 1860. It also amends sections 26, 54A, 154, 160, 161, 164, 173, 197, 273, 309, 327 and First Schedule of Code of Criminal Procedure, 1973 and also inserts new sections 357B and 357C. It also amends sections 114, 119 and 146 of Indian Evidence Act, 1872 and inserts new sections 53A. It also amends section 42 of Protection of Children from Sexual Offences Act, 2012.

Administration of Criminal Justice in India and Human Rights

The administration of criminal justice system involves the following wings and they are governed by codified laws, Rules and Manuals as well as the Rulings of High Courts and Supreme Court:

1. *Police:* They are responsible for registration and investigation of cases resulting in submission of charge sheets/final reports to courts concerned.
2. *Prosecution:* Their duty is to prosecute cases against accused on behalf of the State. Providing free legal aid to certain accused is also the responsibility of State through selected lawyers brought on panel. Lawyers appearing for the accused are also supposed to cooperate with the system to ensure speedy trial.
3. *Judiciary:* Trial Courts are required to function for dispensation of justice, which should be free, fair and speedy. Appellate Courts have their own responsibilities to ensure justice and also to ensure that the Human Rights of both, the accused and the victims are protected.

4. *Correctional Services: Jails and Protective Homes*—It is the duty of these agencies to ensure that while in imprisonment their rights are not violated.
5. *Certain rights of undertrial prisoners* are to be protected by the Prison authorities, Police and the Courts.

We now examine the difficulties, lack of transparency and disclosures at the level of the above agencies, which results in violation of Human Rights.

At Police Level

1. *Non-Registration of cases, minimisation and concealment*—Section 154 Cr. PC lays down that every information relating to the commission of a cognizable offence given at a police station must be recorded and a copy be given free of cost to the informant. In case of refusal at the Police Station level the aggrieved person can approach the District Superintendent of Police, who after enquiry will get the FIR lodged. The informant, if aggrieved by the refusal on the part of police, may also approach the court concerned to get the FIR registered and have the case investigated by the police.

The reasons for non-registration of cases are:

(1) There is tendency of not registering the FIRs as the annual crime figures get inflated as compared to previous years and it may invite the wrath of the seniors, Government and the media. It is a double edged weapon as State Government's claim that they have successfully controlled the crime and the opposition parties quote the crime figures as failure of the ruling party on crime and law and order front. Resultantly the victim of the crime is the sufferer, though law envisages that State will take care of his/her legal rights including safety and security. Computerisation and e-mail inter linking of all police stations in India is underway and let us hope that things may improve in the times to come.

(2) There is shortage of Investigating Officers, hence to avoid the over burden of investigation, they avoid registering FIRs.

(3) The rate of success in certain cases, particularly in property offences is much less, which reflects adversely on the performance of police, hence police avoid registering such cases.

(4) Heinous property offences like dacoity, loot etc. are discouraged for registration because such cases attract adverse publicity. There is tendency on the part of the police to register such cases under mild sections, for example a case of dacoity is registered as of robbery.

(5) In 1970-71 UP Police launched a drive to register each and every case as it was reported. This resulted in exaggerated reporting by the informants, particularly under robbery as cases of simple quarrels were reported under these sections to make them cognizable and also to exert pressure on police to book the persons against whom such cases were reported. A subsequent study showed that about 45 per cent of robbery cases reported were either false or were wrongly reported under more serious sections of law.

2. *Investigation of cases:* Following commissions and omissions by the police result in Human Rights violations:

1. The police officers do not take adequate precautions about interrogations, arrests and detentions of women, children and others as per requirement of law.
2. The investigating officers at times exceed their limits in respect of search and seizures, thus violate the law and also infringe the Human Rights of such persons.
3. Custodial torture and deaths—The investigating officer gets only 24 hours for interrogating the suspect, which is much less, hence they use third degree methods, though illegal, to extract confessions so that the cases are worked out promptly. Despite state prohibitions against torture and custodial misconduct by the police, torture is widespread in police custody, which is a major reason behind custodial deaths. The police often torture innocent people until a 'confession' is obtained to save influential and wealthy offenders. G.P. Joshi, the programme coordinator of the Indian branch of the Commonwealth Human Rights Initiative in New Delhi comments that the main issue at hand concerning police violence is a lack of accountability of the police.
4. *Corruption*—Police corruption is another major factor which deprives the victim of the crime of his/her legitimate right to get relief from the State. The secrecy maintained by the

investigating officers, gives further rise for suspicion and injustice. The accused has no right to claim the copies of the documents/statements collected by the police during investigation. One can get the copy through court only, that too mostly after the investigations are over.

Prosecution

Following points are mostly responsible for lack of prosecution of accused and also of the State:

1. Panel of Public Prosecutors prepared under Section 24 and 25 Cr.PC by the State Governments is mostly based on considerations other than merit. Such lawyers do not meet the requirements of the job and thus are not able to take care of the prosecution and the interest of the State and justice.
2. The defence lawyers also do not cooperate with the courts and unnecessarily seek adjournments and thus delay the disposal of cases.
3. Free legal aid at the cost of State is also not ensured very often and the poor person keeps on languishing in jails.

Judiciary

Following are the expectations from the judiciary:

1. Presiding officer must be free from motivations, political and personal.
2. Magistrate not to be mute spectator to the foul play. He has to act as unbiased umpire and blow the whistle whenever infringement takes place.
3. Fair trial
   (a) Judge not to preside in case one is personally interested.
   (b) To ensure that counsel must represent the parties.
   (c) Trial in presence of accused.
   (d) Right of cross-examination.
   (e) Right of reasonable decision protection from biased conviction/acquittal.
   (f) Speedy Trials/Limitation as Justice delayed is justice denied.

Sentencing

- Judge to give chance to prosecution and defence to be heard on the question of sentencing.
- Hearing the offender on the nature and quantum of punishment.

Other Factors

1 At times adequate precautions are not taken by the courts, which result in miscarriage of justice.
2 The subordinates responsible for giving dates in cases, often keep it close to their chests so that they could ask for money for revealing that information. The payment of *dasturi* to court staff is a very old practice and mostly practiced under the nose of the presiding officers. It will be better if cause lists of the cases are put on web-sites resulting in disclosure and transparency.
3. Courts do not care much for the welfare of accused, while they are under custody.

Human Rights of the Undertrails

Main problems faced by the undertrials, which result in infringement of their rights are:

1. Non-availability of free legal aid—For some of the undertrials there nobody from their family members to help them as such they need free legal aid.
2. Frequent absence of panel lawyers appointed for providing them free legal aid, which results in undue delay in trials adding further to the woes of undertrials.
3. Request for early disposal of cases as they keep languishing in jail for several years.
4. Absence of prosecution witnesses especially the Police personnel and Medical Officers during trials leading to undue delay in the disposal of the case.

Suggestions

The following suggestions are given for ensuring implementation of Human Rights of the undertrials:

1. The data about summoning of the undertrials in courts be Computerisation and properly utilized by all concerned.
2. Police escort personnel should reach the jail on time to receive them for escorting to courts.
3. Video conferencing system be introduced as early as possible.
4. District monitoring committee must visit jails as per schedule and sort out problems.

Police

Prison Vans—To overcome the problems of prison vans it is suggested that: (1) adequate number of vans be provided, (2) separate vans be arranged for escorting females, so that they are not made to travel and sit with males, (3) at many places courts have started functioning at Tahsil Hq, hence separate escort vans should be provided for those places.

Police Escort Parties

- Guards and Escort Rules be revised on priority basis and suitable amendments be made so as to reassess the scale of escort personnel.
- Police personnel be suitably briefed at the jail by the jail staff at the time of handing over the prisoners to them.
- Escort personnel be punctual while reporting in Police Lines, at jail and then at lockups, so that no delay is caused in producing before the Courts.
- Escort personnel have to perform very long hours of duty. If the system of readmission in jails of the undertrials whose hearing is complete by lunch time is introduced this problem is likely to be sorted out to a great extent.

Judicial Lockups

1. At some places lockup buildings are old and risky as they may crumble any time and thus keeping undertrials in them is not safe.
2. There is acute shortage of space in the lockups and the undertrials have to remain mostly in standing position for long hours.

3. Average daily attendance is much more than the space available in the lockups thus resulting in congestion and over-crowding.
4. Very few districts have separate lockups for females, therefore, they are kept in verandahs facing the rooms where men are lodged. At places where female lockups are available their locations are unsuitable as they are within the view of males and their privacy is disturbed.
5. In several districts due to the shortage of space in lockups the undertrials are kept waiting in police prison vans, which is not only inhuman but also in violation of Rules, as they have to face rough weather conditions of summer, winter and also rainy season.
6. In many districts new courts have started functioning at Tahsil Hq. and some more districts are going to have such courts in near future. It is suggested that new lockups be constructed at all such places.
7. At some places lockups get water logged during rains and the undertrials have to remain standing there.
8. Toilets and sanitary conditions of the lockup rooms are far from satisfactory. Some rooms do not have any toilets. At several places the facilities of running water in toilets are wanting. For want of daily and routine cleaning, the toilets stink badly and it is miserable to be there for the whole day.
9. At most of the places there are no arrangements for offering drinking water to undertrials in lockups. Wherever, the water taps are available in rooms, they are very close to the toilets which is unhygienic. A bucket and a mug is kept in the lockup verandahs. The water is normally drawn from the hand pumps available inside the compound either by the police escort parties or the undertrials.

Suggestions for Improvement

- Construction of cemented benches alongside the walls inside the lockup rooms so that undertrials may sit on them instead of squatting on the floor or remain standing for long hours.
- Provision of separate lockup rooms be made for females.
- Staggering of hearings in courts. Those coming for grant of remand only be brought first, kept in the lockup, taken to court for grant of remand by lunch time. Thereafter,

undertrials whose presence is no longer required be taken back to jail and be admitted there. This will reduce congestion in the lockup rooms in the post lunch session and will give sufficient space for the remaining prisoners.

- The computerization of data about remand cases will help.

Sanitation and Drinking Water

- Arrangements be made for daily cleaning of the lockup premises, verandahs, rooms and toilets either in the evening after departure of prisoners when the rooms get empty or early in the next morning before arrival of the undertrials. In any case it be done under the supervision of some responsible official of the court who may ensure that no article of offence, explosion or wall breaking implements etc. are pianted during the cleaning exercise.
- Wherever possible *Sulabh Shauchalayas* could also be arranged, or cleaning could be outsourced. The design of such toilets be suitably prescribed to ensure security and safety. The suitable design of such toilets be prescribed to ensure security and safety.
- Immediate arrangements are required for offering drinking water to the undertrials in lockups. Hand pumps be installed inside the compound of the lockup and a daily wager be provided for fetching water and offering it to those in lockups.

Police Escort Parties

Criminal background of each and every undertrial be traced and kept on record. The escort personnel be very carefully briefed about each one of them and the risks involved not only for them but also to the persons escorted. This should be done by the SI in-charge of the escort party and wherever, need be by a Gazetted Officer in-charge of these duties.

Main problems faced by the escort staff are:

(1) Very long hours of duty say 12 to 16 hours,
(2) no time and facility for food,
(3) no place for rest at lockups,
(4) no office accommodation available hence they work in verandahs of the lockups,

(5) no relief or change of shift from the time they leave the Reserve Police Lines and till they return back late in the evenings.

Remission/Suspension/Commutation of Sentences/Mercy Petitions

Such matters are often decided on political considerations. It is suggested that Government may do it only on merits and in the interest of justice. Actions to be taken by Governments in such matters be made public in advance and if need be, public opinion be invited.

Human Rights of the Crime Victims

Everybody talks about the rights of the accused, who is presumed to be innocent unless proved guilty but the victims who suffered as a consequence of the act of the accused are forgotten. The only solace is that the State contests the case/s against the accused but there is no provision for monetary compensation of the loss suffered by the victim, including expenses incurred on treatment of ailments inflicted during commission of crimes. The fine in some cases, wherever and whenever it is imposed under the law is deposited in the state exchequer but the victim does not get any compensation. Some provisions have been made in the Rules of 1955 to compensate the victims of the Scheduled Castes and Scheduled Tribes (Prevention of Atrocities Act) 1989. Similar provisions with certain modifications, need to be made to compensate the victims of serious offences but care has to be taken to curb the tendency on the part of informants of wrong reporting of crime just to get compensation.

Efforts to Educate People

Public access to, and understanding of, national law is crucial to any functioning democracy. Sushant Sinha launched *(www.judis.nic.in)*, Indian Kanoon in January 2008. The website indexes judgements from the Supreme Court, the High Courts and various tribunals and links them to the relevant statutes. Importantly, it provides all these tools free of charge. Sinha explained: "Even when laws empower citizens in a large number of ways, a significant fraction of the population is completely ignorant of their rights and privileges. As a result, common people are afraid of going to the police and rarely go to court to seek justice. People continue to live under the fear of unknown laws and a corrupt police." Indian Kanoon is now helping to remedy that situation. It is used by approximately half-a-million unique users per month, widely promoted on Twitter and Facebook, and since March 2012 a mobile version has been available.

Human Rights Day and the Link to Anti-Corruption

Human Rights Day 10 December follows closely on the heels of Anti-Corruption Day, 9 December, which is not just a coincidence. They stand together because *human rights are far more likely to be safeguarded in a world where there is no corruption.* The human rights campaigner and the anti-corruption activist both work to eliminate corruption and petty bribery that denies ordinary people the public services they are entitled to, their human rights. The pursuit of integrity and the need to bring business dealings out of back rooms into the public domain is more necessary than ever. Furthermore, preventing corruption needs to be prioritised in efforts to eliminate poverty, inequality, human rights violations and social instability. Only by tackling corruption we will be able to effectively respond to these issues.

Conclusion

Let transparency and disclosure be the guiding principles of every Government for healthy administration. That will go along a way in ensuring the protection of Human Rights. Let it be known to all that any body who dares to violate this 'one would not go unnoticed and unpunished'. It may be that the *right to information, like a muscle, needs frequent and vigorous exercise in order to function as effectively* as possible. Regular requests remind governments that transparency is the rule and not the exception and that every citizen has the power to expose dishonest or abusive systems. Although the role of the internet in realising and strengthening this power is not always a straightforward one, information technologies can be extremely valuable tools for promoting transparency and empowering citizens. Human Rights violations could be ensured to a great extent if the Governments and the departments concerned make easy disclosure of information to the public and transparency and disclosure is ensured at every level. Those failing to ensure be taken to task so that it becomes a lesson for other defaulters.

16

Ensuring Transparency and Disclosure in Justice Delivery System

Lessons from Formal and Informal Justice Systems

Mridul Srivastava

Introduction

Over the years, the international community has been actively engaged in the reconstruction of justice by focusing its work on the formal structures, e.g. court systems, police forces and penitentiaries and legislative processes. This reflects our understanding of justice—formal, predictable, and equitable, with strict procedures and accountability at every level. This, however, does not reflect the prevailing conditions on the ground, which are marked by lack of resources, training, infrastructure, credibility and authority (Thorne Kristina, 2005).

There may be divided opinions on this point, but largely before the introduction of the published laws and formal justice system, societies were managed by traditions, culture and self-defined regulations. The deviancy was very little and even after the judgment is passed by the *Panchayats* the accused and victims became friends. One can say it was possible because of the close knitted society with homogeneous characteristics that was prevailing at that time. Another view on this point is that there is proper transparency and disclosure mechanism among all the stakeholders present in the informal justice systems.

Benefits of the Proper Disclosure in Criminal Justice System

Proper and timely disclosure is the lynchpin of our criminal justice process. It provides the accused with knowledge of the case the prosecution proposes to make against them and so is the foundation of a fair trial. If a trial is not fair the conviction may be set aside and the accused discharged (Dietrich, 1992).

Martin Moynihan explains the benefits of proper disclosure in criminal justice system in the following terms:

(1) It provides an accused and his lawyers with knowledge about:

- the events alleged to constitute the offence or offences;
- the issues which arise relating to those events that have to be dealt with to progress the matter to resolution;
- the identification and access to the evidentiary material bearing on those issues;
- the prosecution case will present so providing a basis for the lawyer to obtain instructions and give advice to an accused.

(2) It puts the Office of Public Prosecutions in a position to gauge the strengths and weaknesses of the prosecution case so as to consider whether:

- there should be further investigation and collection of evidence;
- the charges should be modified;
- the matter should be pursued.

(3) It provides a platform for decisions by prosecution and defence so as to progress the case to resolution, for example by:

- negotiation;
- a timely plea of guilty;
- identifying issues of law to be determined at committal court proceedings or by way of a pre-trial ruling in the Supreme or District Courts;
- the conduct of the trial.

(4) It provides a platform for court control of the progress of the case to resolution with the minimum but necessary use of public resources, for example:

- time limits can be imposed, compliance monitored, founding focussed court intervention to progress the matter to a conclusion;
- directions can be given, monitored and enforced.

Timely disclosure minimises delay and supports the effective use of public resources. It fosters early pleas of guilty, founds negotiation and reduces wasting of resources.

Concept of Swift and Sure Justice

The public has a right to expect the justice system to be swift and sure:

Swift: so that the low-level, straightforward and uncontested cases, where a quick response is appropriate, are dealt with promptly and efficiently; and

Sure: so that the system can be relied upon to deliver punishment and redress fairly and in accordance with the law and public expectation.

A criminal justice system which fails to command public confidence in this way has fallen at the first hurdle. Our focus on crime prevention is as integral to our efforts to deliver swift and sure justice as is the need for a robust response when offending occurs. Preventing crime is the right thing to do for victims, for society and for potential offenders. When crimes occur, the response must be swift if it is to be an effective deterrent. However, despite a falling case load the criminal justice process remains slow and cumbersome. There is a cultural tolerance of delay. It takes an average of five months from an offence for an offender to be sentenced in the magistrates' courts. Witnesses still have to wait an average of two hours before giving their evidence in the Crown Court and an hour and a half in the magistrates' courts (Ministry of Justice, 2012).

Efficient Justice Through Technology

Technology has a critical role to play in delivering efficient criminal justice. Huge sums of money have been spent on IT in the criminal justice agencies during the last decade, in particular under the CJS IT programme, but the public did not secure sufficient return on these substantial investments. We have to speed up processes, and enable swifter justice through exploiting the IT. It also has a role to play in supporting other elements of our reform programme, for example, improving transparency and accountability through online local crime maps, local court performance information and the broadcasting of proceedings. New social media websites also provide an opportunity for local criminal justice services to reconnect with their communities.

Transparent Justice

The criminal justice system is criticised for being opaque, remote and impenetrable. De-mystify the workings of the criminal justice system can be obtained by:

- Publishing relevant and easily accessible information about local crime, and its outcomes, the performance of local criminal justice services, and the reoffending rates they achieve; and
- Broadcasting what happens in courts.

The operation of the criminal justice system can be a mystery to victims and the public, and it too often fails to engage local communities or reflect their priorities. Our first responsibility is towards victims, yet they feel ignored by a system that seems to be built around the needs of offenders and their lawyers. The criminal justice system is a monopoly: victims and the public cannot choose to be protected by anyone else. If we are to ensure that services improve and deliver the best outcomes it is essential that their workings are exposed to public view. Only when armed with the right information and given the chance to observe how the system works in practice can the public hold the criminal justice system to account.

Accountable Justice

Accountability on the part of executive and judiciary is the most desired task in the criminal justice system. Constitution of India, Third Schedule, Part IV lays down the following oath for the Supreme Court Judges:

> "I, *(name)*, having been appointed Chief Justice of the Supreme Court of India do swear in the name of God/ solemnly affirm that I will bear true faith and allegiance to the Constitution of India as by law established, that I will uphold the sovereignty and integrity of India, that I will duly and faithfully and to the best of my ability, knowledge and judgment perform the duties of my office without fear or favour, affection or ill-will and that I will uphold the Constitution and the laws."

The Transparency Accountability Initiative of USA (2011) has prepared a document named "Opening Government" which illustrates the following major sectors in which transparency and disclosure is required:

1. Asset Disclosure
2. Budgets Disclosure
3. Electoral transparency, participation and accountability
4. Environment transparency, participation and justice
5. Financial sector reform
6. Forestry and Land transparency
7. Disclosure of Military and intelligence budgets
8. National security transparency and accountability
9. Open government data
10. Police and public security
11. Right to information
12. Judicial Accountability
13. Service delivery

The criminal justice system is an essential component of the Rule of Law. An effective criminal justice system should provide equal justice to all according to law by disposing of cases impartially, fairly, expeditiously, with the minimum unavoidable delay and with the minimum but necessary use of public resources. (Moynihan, 2008).

White paper on Justice Reforms (2012) discusses three kinds of change: Our justice system needs reform to make sure these expectations are met. The timing is right: in support of reform, there is clear opportunity for positive change in several areas, and strong will across the system. It is clear that our justice system must be strengthened in three ways. Our justice system must be *transparent, timely and balanced.*

The main elements of these three aspects of good justice system are illustrated below:

Transparent: Clear Governance, Common Understanding, Performance Focus

Timely: Efficient Case Management, Early Assistance to Citizens, Smart Choices at the Start

Balanced: Integrated Approach, Programme Based on What Works, Citizen Focused Services

The Role of Information Technology in Justice System Accountability

A key to using information technology to deliver transparent, timely and balanced justice is management's capacity to see and understand how the system operates. This requires: (a) collecting the right data to know the costs and outcomes of justice services; (b) business intelligence to be able to use data to learn how the system functions; and (c) performance reporting, i.e using business intelligence to let citizens see for themselves how the system is working.

As part of the Justice Reform Initiative, British Columbia Government commissioned three reports between February and August 2012: the Cowper Report, the McCuaig Report, and the Legal Services Society Report. The tables below summarize the government's response to some of the recommendations made through these reports and consultations.

Table 16.1: Objective of Reform and Required Action

Objective of Reform	*Required Action*
Advance family justice reform	Early assessment, information, and referral
	Family legal aid reform
	Revised child support process
	Adult Guardianship
Transform dispute resolution	Civil Resolution Tribunal
	Road Safety Systems
	Tribunal transformation
Improve early criminal processes	Improvements to the charge assessment process
	Enhancing system-wide knowledge of risk assessment
	Criminal legal aid reform
	Restorative justice

(Contd.)

Objective of Reform	*Required Action*
Undertake public safety reform	Examine options for models of policing Crime prevention Crime reduction initiative
Protect marginalized women	Prevention and protection Modernize reporting and tracking of missing persons Improve criminal investigations of missing persons Vulnerable witnesses and victims
Respond to domestic violence	Domestic Violence Action Plan Domestic violence units Domestic violence courts
Require the use of evidence-based approaches	Measurement is an essential part of reform Monitor and evaluate Applying rigour to reform Implementing "what works"

Making the data of the Criminal Justice systems public requires some principles that must be followed because of its sensitive nature. The first principle requires that personal data should be processed fairly and lawfully. The publication of personal information about convictions is "perfectly possible, without compromising legal provisions... or placing individual members of the public at risk" as long as "due consideration [is] given to all of the implications and consequences that may impact upon the different parties involved". The second principle regarding the disclosure is that disclosure should generally be 'fair', because people who have been convicted of offences can expect that the fact of their conviction will be made public, and there is a legitimate public interest in doing so; disclosure by relevant public authorities will generally be 'lawful', because it will normally be made by a public authority in connection with the exercise of its functions. The third principle requires that data should be adequate, relevant and not excessive; the fourth principle requires that data should be accurate and up to date; and the fifth principle requires that data should not be kept for longer than necessary (Ministry of Justice, June 2011).

Governments can bring the change in the process of transparency and disclosure in justice delivery system through considering which cases the public wants to know about; developing a local policy framework; trusting the public with information; using the 'you said, we did' format in communications; using practical safeguards to protect information online; using leaflets and newsletters; using all sources of information on convictions; considering use of social networking sites; making use of examples of good practice, etc.

In the United Sates, a bill entitled the Supreme Court Transparency and Disclosure Act of 2011 (the "Transparency and Disclosure Act"), which was introduced in 2012 in the House of Representatives, proposed that (1) Supreme Court Justices be held to the ethical Code of Conduct; (2) there be a process for review of complaints alleging that a Justice violated the Code; (3) a Justice disclose publicly the reasoning behind his or her recusal from a case or refusal to withdraw in response to a motion to disqualify; and (4) there also be a process for reviewing these decisions. These proposed restrictions on a Justice's conduct would supplement ethics laws already in effect. Those laws apply to the Court and mandate recusal under certain circumstances and subject Justices to the federal government-wide financial disclosure and gift regulations (City Bar Association Committee on Government Ethics September 28, 2012).

Transparency and Disclosure in Informal Justice Systems

The reconstruction of justice, both of its institutions, their functionality and of the population's trust in them, is a precondition for peace and sustainable development to take root after a conflict situation. Often, however, actors shy away from investing time and resources in this sector for a variety of reasons. The term "informal justice system" is contested in the sense that to some, it seems to implicitly accord a formal status to a mechanism that generally exists without official sanction. Different cultures also have a different understanding of what constitutes an "informal system" (Thorne Kristina, 2005).

Why don't the Poor Use Formal Justice Systems?

Lena Hasle has explained why the poor women do not use formal justice system on the basis of her study in Bangladesh. The main points highlighted by her are:

- Mistrust of the law, fear, intimidation;
- Lack of understanding — language issues, unfamiliarity of formal procedures and court atmosphere, low legal literacy;

- Unequal power relations;
- Physical and financial inaccessibility;
- Formal systems are culturally 'uncomfortable';
- Formal system lacks legitimacy — can be complicit in conflict and past oppression, corruption;
- It usually takes a long time to process cases, opportunity costs;
- Going through the formal system may lead to more problems between the disputing parties.

Common Characteristics of Informal Justice Systems

Leeuwen *et al.* (2005) in a study of Burundi highlight the common characteristics of informal justice system:

- The problem is viewed as relating to the whole community as a group — there is strong consideration for the collective interests at stake in disputes;
- Decisions are based on a process of consultation;
- There is an emphasis on reconciliation and restoring social harmony;
- Arbitrators are appointed from within the community on the basis of status or lineage;
- There is often a high degree of public participation;
- The rules of evidence and procedure are flexible;
- There is no professional legal representation;
- The process is voluntary and the decision is based on agreement;
- They have a high level of acceptance and legitimacy;
- There is no distinction between criminal and civil cases, informal justice systems often deal with both;
- Often there is no separation between informal justice systems and local governance structures — a person who exercises judicial authority through an informal justice system may also have executive authority over the same property or territory; and
- Enforcement of decisions is secured through social pressure.

A UNDP sponsored project on Informal Justice systems in the state of Madhya Pradesh, with which the author was associated, visited extensively 5 districts of Madhya Pradesh. During the field visits, it was found that tribal *Panchayats* are far better in some areas in comparison of our formal justice system. We examined their system of dispute resolution very deeply. In regards to the access of justice, tribal people don't come into conflict with the government departments. Government also in turn ignores the issues related to their traditions like the cases of bigamy and child marriage. People approach the formal system as well. The cases of heinous crimes like murder and rape is generally reported to the police. The reason behind reporting these cases is to build pressure on the other party for the compromise and to extract more amount of money from the accused family.

A Tribal Panchayat entertains all kinds of cases criminal, family matters and property matters. Normally a Tribal Panchayat [of Baigas, Gonds, Sahariyas, Bhil-Bhilalas and Bharias] handles the cases like fighting between brothers, dispute with neighbours, altercations under the influence of liquor, theft, use of abusive language, divorce (Chuta Chutti), adultery, property matters, woman related issues, etc. Tribal Panchayat takes fine from the accused and give it to the victim.

Following other major kinds of disputes are normally referred to Tribal Panchayat:

- Cases of elopement
- Marital dispute
- Land dispute
- Use of abusive language
- Altercations under the influence of liquor
- Disputes related to the field boundary or on crossing of boundary by grazing animals
- Petty theft

Exogamous marriage, beating of a wife during menstruation period and use of abusive language in front of women are considered as serious crimes among Gond. Serving tested food by wife to husband, rape of a married woman, and murder of a cow are considered as serious crimes among Sahariya. Rape and murder are considered to be the most heinous crimes among Bhil, Bhilala and Bharia. In case of Bharia, women related issues, attack with arrow or *falia*, and theft are serious crimes. In women related cases elopement and the pregnancy without marriage are more serious crimes. Tribal Panchayat refers cases of serious crime such as murder and rape to police.

Sometimes, people approach Tribal Panchayat when police does not register a case. Sometimes, tribal people approach formal justice system for creating pressure on other party. After reporting the case at police station, a panchayat meeting is called for solving the dispute by charging fine and compromise. Only on the request of the concerned parties or the family members of the concerned parties a panchayat meeting may be called. Once the meeting is finalized, it is the responsibility of Kotwar to inform all villagers. Women can take their issues directly to the panchayat but during most of the time her father or other family members call the panchayat meeting. Tribal panchayat takes care of the disadvantaged groups too. If anybody is sick and whose presence is necessary in the panchayat then members visit his place otherwise somebody who is directly or indirectly associated with the dispute has to attend the case hearing. Normally by tradition, members of Tribal Panchayat are all men. Women are not given representation in the panel of members. There are many reasons behind it. One is that it is a patriarchal society and other is the working environment in the panchayats. There is always possibility of hot discussions, heated exchange of arguments, frequent use of abusive language, chances of attack and fight, and use of weapons also. Hence, women like to refrain away from Panchayat meetings.

Baiga and Gond people do not believe in formal justice system and do not at all want to refer their cases to police. First priority is always given to Tribal Panchayat system. Baiga shared one of the saying as *'Bakari Ke Chare aur Kachahari Ke Chadhe Kabhi Nahi Panapate'*. It means those who approach court never prosper in their life. When a relative of any member of panchayat is involved in a dispute, he is not supposed to participate in the particular meeting as a *panch.* He can participate as a common man.

In some villages, members of Gram Panchayat can also participate in the meeting as a villager. No any significance is given to his opinion. Gram Panchayat members also do refer cases to Tribal Panchayat. In Bhil and Bhilala there are two famous saying in Hindi, i.e.

> *Roti Vyavahar hai lekin beti vyavahar nahi*
> (can eat together, but can not marry in other caste).

Kal se nahi to bal se (if not possible to handle a woman with *saam, daam, dand, bhed* then they use force).

Any outsider is not allowed to influence the process of giving justice through Tribal Panchayat. People do take advice of NGO representatives working in the area, but ultimately decisions are taken by Tribal Panchayat. Disputes that can be solved by Tribal Panchayat are not referred to NGOs working in the area.

Decisions are generally taken by consensus in Tribal Panchayat. So there is no question of showing dissatisfaction over the decisions taken by Tribal Panchayat. When any of the disputants are not satisfied with the decision given by Tribal Panchayat, they can further refer their case to police.

Section 222 of M.P. Land Revenue Code talks about the selection process of a *Patel.* If a person dies or doesn't want to be a *Patel* then either his son or brother will become the patel but all villagers must agree on his selection. *Patel* is very important person in the village and he has a say in the village. He has been made in-charge of the village boundaries and is responsible for revenue collection. The villagers started coming to him for their dispute resolution also. The report of 1935-41 and the MPRLC don't give the power to settle the dispute to a Patel. But the villagers consider him part of the government and show faith on him. This is also now reflecting with the introduction of *Panchayati Raj*. The *Sarpanch* also became an important person and as he is also a part of the chain between villagers and government, villagers also included him in their traditional *panchayats*. This brought more legitimacy to the traditional panchayat system. In fact, there are some differences between the *Patel* and *Sarpanch* but that are not reflecting overall because of the social pressure. To increase the faith in formal system quick decision and awareness is needed. There is need to divert the minds of the tribal people from disputes towards development. The position of *Patel* or *Mukhiya* is very powerful and strong at the village level. Although it is only a compromise and compensation method. *Patel* or *Mukhiya* gives the last decision. In their own cases either a case of *Patel* or *Mukhiya's* family or the *Sarpanch's* family they cannot be a judge in the panchayat, The other *Panchs* alongwith *Patel* or *Mukhiya* or *Sarpanch* solve the case.

Procedures Followed by Tribal Panchayat

Traditionally, there is one Tribal Panchayat for every village. Any outsider can not influence decisions taken by Tribal Panchayat. In fact, during Tribal Panchayat meetings intervention by any outsider is not allowed. A Tribal Panchayat meeting is announced on the day suitable for all. The time is decided as per convenience of all villagers. The place is decided on the basis of character of disputants. If *Panch* feels that disputants are dishonest, then they choose a place where no one lies and speak out truth only. It may be a temple, religious tree, cowshed etc. They use *dindori* (Dhol) to inform all villagers regarding the panchayat meeting. In cases of Bhil and Bhilala tribe they prefer the morning time because in the evening they prefer drinking. Normally a case hearing is conducted in the morning at a common place or in a cow shed which is supposed to be a sacred place. Among Sahariya, a tribal panchayat meeting is generally conducted during night and the time is decided as per the convenience of all villagers. The place is fixed and normally it is located at the centre of the village.

There is a common procedure for resolving all kinds of disputes. Fees are not charged to hear the case. Disputants are supposed to provide tea and *pan-supari* to members and all those who participate in the meeting. In Bhil and Bhilala tribe disputants provide money for the *Tadi* (local wine) for the participants and sometimes the party of the Bhokda (Bakra) is also there in the elopement cases. The traditional panchayat don't entertain old cases, only recent cases of maximum one month are taken to the traditional panchayat. Sometimes a case is taken for hearing by tribal panchayat after certain period which is necessary to reduce the anger of both the parties.

The presence of both the disputants is compulsory while hearing a case. Both parties are given a chance to explain the matter in front of Tribal Panchayat members. Normally, the disputants themselves plead their cases but in case of women or disabled, the family members can also plead on behalf of them. If anybody is so sick that he/she can not come to the panchayat then members go to his/her place to record the statement.

Method of Investigation

The main method of investigation is taking the statement from all the persons related directly and indirectly with that particular dispute. Tribal Panchayat gives importance to the oral statements more than any other evidence. Evidences are cross checked by using method of confrontation and conducting cross examination of witnesses. There is no trial by ordeal system present and after the dispute settlement they take oath by taking grains or water in hand that they will not involve themselves in dispute later. Sometimes, oath is given to put pressure on individual to speak truth and to confirm the statement given by a person. Whenever villagers/members feel that the disputants are dishonest, they ask disputants to swear of their god. Baiga swear on *Thakur dev*, or *Jal (*Water*),* or *Agni* (Fire) or *Vayu* (Wind) or *Anna* (Foodgrain) or *Lakshmi (*cow) or any religious tree like Banyan/Sal/Peeple tree. Gond people use *Ramayan*, a holy religious book, or Saja tree for the same purpose. Sahariya ask disputants to take swear on *Gangajal* (holy water), or coconut. They keep sesame, rice and coconut at the place of panchayat meeting. These are considered as holy objects. The Bhil and Bharia prefer the oath of the Bada Dev (Tree of sal).

All the members and the villagers continue the meeting until the matter is resolved. If the case is complicated and members do not come to the consensus then they follow the practice that every member will go to a different direction, think and come back. But at any cost, decisions are taken whatsoever be the matter. Sometimes they sit two three consequent days to resolve the matter. If any of the disputants is not satisfied, they may call the meeting the next day. But it happens very rarely. If the accused refuses to come for the meeting, he is advised and convinced for attending the meeting. But still if he fails, then he is ex-communicated. If the person is not happy with the decision, he is convinced and guided by the elderly members to follow the decision taken by the panchayat. But he is free to go to police for registering his complaint. Decision of *Panchayat* differs from case to case.The amount of fine depends upon the crime committed, the economic condition of the person, and the source of livelihood. The fine has to be deposited itself in the meeting. If the accused has no money at that point of time, then he is given some time period and one member has to take the responsibility to get the fine deposited.

Keeping Records

Tribal Panchayats of Gond and Baiga hardly keeps any record but the Bhil, Bhilala and Bharia keep records of the decision in some cases where they mention the final decision and the punishment provided to them and also they mention about the punishment applicable if both the parties don't follow their decisions. It was observed in Sahariya that their *Panchayats* are keeping record. The records are written either on a plain paper or on the letterhead of

Gram Panchayat as it is the legalized institution. This is also because usually they send this record (*Panchnama*) to the nearest police station for their information. In most cases, police try to mint money from both disputants and hence they take the precaution and send the *Panchnama* to police and leave no possibility of exploiting people. Generally decisions are taken on the basis of decisions taken previously in similar kinds of cases. If a person repeats his/her mistake, then amount of fine is increased gradually.

Decisions are not taken in the absence of either of the party. Both the parties are forced to attend the hearing. Decisions are by and large taken by consensus. It is the responsibility of *Mukhiya/ Patel* to facilitate the process, take opinion of all members and other participants and then draw a conclusion that is acceptable to both parties. People sometimes try to put pressure on members of Tribal Panchayat, but as the process is open for all to participate, such pressures are of no use. In some villages, it was informed that influential persons use pressure tactics to pressurize the members.

If villagers feel that any member is giving his opinion under the influence of any pressure, then they raise an objection and condemn the member for wrong conduct. Thus, Tribal Panchayat takes decisions independently and does not succumb to any pressure. Women are given a chance to give her statement in front of all. It was shared in all villages that dignity to certain extent is shown while discussing matters related with women's character. Normally women are not cross questioned. When a case is related with a woman's character, other elderly women from the village talk to her separately and then they explain the case to Tribal Panchayat members.

The disputes are resolved in 3-4 hours or a Tribal Panchayat meeting is continued till the *Panch* and disputants both agree on a final conclusion. If Tribal Panchayat is not able to arrive at a final conclusion in a single meeting, then a series of meetings are called till the final decision is taken. The interval between the meetings depends on the situation. If there is no consensus among members then the Patel's or Mukhiya's decision is respected as final decision. If the panchayat don't reach the solution then only there are chances of the matter being referred to the police. The decisions are taken as per the situation. They also consider judgment given previously. There are no written documents of rules to refer.

Nature of Punishments

There is no system of corporal punishment. The only punishment is fine and social boycott. The fine/punishment is levied as per situation and it is different from case to case. There are no written norms/ specifications for charging fine. Normally cases are solved by asking the disputants to sacrifice a pig/goat/chicken depending on the seriousness of the case and distribution of Mahua liquor. Fine is always charged considering economic status of an individual. In most of the cases, fine up to Rs. 4000 is charged. It seems that this amount is flexible. Sahariya informed that they charge fine up to Rs. 20,000. In the case of rape Bhil charge fine up to Rs. 60,000 and if the parents agree then they marry the girl with the same person. Recently, there is an increase in the fine amount. There are two reasons behind the increase of the fine amount. One is increasing prices and the other is to make deterrent effect on others to prevent crime. The main criterion is the fault and not the economic condition of the accused. Amount of fine is utilized in drinking liquor and eating meat. In some of the Gond villages it was informed that now people have understood the ill effects of drinking liquor and hence any kind of *Mithai* (sweetmeat) is distributed. In case of Sahariya tribe, there are two ways of spending the fine amount collected—either on the cultural functions or giving money to the needy as a loan without charging any interest.

There is a system among Bhils that if a Bhilala boy marries a Bhil girl then villagers will not accept and they will socially boycott the family, but if the family gives party to the villagers then they again include the family in their community. If a girl becomes pregnant before marriage, then they beat the girl and if the boy is unmarried then either they marry her with that boy or settle the issue with money exchange but if the boy is married then they ask the girl to abort the child and if abortion is not possible then they leave the child anywhere after the birth. Tribal Panchayat charges fine only and sometimes they beat a woman as that is the only punishment for women. Beating women is very rare. The fine money goes to the victim. The decision of panchayat is binding on men and women equally. There is no punishment which affects their dignity. Women are normally not charged fine in terms of money. If a woman is found guilty, the money is taken from her parents or husband. Sahariya tribals informed that in case of adultery, even the physical punishment is given to the man involved like slapping, and the accused has to pay for the expenditure on bidi and tea. He is also asked to donate some money in the name of village deity.

In rare cases among Baiga, women's as well as men's hairs are cut using heinous practices. Urine of all members of Tribal Panchayat is collected in a bottle, it is put on hairs of the accused, and then hairs are cut in front of all villagers. Except the punishment of cutting hairs using heinous practices, women are generally satisfied with the kind of justice given by Tribal Panchayat. When a disputant refuses to accept a decision, he is boycotted, and villagers stop keeping any relations with him till he accepts the decision. A social ban is announced if any disputant denies the Panchayat decision. The socially banned disputant and his/her family members could not participate in any village function and social rituals. Villagers do not allow the socially banned family in any individual or common function in the village. No one talks with socially banned family and avoid keeping any relation with them. There is no change over the years in terms of kind of cases handled by Tribal Panchayat. In cases of child marriage the district administration takes action only on the written complaints received and they stop the marriage and arrest the parties. But without written complaints they don't intervene. In such cases there is political pressure on government administration so most of the time they are not able to take any action.

Assessment

Tribal people still strongly believe in Tribal Panchayat system. In more than 99 per cent of disputes, Baiga/Gond/Sahariya/Bhil/Bharia people do not approach police. In fact, most of the people have not yet seen court. Even young people believe in Tribal Panchayat system and are afraid of formal justice system. As far as the matter of belief is concerned youth also believe in traditional system because of the social pressure. There are hardly any cases that are first referred to police by tribal people. They refuse to approach police, as police does not give them a dignified treatment. Police always use abusive language, give harsh treatment and ask for money and liquor. In tribal people's opinion the formal justice system is exploitative, time consuming and expensive. There are very rare instances where dispute is first reported to the police. In such cases, tribal panchayat do not interfere in the matters on its' own. Panchayat handles the cases that are referred to police, only when one of the disputants approaches them to resolve the dispute. Many a times police themselves direct certain cases (particularly non cognizable offences) to traditional Panchayats to solve the dispute. Tribal people oppose police to handle the cases and try to solve the dispute on their own. People believe that the dispute resolving process is so transparent that there is no corruption. Even if dispute is among two persons belonging to 2 different villages, same procedures are followed by involving members from other villages. Tribal people have not yet included procedures of formal justice system in the Tribal Panchayat meetings.

People expressed overall satisfaction with the way Tribal Panchayat system is handling cases. The reasons given for it are as follows:

- Both parties are listened.
- Disputes are solved at village level
- Dignity of both parties is maintained.
- Equal treatment is given to both parties.
- Tribal Panchayat system is less expensive, hence more affordable as compared to formal justice system
- Tribal Panchayat system is less exploitative and even in the case of rape it is sympathetic towards women.
- Tribal Panchayat system is more easily accessible, resolves disputes in lesser time as compared to formal justice system

Thus, Tribal Panchayat system is better suited for tribal people. Women also feel that Tribal Panchayat system is better for them as they can easily approach it and their voice is heard. Women feel that traditional system gives justice to them and cases are also handled with sensitivity. Women feel that Tribal Panchayat system treats both men and women equally. Women expressed strong resentment over the custom of cutting hairs by applying urine of members.

Mukhiya and even women feel that women shall never be given representation on panel of members of Tribal Panchayat because of the following reasons:

- Use of abusive language in panchayat meetings. As per tribal norms, women shall not listen to it.
- Role of a panch requires him to attend meetings, talk to people, invite them for meetings, etc. and women are not supposed to mix up freely in the society. Hence, women shall

not act as members. Only concerned women can participate in the Tribal Panchayat meetings when it is required.

Tribal Panchayat system should not be linked with formal justice system. There is a possibility that drawbacks of formal justice system would enter Tribal Panchayat system. People have categorically demanded that decisions taken by them should get some approval from the government and should be considered authentic. If the matters are solved by panchayat, then it shall not be reopened by the police. They feel that government can approve decisions taken by Tribal Panchayat, but shall not intervene in the decisions taken by Tribal Panchayat. Tribal Panchayat system is supportive to some extent to formal justice system as it is addressing cases of minor altercations, petty thefts, etc. at village level and not increasing burden on formal justice system. Tribal Panchayat system is not creating problems for formal justice system, as it is not handling criminal cases at all. Due to the education and exposure now a day people have started approaching the formal justice system especially in case of serious crimes.

The fundamental difference in the traditional and formal justice systems is the procedure, customs and complicity. The positive points of the traditional systems are it is less expensive, less time taking, quick decision-making, they have faith in that, small disputes solved readily and it maintains the peace and hormonal relations afterwards also. The negative points are that the panchayat don't take proactive role like when outsiders are cutting trees from jungle, spend money in the party, due to heavy fine the poor become more poor, interested parties including judges are in the direct link that can affect the decision. To pay the fine people might have to sell their lands, ornaments and need to borrow money from the money lenders.

Merits of Tribal Panchayat System

- Informal Justice System is better than formal justice system for tribal people as it is easily accessible, less time consuming, cheaper and non-exploitative.
- Both parties involved in the disputes get satisfaction and have faith in the Tribal Panchayat system.
- Formal Justice System is more exploitative, time and money consuming. In this system Tribals neither get justice nor even satisfaction.

Tribal panchayat are solving the offences that comes under sections 294, 223. It saves time and money of poor tribal people.

Demerits of Tribal Panchayats

- It involves the punishments like social ban on families, most of the times disputants are asked to give dinner to community members (it necessarily involves offering of meet and liquor) and sometimes humiliating practices are followed during *Jat Miloni.*
- The punishments/fine charged are over estimated. The deprived tribal people face difficulties in arranging the money.
- In Tribal Panchayat system, women are treated as equal as men, but it is not always true. Women could not express their opinion due to pressure of her husband and society in general.
- In cases like section 125,498, women could not talk freely/ openly.
- Women are not involved in decision-making.

The strengths and weaknesses of Tribal Justice System are summed up in Table 16.2:

Table 16.2: Strengths and Weakness of Tribal Justice System

Positive Aspects/Strengths	*Negative Aspects/Weaknesses*
Understandable and culturally 'comfortable'	Unequal Power Relations and Susceptibility to Elite Capture
Focus on consensus, reconciliation and social harmony	Unfair and unequal treatment of women and disadvantaged groups
Informal justice systems can be good partners with the formal justice system	Lack of accountability
Swift solutions	Opaque interface between informal and formal justice
Social legitimacy, trust and understanding of local problems	Non-adherence to international human rights standards
Informal justice systems often survive violent conflict	Unsuitable for certain disputes that are important for security and sustainable development

(Contd.)

Positive Aspects/Strengths	*Negative Aspects/Weaknesses*
Geographical and financial accessibility	
Problems get solved at village level.	Records are not maintained
No external agency required.	Fine charged is based on whims of members of Tribal Panchayat. No standardized procedures.
Time required much lesser.	Kinds of disputes addressed are limited
Easily approachable and affordable.	Women not given representation as members on panel of panch
Less humiliating as compared to treatment received from police	Treatment given to women in certain cases (during jat-miloni, accepting a woman back to her original tribe group) is humiliating and disgraceful.
No economic exploitation	Use of fine amount—it is used for consumption of liquor and meat. Not used for any constructive developmental work
Disputes resolved within the framework of social traditions that are acceptable to both parties	Many times the judgment of the panchayat is biased in case of inter tribal disputes.
Political influence not considered while giving decisions.	The fine money in *bharia* tribes is utilized by the panchayat only. No provision of disbursement of fine money for the victim.
Strong hold on people's mind. People still have a strong faith.	In Dhar, there is much more effect of urbanized culture and the effect of the traditional panchayat is vanishing but in bhil, bhilala and bharia tribes it is strongly functioning.
No infrastructure required	Village politics due to the Panchayti Raj has weakened the old system.

Several factors, such as, respect for and acceptance of local culture, could be invoked to support the locally rooted informal judicial systems. They are complementary in the sense that they cover the gaps left by it. They may overlap with the formal system in some cases. For the most part, though, they provide a modicum of justice and security to the population in areas where the formal system cannot. Furthermore, when other sectors are prioritised, and any given activity will only be allocated a small amount of resources, it would seem a waste not to take advantage of existing local structures. The fact, these may not correspond to our concept of justice, or fully comply with international standards, is in reality only another reason why we should engage them. If we are seeking to guarantee a quality of justice rather than just recreating a formal structure, work with the informal structures becomes an imperative.

On the basic level, authority and credibility are vital for any justice system. In peaceful societies, it could be argued that the resort to informal systems is an expression of the lack of trust in formal structures. Taken to the extreme, this lack of trust might even be a reason for the formal structures to collapse or for the society to slide into conflict. When we talk about reconstructing the rule of law in post-conflict settings, we therefore, envisage reconstructing the people's trust in the institutions involved in providing justice services be they formal or informal. Both reports provide certain basic recommendations for action. Whereas, the Somalia report voices this in terms of a six-point package, the Burundi one makes several recommendations and targets three priority actions at various actors, national and international alike. Certain themes are contained in both sets of recommendations, e.g. the need for any action to be comprehensive, or at least complementary to other activities; the need to sustain assistance efforts; and to implement them on the scale that is needed (Thorne Kristina, 2005).

How to Engage with Informal Justice Systems?

The normative framework can be either formal or informal in nature. Formal norms are reflected in the Constitution, national legislation, regional regulations and jurisprudence issued by the courts. Informal norms evolve through social interaction and reflect customs and accepted behaviour within a particular group or community. The normative framework has the capacity to both protect and defend the interests of the poor, or in fact perpetuate injustices and inequities.

Legal awareness is critical for securing access to justice. Poor and disadvantaged groups often fail to make use of laws and rights precisely because they are not aware of them. Poor communities need to be aware of the law, of available remedies and how to access those remedies.

Once equipped with legal knowledge, the poor and disadvantaged require adequate access to both informal and formal justice systems to seek remedies.

Although physically more accessible informal systems often reflect the social and political inequities which define many poor rural communities. The poor, women and ethnic minorities face challenges in accessing informal justice due to a lack of neutrality, unclear standards and guidelines and sometimes a lack of capacity on the part of informal justice actors. Building access to these systems includes establishing oversight mechanisms; ensuring representation for disadvantaged groups in local-level institutions; capacity building for informal actors; and building bridges between formal and informal systems.

Public confidence in legal institutions is dependent on timely, independent and consistent application of applicable norms, free of political intervention and corruption. It also requires accountability to the public for performance against agreed service standards.

Public monitoring and scrutiny of formal and informal justice systems is fundamental to achieve the goals articulated above (Wojkowska, 2005).

To conclude, we may sum up the main lessons from formal and informal Justice Systems:

- Identify the claim holders — those who are most vulnerable. Policies and programmes need to ensure an explicit focus on the poor and disadvantaged. People's perceptions of justice, the obstacles they face and the ways they address them need to be understood;
- Identify the duty bearers — the ones accountable for addressing the issues (including institutions, groups, community leaders);
- Assess and analyse the capacity gaps of claim holders to be able to claim their rights and duty bearers to be able to meet their obligations and use analysis to focus capacity development strategies;
- Capacity development for access to justice;
- Find solutions for problems instead of imitating models;
- Work together with a truly representative section of the national community to as great an extent as possible;
- Recognize that it is impossible to remedy at once all the

shortcomings of informal justice systems;

- Clarify and socialize dispute resolution procedures;
- Support legal empowerment programmes;
- Support legal awareness activities;
- Develop the capacities of informal justice actors to provide information;
- Employ popular education;
- Support para-legalism;
- Professionalize para-legal work;
- Introduce law students to informal justice systems;
- Increase the availability of information about legal services and dispute resolution methods beyond the informal justice systems;
- Support capacity development of civil society organisations engaged in the provision of legal and quasi-legal services;
- Provide summarized and simplified versions of key legislation to informal justice actors;
- Provide literacy training to informal justice actors where necessary. Means of representation for women and marginalized groups must be developed;
- Provide support to development of policies to improve practices of informal justice systems;
- Support capacity development for informal justice actors in the areas of mediation techniques and citizens' rights;
- Support to civil society organizations working to improve access to justice through informal mechanisms;
- Empower community members Support monitoring of informal justice mechanisms by government and civil society organizations;
- Advocate for the production of written records of informal decisions.

REFERENCES

Blackstone, William, *Commentaries on the Laws of England*, Claredon Press, Oxford.

Committee on Government Ethics (2012), *Supreme Court Ethics: The Need For Greater Transparency—In A Justice's Decision To Hear A Case,* New York City Bar Association, New York.

Cowper Report (2012), *A Criminal Justice System for the 21st Century, http://www.ag.gov.bc.ca/public/justice-reform/CowperFinalReport.pdf*Dietrich v R (1992) 109 ALR 385 per Mason CJ and McHugh J at 388 citing Jago v District Court of New South Wales (1989) 87 ALR 577; 168 CLR 23, per Mason CJ at 29; Deane J at 56; Toohey J at 72; Gaudron J at 7.

Government of British Columbia (2012a), *Charge Assessment Review, http://www.ag.gov.bc.ca/public/justice-reform/CowperFinalReport.pdf* (Schedule 11).

Government of British Columbia (2012b), *Making Justice Work: Improving Access and Outcomes for British Columbians, http://www.lss.bc.ca/assets/aboutUs/reports/submissions/makingJusticeWork.pd*

Hasle, Lena (undated), *"Too poor for rights? Access to justice for poor women in Bangladesh: A case study."*

Leeuwen, Mathijs van, and Linda Haartsen (2005), *Land Conflicts and Local Conflict Resolution Mechanisms in Burundi*, Research for CED-CARITAS, Burundi.

Martin Moynihan (2008), *Review of the Civil and Criminal Justice System in Queensland,* Queensland Government, Australia.

Ministry of Justice (2011), *Publicising Sentencing Outcomes—Guidance for Public Authorities on Publicising Information (Including Via The Internet) About Individual Sentencing Outcomes Within The Current Legal Framework, Neighbourhood Justice and Courts Strategy.*

Ministry of Justice (2012a), *Provisional Statistics on the Timeliness of Criminal Court Cases.*

Ministry of Justice (2012b), *White Paper on Justice Reform Part One: A Modern, Transparent Justice System,* Government of British Columbia.

Thorne, Kristina (2005), *Rule of Law Through Imperfect Bodies? The Informal Justice Systems of Burundi and Somalia.*

Transparency and Accountability Initiative (2011), *Opening Government—Guide To Best Practice In Transparency, Accountability And Civic Engagement Across The Public Sector.*

UNDP, *Mapping the Informal Justice Systems in the State of Madhya Pradesh,* Bhopal.

Wojkowska, Ewa (2006), *Doing Justice: How Informal Justice Systems Can Contribute*, United Nations Development Programme Oslo Governance Centre, Oslo.

17

Transparency, Disclosure and Human Rights

International Standards and Local Practices

Suchismita Goswami

Introduction

United Nations at its very inception in 1946 recognised that "*Freedom of Information is a fundamental human right and the touchstone for all freedoms to which the United Nations is consecrated.*" Until and unless we have full information from the government it is difficult to realise other rights. The regime of secrecy needs to be replaced by the regime of transparency to ensure human rights to all.

Right to Information Act was first passed by Sweden in 1766. They granted public access to government documents and it became integral to the Swedish Constitution. At that time it was known as "Principle of Public Access" meaning the general public is to be guaranteed an unimpeded view of activities pursued by the government and local authorities. This practice then gradually spread across the world. India passed its Right to Information Law in 15th June, 2005 and it came into effect on 12th October 2005. It marks a revolutionary milestone in the democracy of the country. The Right to Information Act in India passed after people's struggle for their basic rights for securing transparency, accountability and participation. Though the Right to Information Law is not enshrined explicitly in our Constitution it was recognised since 1973 by the Supreme Court of India as a concomitant of the fundamental right to freedom of speech and expression guaranteed under Article 19 (1) (a).

Right to Information Act is a tool for transparency and disclosure given to us by the state as a matter of right. Our democracy is made stronger by the presence of such an Act as now the citizens can keep a check on performance of the government. Any democracy calls upon informed citizenry where the people can ask questions about the money spent on their behalf from the government directly. If the Right to Information is denied in any democracy, then it actually denies its people to realise the full range of human rights. An individual is aware of the violation of his rights only when he gets enough information about the government spending and his rights that are earmarked by the government in its spending. Information is always seen to be the subject to be held by the government and its officials. This paradigm needs to be changed and efforts should be made to make information accessible to the poor, the disadvantaged and the minorities. By not disclosing information to the citizens the government actually violates the right to participation, which is a major violation of right in a participatory democracy. "Everyone has the right to freedom of opinion and expression; this right includes freedom to hold opinions without interference and to seek, receive and impart information and ideas through any media and regardless of frontiers." This establishes the importance of transparency and disclosure in order to preserve the right to speech and expression.

The right to access information underpins all other human rights. For example, freedom of expression and thought inherently rely on the availability of adequate information for informed opinion. The realisation of the right to personal safety also requires that people have sufficient information to protect themselves. Apart from freedom of expression it is seen that most of the rights are fundamentally dependent on the Right to Information. Though Right to Information is found to be a favourable tool by the human rights activist to ensure transparency but this also has number of challenges as discussed below.

Challenges in Transparency and Disclosure through RTI

Though Indian citizens have been given a legal right to information through the RTI Act 2005, several challenges remain in its effective use for ensuring transparency and disclosure in government's functioning. These are briefly discussed below.

Delay: A person who files RTI request has to wait for thirty days before he gets any information. This delay in receiving information often violates the basic human rights of a person. It is also seen that the delay is usually much longer and one applicant has to go through first and second appeal. A person coming from a disadvantaged background hardly has the practical knowledge to go through this complicated process and further they do not have the resources to seek information in this long process. It has been pointed out by the RTI activists that there are discrepancies in the rules themselves. Since there is no rule to fine the appellate authority if it does not respond within a certain timeframe, authorities take their own sweet time even to drop cases.

Language: The information that is given through RTI is usually in a very official language which is difficult for a person to decipher. Local language should be used to give information. Special arrangement needs to be made for people who are differently challenged.

Expensive: To exclude more and more people from the purview of RTI it is seen that the application process to apply for RTI is itself made very difficult and expensive. Sikkim and Allahabad High Court charge Rs. 500 as fees for seeking information. In Haryana and Gujarat the application cost is Rs. 50 and Rs. 20 respectively. These hurdles and policies actually make the access to information much more difficult.

Difficult Process: The process usually never ends with filling of RTI application. It is usually dragged up to the level of first and second appeal which further increases the expense of a common person and it is also difficult for the unlettered population to follow such a complicated process. The Supreme Court in its series of judgment actually undermined the worth of Right to Information Act.

Attitude Towards Transparency: The former Prime Minister of our country Dr Manmohan Singh expressed his opinion about Right to Information Act as 'frivolous and vexatious". Most of the time, the Central Information Commission does not give judgment in support of transparency. The appointment of the commissioners is shrouded in secrecy and is usually political in nature. The overall attitude of the government is usually against transparency so it is much difficult for the civil society to fight against the backlash of this anti corruption law.

Pendency Rate: The pendency rate in the state as well as in the central commissions has been high. This is due to lack of apathy towards quick judgment and viewing right to information as a basic human right. This situation needs to be changed with immediate effect and the importance of right to information should be realised by the RTI commissioners. Further as there is no rules to fine the appellate authority to follow the time line it is seen that most of the time they do not comply with the time line. The efficiency of the commissions also plays a great role in disposing the pending cases.

Weak Compliance Mechanism: The RTI Act does not have a strong compliance mechanism to bring the law breakers to justice. In accordance with the RTI Act 2005 the public authority is mandated to disclose information *Suo motu* to the public at regular intervals through different means of communication. This clause is hardly complied by most of the public authority though it is a important clause for a country like India whose majority of the population lies under poverty and illiteracy.

Threat to RTI Activists: In the recent times it is seen that a number of RTI activists have been killed or harassed because they dare to seek questions about the governance of the country and expose corruption. The rich and powerful and the government representatives are causing threats to their lives. The sad part is that neither the government nor the information commission acknowledges such crimes related to RTI. The Whistleblower Act has also not taken up by the legislatures which are being pushed by the civil society very strongly.

Transparency and Human Rights

The Right to Information Law has its own challenges, but it is a potentially powerful weapon for ensuring human rights. The basic human rights can only be successfully accomplished if we have a transparent and free flowing information system. In order to ensure the convolution we need to critically analyse the international standards and the local illustration of human right situation.

Right to Water: Accessibility to water includes information accessibility, i.e., right to seek receive and impart information concerning water issues (ICESCR General Comment 15, 2002 [Art. (9)(c)(3)]. It is seen that to implement clean drinking water it is important for the beneficiaries to know about the schemes and programmes that are run by the government as well as to know the city planning details.

Right to Adequate Food: States have an obligation to formulate and implement national strategies for the right to food in full compliance with the principles of accountability, transparency and people's participation (ICESCR General Comment 12, 1999 [Art. 23]). Right to food can never see the light of the day without the implementation of right to information. This starts from transparency in the ration shop to publishing the list of beneficiaries for schemes. The transparency at all these levels gives rise for right to food at all levels.

Right to Health: Accessibility to the highest attainable standard of health includes information accessibility, i.e., right to seek, receive and impart information concerning health issues subject to confidentiality of information about personal health (ICESCR General Comment 14, 2002 [Art. (12)(b)(4)]). In developing countries like India the multinational companies reap a huge profit margin even in life saving drugs. Private hospitals take huge acres of government lands at very nominal prices with the promise to give free treatment to deprived families. Without free access to information it is difficult to keep ensure right to health for all.

Right to Adequate Housing: In the case of evictions appropriate procedural protection and due process of law includes information on the proposed eviction and the alternative purpose for which that land or housing is to be used (ICESCR General Comment 7, 1997 [Art. 15]). In the recent times displacement is the major concern for any development practitioner. According to Prof. Amartya Sen to make such decisions the people who are being displaced should be able to make informed choices. Informed choices can only be made if the person gets information of all possible choices prior to displacement. Relevant information like the environment impact report are also not proactively published by the government and the people have to fight it out in courts to get access to the environment impact report which usually needs lots of resources from people with merge resources.

Right to Education: States have an obligation to maintain a transparent and effective system to monitor educational standards in educational institutions. Non-adherence to this duty is violation of right to education (ICESCR General Comment 13, 1999 [Art.49, 54 and 59]). Philosophically, right to education and right to information complement each other. Both of these rights cannot be achieved if the other is not implemented seriously. Education is a political weapon for most of the governments from syllabus to the policies involving its implementation. This can be monitored by the people only by free flow of information.

Taking Right to Information to the People

Right to Information has opened up a new era of progressive democracy in our country, but to ensure human rights through transparent governance, it is not enough. To address the rights of the minorities, disadvantaged, women and prisoners we have to work on all systems of transparency to preserve their human rights. There should be public hearing and the panchayat should hold meetings especially for the women and other disadvantaged sections of people. The Scheduled Caste and Scheduled Tribes whose participation is usually minimal in these meetings should be also included. The schemes and other social benefits meant for them should be disclosed to them.

The prisoners are kept in a closed environment and it is seen that the maximum human rights violation is done with them. This is possible because they themselves are not aware of their own rights due to illiteracy and poverty and the families also do not get to know about the violations. The D.K. Basu guidelines are hardly followed in the prison reform system and the rate of custodial violence is increasing. These institutions needs to be opened up and more transparency should be ensured among them.

The dismal scenario in the criminal justice system needs to be reviewed and this can be achieved only by ensuring transparency at all levels.

Wall painting is an amazing initiative to bring upon information to more and more people. Commonwealth Human Rights Initiative along with their local partners started this initiative in a small village in Malav to paint information of the local government on the wall. Most of the people in this village are unlettered and poor. All the information regarding subsidy schemes, services, complains and contact of point persons are displayed and given out by the government by painting all these relevant information through wall painting in the government buildings. The information commission of Gujarat and the local administration supported in the initiative and later it was replicated in other areas.

Newspapers, televisions, radios and even social media should be used to inform people of government advertisement and other policy moves that are undertaken by the government. In the village areas such announcement is usually made by beating of drums and loudspeakers.

Pro-Active Disclosures

Under Section 4 (b) of the Indian Right to Information it is the obligation of the public authority to publish the following information at regular intervals:

(i) the particulars of its organisation, functions and duties;
(ii) the powers and duties of its officers and employees;
(iii) the procedure followed in the decision-making process, including channels of supervision and accountability;
(iv) the norms set by it for the discharge of its functions;
(v) the rules, regulations, instructions, manuals and records, held by it or under its control or used by its employees for discharging its functions;
(vi) a statement of the categories of documents that are held by it or under its control;
(vii) the particulars of any arrangement that exists for consultation with, or representation by, the members of the public in relation to the formulation of its policy or implementation thereof;
(viii) a statement of the boards, councils, committees and other bodies consisting of two or more persons constituted as its part or for the purpose of its advice, and as to whether meetings of those boards, councils, committees and other bodies are open to the public, or the minutes of such meetings are accessible for public;
(ix) a directory of its officers and employees;
(x) the monthly remuneration received by each of its officers and employees, including the system of compensation as provided in its regulations;
(xi) the budget allocated to each of its agency, indicating the particulars of all plans, proposed expenditures and reports on disbursements made;
(xii) the manner of execution of subsidy programmes, including the amounts allocated and the details of beneficiaries of such programmes;

(xiii) particulars of recipients of concessions, permits or authorisations granted by it;

(xiv) details in respect of the information, available to or held by it, reduced in an electronic form;

(xv) the particulars of facilities available to citizens for obtaining information, including the working hours of a library or reading room, if maintained for public use;

(xvi) The names, designations and other particulars of the Public Information Officers;

(xvii) such other information as may be prescribed; and thereafter update these publications every year;

Under Section 4 (c) of the Indian Right to Information it is the obligation of the public authority to publish all relevant facts while formulating important policies or announcing the decisions which affect public

Section 4 (d) provides giving reasons for its administrative or quasi-judicial decisions to affected persons.

These provisions are hardly implemented in reality. We should try to follow the best international practices for disclosing information proactively.

Suggestions

The following suggestions are given for making information available to people in a comprehensible and timely manner at an affordable cost:

- *Findable:* The information that are proactively disclosed by the government are hardly popularised. They hardly reach out to the people to inform them through informal means. Crucial information are found to be in the corner of a newspaper which is usually difficult to locate. The information which are crucial and ensures human rights should be stored in such places which could be accessed easily without much problem. In the walls also if paintings are done it should be in prominent places of the village which would catch attention of all the villagers.
- *Comprehensible:* Most of the time it is seen that the information that are published are difficult to comprehend

by common people. The information which is published should be delivered in a manner which is well understood by concerned people and beneficiaries. It is seen that the government just publishes the whole copy of the budget when budgetary allocations are asked for. How is a common man supposed to decipher the complicated figures that are published in the budgets? It is the duty for the government to make the data comprehensive which could be used by the people to access information.

- *Up-to date:* The data which are proactively disclosed in the websites as well as in the public spaces are usually very old and out dated information. These information needs to be updated to be of any use to the citizens. The information should reach the public on time so that they can use it. The system needs to be updated with new information.
- *Free:* Most of the information which are proactively disclosed should be by principle and by law done free of cost. The information that is detailed out in Section 4(b) are the basic information needed to include the people in informed participation. The people should not ask or spend any money to access such information. It is directly related to the citizens exercise of development and human rights through information. Most of the time by using right to information it is seen that the expense just gets increasing. It just never ends in filing an RTI application with Rs. 10. It is usually denied and one is forced to file the first and second appeal which ends up being much more expensive and even after this there is no surety if the information would be at all given to the information seeker.
- *Language:* The public authorities should be very particular to disseminate the information in local languages and in multiple languages which are prevalent in those areas so that maximum number of people can take advantage of the information.
- *Compliance:* The biggest drawback of the Right to Information Act in India is that there is no agency to check the compliance of proactive disclosure as stated in 41(b). In most of the countries it is seen that there is a compliance mechanism to monitor the implementation of proactive disclosure. The lacking of such a provision makes the clause of proactive disclosure much week in nature.

REFERENCES

CHRI (2003), *Open Sesame: Looking for the Right to Information in the Commonwealth.*

Sathe, S.P. (2006), *Right to Information:* Lexis Nexis, New Delhi.

Stiglitz, Joseph E. (2007), *The Right to Know,* Columbia Press University, New York.

Index